BECOMING PRESENT

STUDIES IN PHILOSOPHICAL THEOLOGY, 30

1   H. de Vries, *Theologie im Pianissimo & zwischen Rationalität und
    Dekonstruktion*, Kampen, 1989
2   S. Breton, *La pensée du rien*, Kampen, 1992
3   Ch. Schwöbel, *God: Action and Revelation*, Kampen, 1992
4   V. Brümmer (ed.), *Interpreting the Universe as Creation*, Kampen, 1991
5   L.J. van den Brom, *Divine Presence in the World*, Kampen, 1993
6   M. Sarot, *God, Passibility and Corporeality*, Kampen, 1992
7   G. van den Brink, *Almighty God*, Kampen 1993
8   P.-C. Lai, *Towards a Trinitarian Theology of Religions: A Study of Paul
    Tillich's Thought*, Kampen, 1994
9   L. Velecky, *Aquinas' Five Arguments in the* Summa Theologiae *Ia 2, 3*, Kampen,
    1994
10 W. Dupré, *Patterns in Meaning. Reflections on Meaning and Truth in Cultural
    Reality, Religious Traditions, and Dialogical Encounters*, Kampen, 1994
11 P.T. Erne, *Lebenskunst. Aneignung ästhetischer Erfahrung*, Kampen, 1994
12 U. Perone, *Trotz/dem Subjekt*, Leuven, 1998
13 H.J. Adriaanse, *Vom Christentum aus: Aufsätze und Vorträge zur Religions-
    philosophie*, Kampen, 1995
14 D.A. Pailin, *Probing the Foundations: A Study in Theistic Reconstruction*,
    Kampen, 1994
15 M. Potepa, *Schleiermachers hermeneutische Dialektik*, Kampen, 1996
16 E. Herrmann, *Scientific Theory and Religious Belief. An Essay on the
    Rationality of Views of Life*, Kampen, 1995
17 V. Brümmer & M. Sarot (eds.), *Happiness, Well-Being and the Meaning of Life.
    A Dialogue of Social Science and Religion*, Kampen, 1996
18 T.L. Hettema, *Reading for Good. Narrative Theology and Ethics in the Joseph
    Story from the Perspective of Ricoeur's Hermeneutics*, Kampen, 1996
19 H. Düringer, *Universale Vernunft und partikularer Glaube. Eine theologische
    Auswertung des Werkes von Jürgen Habermas*, Leuven, 1999
20 E. Dekker, *Middle Knowledge*, Leuven, 2000
21 T. Ekstrand, *Max Weber in a Theological Perspective*, Leuven, 2000
22 C. Helmer & K. De Troyer (eds.), *Truth: Interdisciplinary Dialogues in a
    Pluralist Age*, Leuven, 2003
23 L. Boeve & L.P. Hemming (eds.), *Divinising Experience. Essays in the History
    of Religious Experience from Origen to Ricœur*, Leuven, 2004
24 P.D. Murray, *Reason, Truth and Theology in Pragmatist Perspective*, Leuven,
    2004
25 S. van Erp, *The Art of Theology. Hans Urs von Balthasar's Theological Aes-
    thetics and the Foundations of Faith*, Leuven, 2004
26 T.A. Smedes, *Chaos, Complexity, and God. Divine Action and Scientism*,
    Leuven, 2004
27 R. Re Manning, *Theology at the End of Culture. Paul Tillich's Theology of Cul-
    ture and Art*, Leuven, 2004
28 P. Jonkers & R. Welten (eds.), *God in France. Eight Contemporary French
    Thinkers on God*, Leuven 2005
29 D. Grumett, *Teilhard de Chardin: Theology, Humanity and Cosmos*, Leuven,
    2005

BECOMING PRESENT

An Inquiry into the Christian Sense of the Presence of God

BY

Ingolf U. DALFERTH

PEETERS
LEUVEN – PARIS – DUDLEY, MA
2006

Library of Congress Cataloging-in-Publication Data

Dalferth, Ingolf U.
   Becoming present: an inquiry into the Christian sense of the presence of God / Ingolf U.
Dalferth.
      p. cm. -- (Studies in philosophical theology; 30)
      Includes bibliographical references (p.   ) and index.
      ISBN 90-429-1727-X (alk. paper)
         1. Presence of God. 2. Philosophical theology. I. Title. II. Series.

   BT180.P6D25 2006
   231.7--dc22
                                                                    2005058640

© 2006 – Peeters – Bondgenotenlaan 153 – 3000 Leuven – Belgium.

ISBN-10 90-429-1727-X
ISBN-13 9789042917279
D. 2006/0602/19

With deep gratitude
to the Faculty of Theology at Uppsala
for the honarary doctorate

Preface

This book has taken a long time to become present, and it has changed considerably in shape and argument over the years. What I present now is a reduced version of a considerably larger German original that grew out of the Samuel Ferguson Lectures, which I was invited to give at the University of Manchester in 1995. Professor David A. Pailin, one of Britain's foremost exponents of process thought, made this a very fruitful stay for me. I am grateful for the opportunity of discussing my ideas with him.

At the time I was working on problems in the philosophy of time and in process philosophy and theology[1], and these topics informed the lectures given in Manchester.[2] But when I started to rethink and rewrite the material for publication the argument soon took me beyond epistemology and metaphysics into phenomenology of religion and theology proper.[3] More recently the philosophy and theology of gift and the phenomenology of the 1st-person perspective have become a major challenge to clarify my thoughts on the subject. Some studies I have published[4], and more are in preparation for a German publication. But for reasons of economy I have refrained from discus-

---

[1] Cf. *Gott. Philosophisch-theologische Denkversuche*, Tübingen 1992, especially chaps. 5ff.

[2] Two of them have been published: ›God's Real Presence‹, in: T. Koistinen/T. Lehtonen (eds.), *Philosophical Studies in Religion, Metaphysics and Ethics. Essays in Honour of Heikki Kirjavainen*, Helsinki 1997, 35-59; ›Representing God's Presence‹, *International Journal of Systematic Theology* 3, 2001, 237-256. The arguments of these papers have been completely reworked in chaps. 2 and 6.

[3] Cf. ›Time for God's Presence‹, in: M. Volf/C. Krieg/Th. Kucharz (eds.), *The Future of Theology. Essays in Honor of Jürgen Moltmann*, Grand Rapids, Michigan 1996, 127-141; *Gedeutete Gegenwart. Zur Wahrnehmung Gottes in den Erfahrungen der Zeit*, Tübingen 1997; ›Paradigm Lost. From the Sense of the Whole to the Sense of the Presence of God‹, in: D. A. Crosby/Ch. D. Hardwick (eds.), *Religion in a Pluralistic Age. Proceedings of the Third International Conference on Philosophical Theology*, Bern et al. 2001, 21-48.

[4] *Die Wirklichkeit des Möglichen. Hermeneutische Religionsphilosophie*, Tübingen 2003; ›Alles Umsonst. Von der Kunst des Schenkens und den Grenzen der Gabe‹, in: M.M. Olivetti (ed.), Le don et la dette, Padova 2005, 53-76.

sing the literature extensively and have not incorporated into this book everything interesting and important on these topics but only what is necessary for clarifying my argument and making my point.

A long overdue sabbatical spent in Claremont and in Copenhagen gave me the time to weave the themes together into what I hope is now a coherent pattern. I am deeply grateful to my friends in California whose cheerful creativity makes Claremont such an inspiring environment of research, writing, and living. In the past few months I have had the great fortune of working as a guest professor at the Center for Subjectivity Research in Copenhagen. Its superb working environment and the open exchange of ideas among its members greatly facilitated the completion of the book. I should like to thank my friends and colleagues Arne Grøn and Dan Zahavi for welcoming me as a member at the Center and for not agreeing with most of what I said in most of our discussions. I am grateful to Iben Damgaard, Claudia Welz, Cornelia Richter and all the other research students at the Center for sharing their ideas about phenomenology and subjectivity with me and for doing so much to make that stay a very memorable one for me.

The book would not have appeared without Louise A. Hickman who has made my English accessible to those who know the language, Andreas Hunziker who has compiled the bibliography and checked the footnotes, and Cécile Rupp who has turned a muddled typescript into a readable book. They all have been unfailingly supportive throughout the final stages of producing the book. Readers will be as grateful to them as I am.

Material from the following publications has been reworked and incorporated into the present work with the permission from the original publishers: ›Paradigm Lost. From the Sense of the Whole to the Sense of the Presence of God‹ in: D. A. Crosby/Ch. D. Hardwick (eds.), *Religion in a Pluralistic Age. Proceedings of the Third International Conference on Philosophical Theology*, American Liberal Religious Thought Vol. 7, Bern etc. 2001, 21-48; ›God's Real Presence‹, in: T. Koistinen/T. Lehtonen (eds.), *Philosophical Studies in Religion, Metaphysics and Ethics. Essays in Honour of Heikki Kirjavainen*, Helsinki 1997, 35-59; ›Representing God's Presence‹, *IJST* 3, 2001, 237-256. I am grateful to the publishers.

I. U. Dalferth

TABLE OF CONTENTS

I From the Sense of the Whole
to the Sense of the Presence of God

1. The Paradigm of Rational Religion

Once upon a time people believed in rational religion – a religion entirely of their own making.[1] They were tired of the strife and conflicts of opposing religious sects. But they did not want to give up on religion altogether. They believed that the social consensus needed to produce a stable and well-ordered society must include a sense of the whole, a comprehensive view of the end and purpose of human life in the universe that provides a full account of the nature of humanity, of moral responsibility, and of how people should live their lives. Therefore these believers designed a rational religion that was not »one sect among other sects« but public both in the sense of being »open equally to all« and of being »supported by reasons that are reasons for everyone«[2]. They thought that in dealing with differences of opinion people should be required in all their deliberations to attain neutrality and impartiality by divesting themselves »of allegiance to any particular standpoint and to achieve universality by abstracting« themselves »from all those communities of interest that may limit« their perspective;[3] and they designed their religion to conform to these canons of public rationality. Thus rational religion was not only meant to tell us all we need to know about God, the immortality of the soul, and the requirements of the moral law, it also served as the standard of rationally defensible religion. Religious sects might have deviated from this standard »to varying degrees, the degree of their deviation being a measure of their irrationality«[4]. But in the end rational religion alone and none of the historical religions could stand the test of public acceptance by neutral reason: either one was a rational theist or one's beliefs were not reasonable.

---

[1] In the following I have profited from John Clayton, ›Common Ground and Defensible Difference‹, in: L. Rouner (ed.), *Religion, Politics and Peace*, Notre Dame, Indiana 1999, 104–127. A more elaborate version of the argument of this chapter can be found in Dalferth, *Die Wirklichkeit des Möglichen*. Hermeneutische Religionsphilosophie, Tübingen 2003, 209–256.

[2] Ibid., 109.

[3] Ibid., 109f.

[4] Ibid., 110.

This was a neat and clear-cut alternative, but there was a price to be paid for it: Where rational religion failed to convince, and it increasingly did so in secularised societies, religious beliefs and practices were seen as pre-rational or devoid of any rationality. One simply had to choose: Either one acted rationally and followed the guidelines of reason, or one held a religious belief, stopped being reasonable, and took leave of public rationality.

The only way out for those who did not want to choose in this way was to refute the objections against rational religion and show it to be rationally defensible after all. This gave philosophers and theologians an opportunity of endlessly debating the pros and cons of rational religion and of the reasons adduced in support of one position or the other. But although this debate still seems to be the favourite pastime of many philosophers of religion to this very day, they rarely stop to notice that all they can hope to achieve is a defence of an idealized construction in the line of the tradition-free reasoning of Enlightenment rationalism, whether worked out in terms of Swinburnian probabilism, Reformed epistemology, Hartshornian maximum perfection, or a mix of latter day Thomism and a polished-up version of Calvinism. But the more refined and technical the arguments get, the less they have to say about actual religious beliefs and the further they are removed from the requirements of religious life and the intellectual challenges of actual religious practices or the widespread disinterest in participating in them. These arguments defend a public religion that is of no interest to the public, and hence they fail even where they should succeed. For just as problems in English or German cannot be solved by making everyone speak Esperanto, so problems of rationality and truth in historical religions cannot be solved by rational religion. The paradigm of rational religion offers a wrong solution to a false problem. Hence philosophers of religion should not continue to pursue this line of thought.

2. The Historical Setting of Rational Religion

Rational religion originated in a particular historical situation; the Enlightenment. It was the result of thinkers of this era applying the methodological regimentation of reason in 17th century philosophy (e.g., Descartes, Bacon) to religious belief. *Beliefs* are rational when they accord with certain established rules of thinking, i.e., when they are determined by the mathematical and experimental methods of the relevant scientific disciplines, and *religious beliefs* are rational insofar as they can be construed within the limits of this narrow conception of rationality alone.

In this sense rational religion is defended to this very day[5], but as a universally applicable paradigm of public religion, it has been a failure from the beginning. Schleiermacher decisively criticised it as a useless fiction and unhistorical construction at a time when others still tried to put it into practice. But even in Jefferson's Virginia it had a chance to succeed only under the exceptional circumstances of a homogeneous religious population. There »was not a single Roman Catholic church« in »the whole Commonwealth of Virginia« in Jefferson's time, and »the nearest Jewish congregations were in Philadelphia to the north and Charleston to the south«.[6] So rational religion was a more rational alternative only to Protestant diversity: Eliminating all the distinguishing doctrines of the diverse Protestant groups left only the residue of rational religion.[7] This religion was never neutral, but part and parcel of a particular political program.[8] It had not grown out of an actual religious practice but was an abstract product of the mind that resulted from the philosophical attempt to rebut 17th and 18th century atheism on its own grounds.[9] And it »was able to pass itself off as ›universal‹ only because of the paucity of knowledge about« other religious traditions.[10] In short, rational religion was a theoretical construction in a particular historical situation, and its appeal as a paradigm of rationally defensible religion depends on that particular background.

Today our situation is very different. We know about the forces, chances, and dangers of secularisation. We have political, social, and juridical institutions, which define public space, regulate access to it, and function without an explicit religious backing. And we live within a culture of religious diversity of quite a different order. Our societies comprise, not only a fragmented Protestant tradition, but fragments of

---

[5]   Cf. Chr. Jäger (ed.), *Analytische Religionsphilosophie*, Paderborn 1998; Ch. Taliaferro (ed.), *Contemporary Philosophy of Religion*, Oxford 1998; M. Peterson/ W. Hasker/B. Reichenbach/D. Basinger (eds.), *Reason and Religious Belief. An Introduction to the Philosophy of Religion*, New York/Oxford ³2002; Dalferth, *Die Wirklichkeit des Möglichen*, 211-218.274-332.

[6]   Clayton, ›Common Ground and Defensible Difference‹, 111.

[7]   Ibid., 110f.

[8]   This is also true of deism in Great Britain. Cf. J. Cartwright, *The English Constitution Produced and Illustrated*, London 1823, 147.

[9]   Cf. Dalferth, *Die Wirklichkeit des Möglichen*, 257-335.

[10]   Clayton, ›Common Ground and Defensible Difference‹, 111.

very different religious traditions: Protestants, Eastern Orthodox, Roman Catholics, Muslims, Mormons, Jews, Buddhists, and Hindus, to say nothing of the innumerable psycho-religious sects and new religious movements. New religious groups spring up every day, and keeping track of the individualization and diversification of religious orientations is difficult. Most of the people of these groups hardly know about each other. But even major world religions with long interconnected histories have only in recent times begun systematically to take account of each other, to seek closer contact and exchange, and to communicate across traditional boundaries.

Yet after a century of ecumenical and interreligious dialogues, we cannot close our eyes to the fact that these discussions have not fostered a more rational view of religion or a more liberal attitude towards one's own religion and the religions of others. On the contrary, most religious traditions have seen a rise of fundamentalism in their ranks in recent years[11], and the unexpected progress of »radically conservative movements« around the world has sparked off apocalyptic warnings »against domestic culture wars (Hunter) or global clashes of civilizations (Huntington)« from the liberal establishment.[12] No doubt, »citizens of modern democratic societies share less in common than they had once imagined«[13]. But instead of accepting the fact that what we really share in common is our differences, that what is interesting about our societies is what marks us off from each other, and that our legal, political, and juridical structures must safeguard, not a common sense of the whole, but our freedom to differ, we still largely react to problems of cultural and religious diversity in terms of the classical recipe of early modernity, which is to »privatize difference and cultivate common ground«[14].

This classical liberal strategy in dealing with differences of life(-style), conviction and opinion works only in relatively homogeneous societies with a common historical background, a limited number of options, and a relatively clear (historical) distribution of power between various groups and traditions. Where we abstract from the particular

---

[11] Cf. M. Riesebrodt, *Protestantischer Fundamentalismus in den USA. Die religiöse Rechte im Zeitalter der elektronischen Medien,* Stuttgart 1987; *Fundamentalismus als patriarchalische Protestbewegung. Amerikanische Protestanten (1910-28) und iranische Schiiten (1961-79) im Vergleich,* Tübingen 1990; *Die Rückkehr der Religionen. Fundamentalismus und der ›Kampf der Kulturen‹,* München 2000.

[12] Clayton, ›Common Ground and Defensible Difference‹, 104.

[13] Ibid.

[14] Ibid.

historical setting with its contingent preferences for some views, values, and goals rather than others and where everything is taken to be just as important (or unimportant) as anything else, finding commonly acceptable criteria for privileging one view or one set of values and goals rather than another when defining the common ground which all members of a community should share is hard, if not impossible. Criteria, such as justice, goodness, freedom, equality, or whatever else we take to be basic requirements of good life, are tied up with specific background assumptions of our culture. Their content and force can only be illumined against that background, and they lose their persuasive power to establish fundamental guidelines of common life when they become divorced from the wider cultural tradition to which they belong. If we appeal to them to sustain stable social unity between people who are culturally diverse or have diverse conceptions of the good life, then we are not using these criteria as abstract values, but instead we are interpreting them in the context of a particular cultural tradition. As such, they are taken for granted when we expect, e.g., that our idea of the good life will or should be met with acceptance beyond our own circles, that our own view of shared values and common goals is more convincing than other views, and that not just any other perspective could do just as well as ours in defining the outlines of a common conception of the good life. We move within particular historical traditions when we describe shared values and common goals that should be internalised by the members of a given community and integrated into their personal identity, and only against this background will our plea be found convincing.

Thus classical liberalism had a limited success only by living off the Western heritage, which served as the common background against which it defined its view of the common good of society. On a global scale, this heritage has lost momentum for a number of reasons. However, strategies to maximize common ground need perspectives and background convictions, which must already be shared for the strategy to be successful. Changing the background will enable the same strategy to produce different results; therefore the classical paradigm of rational religion is of little help in dealing with religious diversity today. This paradigm underestimates the force of religious convictions. In addition, it operates with an abstract conception of rationality, ignores the intrinsic historicity of religious practices, and is misled by the paradigm it uses to understand the social function of religion. Let us look at some of these matters in more detail.

3. The Dynamics of Religious Liberty

Consider, first, the separation of state and church in Western societies. Its point was not simply to sidestep religion nor to limit the range of religious activities (as may have been the case in other contexts) nor merely to protest against the establishment of one religion rather than another. Its most important reason was that it was conducive to religious liberty, because it involved no state interference in religious matters or church interference in political matters. The prevailing thought was that, for the good of either side, politics should be kept out of religion, and religion should keep itself out of politics.

This idea was and is, first of all, a principle of practical wisdom (*phronesis*) applied to the realm of politics: It is prudent for the state to keep out of matters that are in principle beyond its power to control because it cannot enforce ideals according to some general rule or law that is legally valid and morally legitimate.[15] If religious beliefs have to be judged by the state at all, then they must be judged individually and in terms of their concrete social consequences, harms, and benefits, not in terms of some general principle about the sense or non-sense of religion as such.

But there was and is also a religious reason for this restraint. In matters of ultimate importance, such as faith which concerns not merely the whole life of a person but his or her eternal standing before God,[16] responsibility must rest solely with the individual person and not with some third party, be it family, church, or state. For religious and political reasons everyone must be left free to pursue his or her own vision of the good life, providing that this pursuit does not impede the ability of others to pursue theirs. It is not the business of the state to promote any one religious view, but to regard all religious and non-religious views as equal. Religions, on the other hand, must be free to compete

---

[15] This is not the only reason for self-restraint on the part of the state. K. Greenawalt, *Private Consciences and Public Reasons*, New York/Oxford 1995 discusses a variety of different principles of self-restraint.

[16] The insight that the »neighbor is one who is equal« with oneself before God, is the religious reason for treating all persons as equal: It is the other's »equality with you before God«, as Kierkegaard has pointed out, which constitutes the equality of persons (*Works of Love* (1847), in *Kierkegaard's Writings*, vol. 16, ed. and transl. by H. V. Hong and E. H. Hong, Princeton, New Jersey 1995, 60). The equality of persons is not an affirmation of an abstract individualism but an implication of the Christian perspective of faith, which views everyone and everything as living and existing before God.

in the market for new members unhindered by »those hostile to religion, or other religious groups or by some agency of government«[17]. Citizens who hold religious beliefs must therefore learn to distinguish between their private and public activities.[18] As private persons, they may proselytize for their religion. In the public realm, however, they must separate »personal belief from civic virtue«[19] and rely exclusively on public, secular, neutral reason. Self-restraint in political choice is the price to be paid for the free exercise of religion in private life.

The trouble is that this idea does not work.[20] Whether someone has this religion or that or no religion at all may not seem to be of public concern, but this lack of concern may change quickly when controversial issues such as abortion, school prayer, or the wearing of headscarves in schools are at stake. Moreover, the difference between public and private life does not coincide with the contrast between a person's public involvement with other persons and his or her standing before God; the private lives of persons are in no way closer to God than their public lives. One's public life cannot be exempt if the whole life of a believer is to be led before God. Not only from the religious point of view is this idea true: The ideal of religious liberty entails being able to hold religious beliefs and engage in worship as well as to act on one's beliefs — in all areas of individual and common life. Religious convictions are all-encompassing and cannot be confined to one's private life only. The free exercise of religion can legitimately be limited only by the proviso that it does not impede the right and ability of

---

[17] Clayton, ›Common Ground and Defensible Difference‹, 106.

[18] Cf. R. Audi, ›The Separation of Church and State and the Obligations of Citizenship‹, *Philosophy and Public Affairs* 18, 1989, 259-296; ›The Place of Religious Argument in a Free and Democratic Society‹, *San Diego Law Review* 30, 1993, 647-675; ›The State, the Church, and the Citizen‹, in: P. J. Weithman (ed.), *Religion and Contemporary Liberalism*, Notre Dame, Indiana 1997, 38-75; ›Liberal Democracy and the Place of Religion in Politics‹, in: R. Audi/N. Wolterstorff, *Religion in the Public Square. The Place of Religious Conviction in Political Debate*, Lanham, Maryland 1997, 1-66; *Religious Commitment and Secular Reason*, Cambridge 2000.

[19] Clayton, ›Common Ground and Defensible Difference‹, 106f.

[20] Cf. N. Wolterstorff, ›Why We Should Reject What Liberalism Tells Us about Speaking and Acting in Public for Religious Reasons‹, in: Weithman (ed.), *Religion and Contemporary Liberalism*, 162-181; ›The Role of Religion in Decision and Discussion of Political Issues‹, in: Audi/Wolterstorff, *Religion in the Public Square*, 67-120; St. Grotefeld, ›Distinkt, aber nicht illegitim. Protestantische Ethik und die liberale Forderung nach Selbstbeschränkung‹, *Zeitschrift für Evangelische Ethik* 45, 2001, 262-284.

others to exercise theirs, not by rigorously excluding it from the political or public realm.[21] Indeed, the »claim that citizens and legislators should rely exclusively on secular grounds«; Kent Greenawalt has pointed out, »is not only wrong but absurd. It invites religious persons to displace their most firmly rooted convictions about values, the nature of humanity, and the universe in a quest for common bases of judgment that is inevitably unavailing when virtually everyone must rely on personal perspectives«[22]. What is needed in public affairs are not reasons that must be acceptable to all irrespective of their most deeply held convictions. Rather the reasons given by legislators must convince those to whom they are addressed, and this may well mean that different reasons have to be given to different groups of citizens in order to make a piece of legislation acceptable to people with widely different background orientations.

But then personal perspectives and religious convictions cannot in principle be banned from the public realm, as Robert Audi would have it.[23] The problem is rather how it is »possible that there may exist over time a stable and just society of free and equal citizens profoundly divided by reasonable though incompatible religious, philosophical, and moral doctrines?«[24] John Rawls's answer is to suggest an ideal of public reason centred on the »criterion of reciprocity«: In the public realm only those reasons for actions are legitimate when we »reasonably think that other citizens might also reasonably accept those reasons«[25]. But this principle asks for more than we can reasonably expect of others. What must be safeguarded is that acting on my religious

---

[21] Clayton, ›Common Ground and Defensible Difference‹, 106.

[22] K. Greenawalt, *Religious Convictions and Political Choice*, New York/Oxford 1988, 258.

[23] Audi, ›Liberal Democracy and the Place of Religion in Politics‹. According to him all arguments in public debates have to follow the *principle of secular rationale* and the *principle of secular motivation*. The first requires »that one has a prima facie obligation not to advocate or support any law or public policy that restricts human conduct, unless one has, and is willing to offer, adequate secular reason for the advocacy or support (say for one's vote)« (25). The second »says that one has a (prima facie) obligation to abstain from advocacy or support of a law or public policy that restricts human conduct, unless one is sufficiently *motivated* by (normatively) adequate secular reason, where sufficiency of motivation here implies that some set of secular reasons is motivationally sufficient, roughly in the sense that (a) this set of reasons explains one's action and (b) one would act on it even if, other things remaining equal, one's other reasons were eliminated« (29).

[24] J. Rawls, *Political Liberalism*, New York 1996, XX.

[25] Ibid., XLVI.

or non-religious convictions does not impede the right and ability of others to act on theirs, not that they must be able to endorse my reasons if they were to perform these or similar actions. There is usually more than one sufficient reason for a given course of action; the reasons acceptable to others are not necessarily those on which I act; and the failure of others to find my reasons acceptable is not enough to reject them as irrational. For all practical purposes, therefore, all that is required of religious or any other reasons offered for a particular course of action is that acting on them does not impede the fundamental rights of other citizens.

All this is not to say that there is no point in distinguishing between private and public activities, practices, and reasons. But the »terms ›private‹ and ›public‹ are notoriously slippery« and can be made to cover nearly everything one wishes, not only in England where public schools are private institutions, but also in the US where nothing seems to be more public than the private lives of politicians.[26] Moreover, the way in which the distinction is often used with respect to religion suggests a view of a neutral public, divested of all interests and generally accessible to all in the same way, which is at best an unattainable ideal and at worst a mirage. When impartiality is (wrongly) thought to require that all distinguishing characteristics of the concrete settings of human life and action be irrelevant, including the specific histories, orientations and aspirations of those who live and act together, universality and neutrality can be achieved only at the cost of being abstract and without a point: The quest for impartiality and the attempt to generate a more encompassing perspective become important precisely in the face of conflicting histories, beliefs, and orientations. Without this background that quest loses its point, for these conflicts define in which respect a more encompassing perspective is to be sought.

Similarly, the distinction between private and public in religious matters must be seen against a particular historical background where it helped to make an important point. But it does not follow that this distinction can or should be used as a general strategy to deal with problems of cultural and religious diversity. Changes of background and context give a different emphasis to this distinction. Publicly accessible common ground can prove to be the very cause of conflict, whereas what is called private may turn out to be unifying.[27] Hence maximizing common ground is not necessarily an antidote to the potentially

---

[26] Clayton, ›Common Ground and Defensible Difference‹, 105.
[27] Ibid., 2.

destructive effects of religious diversity. But neither is it necessary for a common life that we all share the same »common ground« or that the reasons given in public debates for our opinions have to be reasons for everyone. Our reasons »must be contestable by anyone with requisite knowledge«,[28] and hence must be made accessible and not kept in the dark. But actual grounds of decisions and reasons offered in public justification need not be identical. We offer those reasons that we hope will convince those to whom they are addressed. But the reasons we give are not normally the basis of our religious belief. If they are refuted , believers do not stop believing but look for better reasons, for part of what it means to grow up as a religious person is to find other and better reasons for practicing one's religion. Conversely, if faith is lost it is only rarely because of particular critical arguments; more often it is because one realizes that one has stopped practicing the religion for a variety of reasons, not all of which may be expressible in the form of arguments. Religions are more than sets of more or less warranted beliefs; they are complex ways of life, not devoid of reason but neither reducible to reason alone nor to one kind of reason only. In religion, as well as in politics, there is more than one use of reason, both public and private, and the two sets of distinctions (between public and private, and politics and religion) do not coincide.

4. Rationality and Religious Belief

The use of reason, therefore, is not to be restricted to the canons of rationality exemplified by the paradigm of rational religion, which gives little chance to actual religious beliefs to stand up to examination. This paradigm charges them with not meeting the standards of public reason by which we sort out the sound from the unsound, and hence seeks to replace them by something more rational. But a rational belief is not necessarily the product of reason or of reason alone, and religious beliefs do not necessarily rule out rational elucidation nor are they obviously unsound by not conforming to the canons of mathematical-experimental reasoning.[29] The dispute, quite obviously, turns

---

[28] Ibid., 119.
[29] Cf. H. I. Brown, *Rationality*, London/New York 1990; M. Stenmark, *Rationality in Science, Religion, and Everyday Life*, Notre Dame, Indiana 1995; J. W. van Huyssteen, *The Shaping of Rationality. Toward Interdisciplinarity in Theology and Science*, Grand Rapids, Mich./Cambridge 1999, 120ff.

on the question of what can rationally be asserted to be rational. This issue will require some brief elucidation.[30]

First, what is rational is not limited to what we can prove. We may not be able to prove that there is life after death but still have reasons to believe it to be true; on the other hand, even if we have good reasons for believing it to be so, it may be false. A rational belief is not necessarily true, and a false belief not necessarily irrational.[31]

Second, what is rational need not be a self-discovery. We do not have to think up everything for ourselves in order to be rational. Borrowed beliefs are not necessarily irrational, and egocentric reason is not the sole or even main source of rational beliefs. Knowledge is a social product[32], and rationality is not tied to a foundationalist epistemology that begins by dispensing with vicarious information and ends up with cognitive solipsism.[33]

Third, not everything we know must be rational in order to be reasonable. If I am in pain I need no reasons for knowing it. My knowledge is not based on a state of affairs that I have observed or for which I have or lack evidence. Someone observing me, on the other hand, can have reasons to doubt that my pain was really as grievous as my behaviour suggested. However, the possibility of doubt or certainty in a third-person perspective does not imply the same in my first-person perspective. The misapplication of third-person perspectives onto first-person experiences is the cause of much confusion in the debate about rationality. If rationality is intimately bound up with grounds and evidence in a third-person perspective then I am reasonable in going to see a doctor if I am in pain but I am not acting on a rational belief. Where there is no place for doubt and certainty, there is no place for grounds and evidence, and hence no place for rational belief as ordinarily understood.[34]

---

[30] Cf. for the following I. U. Dalferth, *Theology and Philosophy*, Eugene, Oregon 2001, chap. 1.

[31] I. U. Dalferth, *Religiöse Rede von Gott*, München 1981, 507–516.

[32] Cf. M. Kusch, *Knowledge by Agreement. The Programme of Communitarian Epistemology*, Oxford 2002.

[33] Cf. N. Rescher, *The Coherence Theory of Truth*, Oxford 1973, chap. 13.

[34] It is not rational therefore to require that every belief must be justified in order to be reasonable. »Justification is required for *changing* one's state of full belief« as I. Levi points out (*The Covenant of Reason. Rationality and the Commitments of Thought*, Cambridge 1997, 20). However, there is no rational obligation that everyone has »to justify what he or she fully believes«. On the contrary, in »the absence of a good reason to change, the inquirer should retain the commitments he has«; and the »mere presence« of disagreement is not such a good reason« (3). In-

Fourth, rationality is not the sole prerogative of (empirical) science.[35] Scientific rationality, with its canons of generalizable experience and mathematical construction and its procedures of conjecture and refutation, is an important, but by no means the only, form of rationality.

Fifth, rationality pertains primarily to method and not to content. Our beliefs are rational, not because of what they hold, but because of the way they are held. They are, ideally, beliefs that in the light of critical discussion appear to be the most warranted thus far.[36] Of course, what it is for a belief to be warranted, and which methods are appropriate for warranting it, may themselves be matters of dispute. What is appropriate in physics is not necessarily so in theology. But beliefs, in whatever area and of whatever type, may be held dogmatically or rationally. They are rational if they are supported by argument, buttressed by reasons, and established upon evidence;[37] and they fail to be rational if they are held contrary to the rules of logic, the canons of argument, and the criteria of evidence relevant to the area under discussion.

Sixth, the notion of a rational belief can mean that the content of the belief is rational, i.e., that the belief is justified or justifiable; but it can also mean that the way the belief is held is rational, i.e., that the belief is reasonable. The two senses should not be confused.[38] In the first or logical sense a belief is rational if what is believed can be supported by argument and justified by reason,[39] and our concept of ra-

---

deed, we »may tolerate the public expression of dissent while expressing our own contempt for it. But we are not obliged to register contempt either. ... Respect for a dissenting view arises when an agent confronted with dissent recognizes a good reason for genuinely opening his or her mind by ceasing to be convinced of the view initially endorsed which is in conflict with the dissent.« But to »confuse toleration with respect for the views of dissenters can lead advocates of toleration to urge upon us the skepticism of the empty mind« (20). Cf. ›The Ethics of Controversy‹, in *The Covenant of Reason*, 239-254.

[35] Cf. Stenmark, *Rationality in Science, Religion, and Everyday Life*, 199: The »claim that science is *the* paradigm case« for rationality takes »as the lowest level what in fact might be the highest level of rationality which we finite human beings with our limited cognitive resources are currently able to reach«; and this entails that »in almost all other areas in life, people almost always will be irrational.«

[36] Cf. K. Popper, *Objective Knowledge. An Evolutionary Approach*, Oxford 1972, 22.

[37] J. Barnes, *The Presocratic Philosophers*, London ²1982, 5.

[38] Cf. Dalferth, *Religiöse Rede*, 495ff.

[39] R. M. Green, *Religious Reason. The Rational and Moral Basis of Religious Belief*, New York 1978, 14ff.

tionality will be narrow or broad depending on whether we expect those arguments to conform to the requirements of proof,[40] of strict probability[41] or of the nature of a cumulative case.[42] In the second or practical sense it is not the belief, but the believer's believing which is rational because she or he has good grounds, or does not need any grounds for holding this belief.[43] But (practical) grounds for believing are not necessarily (theoretical) reasons for a belief. A person may not be able to justify her belief that God exists, yet be reasonable in believing it. We can share this belief and yet differ widely or even irreconcilably in our grounds for believing it, as is the case with Christians, Jews, and Moslems. We need not deny reasonableness to their believing just because what they offer as grounds is not acceptable to all of us in the same way, for rationality is not primarily a quality of the belief in question but of how the belief is held.[44] A belief is rational if it is held rationally; it is held rationally if we have reasons to believe it; and one, though by no means the sole, kind of reason to believe it is the justification of the belief.

Seventh, if the rationality of a belief depends on the reasonableness of our believing it, it will vary according to the kinds of reason we have for believing it; and if, as is often claimed, we can believe something on internal and/or external grounds, we have to distinguish between internal and external rationality. This distinction is as easy to state, as it is difficult to explain; so it needs to be elucidated.

The distinction between external and internal rationality is grounded in the awareness of the diversity of scientific, moral, religious, political, and other kinds of beliefs and the corresponding diversity of criteria for rationality. Scientific beliefs, for example, are held rationally if they are held tentatively and in proportion to the evidence available. Religious beliefs, on the contrary, are not tentative, but unconditional. Believers do not hold their beliefs with a conviction proportionate to

---

[40] Cf. G. Mavrodes, *Belief in God. A Study in the Epistemology of Religion*, New York 1970, 22ff; T. Penelhum, *Problems of Religious Knowledge*, London 1971, 21ff; Dalferth, *Religiöse Rede*, 520ff.

[41] R. Swinburne, *The Existence of God*, Oxford 1979; J. L. Mackie, *The Miracle of Theism. Arguments for and Against the Existence of God*, Oxford 1982.

[42] B. Mitchell, *The Justification of Religious Belief*, London 1973.

[43] Mavrodes, *Belief in God*, 11ff; ›Rationality and Religious Belief – a Perverse Question‹, in: C. F. Delany (ed.), *Rationality and Religious Belief*, Notre Dame, Ind./London 1979, 40f.

[44] J. Kellenberger, *The Cognitivity of Religion. Three Perspectives*, Berkeley/Los Angeles 1985, 21ff.

evidence, as one hopes is the case with scientific beliefs. Their beliefs are neither probable nor well founded in a scientific sense. For not even their indubitability – as Wittgenstein put it[45] – would be enough in this case because it »wouldn't be enough to make me change my whole life«[46]. Wittgenstein concluded from this observation that religious beliefs are neither reasonable nor unreasonable; they are not the kind of belief to which reasonableness would apply.

Wittgenstein's conclusion, obviously, is too strong. All he can reasonably claim to have shown is that scientific reasonableness does not apply; but it is not clear that this is the only sort of reasonableness. P. Winch,[47] D. Z. Phillips,[48] and others[49] have therefore modified Wittgenstein's view. For them, religious and other kinds of beliefs can indeed be rational or irrational; but the criteria of rationality by which we draw this distinction are embedded in the way of life to which the belief in question belongs. »Religious believers, when asked why they believe in God, may reply in a variety of ways. They may say, ›I have had an experience of the living God‹, ›I believe on the Lord Jesus Christ‹, ›God saved me while I was a sinner‹, or, ›I just can't help believing‹. Philosophers have not given such reasons very much attention. The so-called trouble is not so much with the content of the replies, as with the fact that the replies are made by believers. The answers come from within religion, they presuppose the framework of Faith, and therefore cannot be treated as evidence for religious belief«[50]. That is to say, religious beliefs are rational or irrational in a sense internal to religion or religious life and not according to some objective norm taken from some other doxastic practice; and in order to find out how this distinction operates in a given case we have to pay heed to actual religious practice.

The upshot of this line of argument is that the question of rationality takes on two different forms. On the one hand, there is the question of

---

[45] L. Wittgenstein, *Lectures and Conversations on Aesthetics, Psychology and Religious Belief*, ed. C. Barrett, Oxford 1970, 55ff.

[46] Ibid., 57.

[47] P. Winch, *The Idea of a Social Science and its Relation to Philosophy*, London 1958; ›Understanding a Primitive Society‹, in: D. Z. Phillips (ed.), *Religion and Understanding*, Oxford 1967, 9-42.

[48] D. Z. Phillips, *Faith and Philosophical Enquiry*, London 1970; *Religion without Explanation*, Oxford 1976.

[49] Cf. Stenmark, *Rationality in Science, Religion, and Everyday Life*; C. O. Schrag, *The Resources of Rationality: A Response to the Postmodern Challenge*, Bloomington, Indiana 1992.

[50] Phillips, *Faith and Philosophical Enquiry*, 63.

the rationality or irrationality of a given belief, which has to be decided according to the criteria internal to the way of life to which it belongs. Unless there are strong overriding reasons to the contrary, as W. P. Alston and others have argued[51], religious beliefs are to be justified in their own terms, i.e., in terms of the religious doxastic practice in question and not some other practice. »Our beliefs are rational unless we have reasons for refraining; they are not nonrational unless we have reasons *for* believing«.[52] We are ›innocent until proved guilty‹, as long as our beliefs accord with the communal convictions of a given religious doxastic practice. On the other hand, there is the question of the rationality or irrationality of this whole way of life, including its doxastic practice. For some Wittgensteinians, questions of this sort are illegitimate because all we have are internal criteria, which can be described and expounded in their own terms but not justified in terms of any external criteria taken from other contexts of life, belief, and practice.

This is not to deny that some modes of life have rightly been rejected as irrational.[53] But the distinction between the rational and the irrational is always drawn in terms of criteria internal to a form of life or doxastic practice. If beliefs in trolls are rejected as irrational, then that occurs within, say, a scientific or a Christian practice; and this rejection is perfectly rational as long as we have reasons to assume that the scientific or Christian criteria of rationality are relevant to the beliefs in question. Thus in order to reject a whole practice or form of life, we do not need a specific (objective) set of more fundamental external criteria of rationality by which we assess not only particular beliefs but whole modes of life. All we need are reasons for believing those beliefs to fall into the province of science or the Christian faith, i.e., some second order beliefs about the kind and type of belief in question.

Now it is an essential aspect of our cognitive structure as free and rational agents to have second order beliefs of this sort, and continuously to strive after better ones. The world surrounding us is so complex, and the information accessible to us so manifold, that we have to reduce its complexity and select the information important for us if we

---

[51] W. P. Alston, *Perceiving God. The Epistemology of Religious Experience*, Ithaca, N.Y./London 1991.
[52] N. Wolterstorff, ›Can Belief in God be Rational If It Has No Foundations?‹, in: A. Plantinga/N. Wolterstorff (eds.), *Faith and Rationality. Reason and Belief in God*, Notre Dame, Indiana 1983, 135–186, 163.
[53] Kellenberger, *The Cognitivity of Religion*, 13. Cf. K. Nielsen, ›Wittgensteinian Fideism‹, *Philosophy* 42, 1967, 191–209, 207.

want to survive and act within it. This we do by developing perspectives on the world that select some information and ignore others. We then integrate the information selected into cognitive models of the world that are less complex than the world and precisely for this reason capable of providing orientation and guidance for our actions. This is done in not just one but a multitude of not necessarily homogeneous ways so that we exist simultaneously in a variety of different worlds.

In order to avoid existential schizophrenia, we develop second-order beliefs that enable us rationally to select information, build and relate cognitive models, and choose courses of actions. We distinguish forms of life from each other, identify their distinctive problems, and specify the criteria of rationality valid within them. But this process of compartmentalizing rationality does not stop our various modes of life from forming a network of mutually interdependent beliefs and practices, at least in those areas of our life and culture where coherence and consistency are necessary for survival. We apply our criteria across contextual boundaries if we consider them to be relevant to the problem at stake. We evaluate the internal criteria in the various contexts in the light of what for us are the more basic norms. And we take these norms from those forms of life which we accept as central to our view of the world and our understanding of our place in it because they involve our entire personalities.

Thus to reject the idea of external criteria beyond such formal requirements as consistency, which are generally applicable to all forms of life, and to accept the relativity of rationality is not necessarily to fall into the trap of an amorphous pluralism and relativism according to which anything goes. Rationality is not tied to one form of life or one doxastic practice only, but neither are our practices isolated from each other, nor is every form of life as central to our individual and common way of life as any other.

It follows that the distinction between internal and external rationality is ambiguous, and the whole debate consequently confused, because to believe something on internal grounds can mean a number of different things, not all of which are equally acceptable. At least three cases are to be distinguished. A believer may hold his or her belief on grounds that are part of the very belief in question;[54] or on grounds which are part of the same system of beliefs or forms of life; or on

---

[54] H. E. Root, ›Beginning All Over Again‹, in: A. R. Vidler (ed.), *Soundings. Essays Concerning Christian Understanding*, Cambridge 1962, 13.

grounds which are part of the same believer's system of belief or »noetic structure«.[55] The first case is not a case of rational belief at all because it blurs the vital distinction between a belief and the reasons for a belief. If belief in Christ were the only ground for belief in Christ, it would be an arbitrary, irrational, even trivial belief. This is not so in the second case. It is perfectly rational to accept a belief on the basis of other beliefs that belong to the same practice. Christians characteristically believe in the resurrection of the dead on the basis of their belief in the resurrection of Christ, and there is nothing irrational about this way of grounding their belief in the resurrection. Similarly in the third case, if a belief is supported by the beliefs that form the foundation of one's system of beliefs, it is rational (Alvin Plantinga).[56] But foundational structures of belief-systems, for all their structural similarities, can and do differ from person to person. If belief in God is basic to my system of beliefs, it can provide grounds for my believing in the resurrection of Christ and for my believing that the sun will rise tomorrow. But this will not be the case for one who does not believe in God; whereas he or she may have other reasons for believing in tomorrow's sunrise, this is most likely not so for the resurrection of Christ. Consequently, what is rational for me is not necessarily so for somebody else,[57] but if it were, it might be for different reasons. That is to say, rationality is relative, not only to a particular system of beliefs and practices, but also to a particular person; and the two kinds of rationality do not necessarily coincide.

Thus claims to believe something on internal grounds may refer to the criteria of rationality operative within the form of life to which the belief in question belongs, and this is how such claims are usually understood by Neo-Wittgensteinians. But these claims may also refer to the criteria of rationality operative within the complex system of beliefs and practices of a particular person, and this is something quite different. The difference is that in the first case it is a form of life; in the second, a particular person has basic beliefs that may be adduced as grounds or evidence for other beliefs. But whereas a form of life comprises a relatively homogeneous set of beliefs so that basic beliefs in a

---

[55] A. Plantinga, ›Is Belief in God Rational?‹, in: Delany, *Rationality and Religious Belief*, 12f.

[56] Plantinga, ›Is Belief in God Rational?‹; ›Is Belief in God Properly Basic?‹, *Nous* 15, 1981, 41–51; *Warranted Christian Belief*, New York/Oxford 2000, chaps. 8–10; cf. G. Gutting, *Religious Belief and Religious Scepticism*, Indianapolis 1982, 79–82.

[57] Kellenberger, *The Cognitivity of Religion*, 102f.

system are not of a completely different kind from the other beliefs of the system, this is not so with persons who exist in a plurality of diverse forms of life. A person may, on the basis of his or her beliefs or noetic structure, have grounds for the belief in the resurrection that are not part of, or even at odds with, those acceptable in standard Christian forms of life. So what seems to be an external ground from a Christian perspective can be an internal ground from the personal perspective, and vice versa. Consequently, the internal rationality of a system of beliefs is not to be confused with the internal rationality of a believer's system.

In short, there are many forms of rationality, for human life and reasoning does not constitute a monolithic activity.[58] All forms of rationality are relative to reasoning both in contexts of beliefs and practices and in contexts of personal appropriation of beliefs and practices. Yet there is no reasoning without reasons, concepts, and patterns of inference and therefore some rudimentary form of rationality; and rationality begins to flourish in an atmosphere of argument and discussion in which we learn to communicate and critically evaluate, not only our beliefs, but also our reasons for and against our beliefs.

This procedural, argumentative form of rationality is not the only form of reason and reasonableness, as we have seen. But it is basic to all rational activities, including religion and theology. Religions are not more or less obvious failures to conform to the standards of public, neutral, and universal reason, as the paradigm of rational religion would have it. They are better understood as »*localized rationalities,* i.e., ... largely coherent instances of group-specific reasoning«[59]. Theologians – unless they are very bad theologians – do not revel in pronouncing mystery and paradox, nor do they set out to construct systems of ultimate truths. What they are trying to do is to solve problems that arise within the perspectives of a given religious practice by argument and reasons.

In this weak but significant sense, many religious traditions are rational. They comprise rational strands, which present reasoned beliefs, not non-debatable dogmas for the faithful to believe and the godless to ignore, which proceed by argument and which seek to convince by reasons. But their style of argument is context-sensitive and resembles

---

[58] Cf. N. Rescher, *Rationality: A Philosophical Inquiry into the Nature and the Rationale of Reason,* Oxford 1988; *Pluralism: Against the Demand of Consensus,* Oxford 1993.

[59] Clayton, ›Common Ground and Defensible Difference‹, 113.

the arguments of legal and rhetorical debates more closely than the mathematical-deductive or experimental-inductive types of reasoning idealized in the Enlightenment paradigm of public, neutral, and universal reason.[60] The proper task of philosophy of religion, therefore, is not to lay the epistemological foundations of rational religion according to the Enlightenment paradigm, but to explore and elucidate the reasonableness of actual religions and religious traditions. This task would involve attention to »the practical operations of reason in specific contexts«,[61] and »entail a shift from focusing on reasons as grounds to focusing instead on reasons as motives and reasons as goals«[62]. The result would be, not a rational religion, but a deeper insight into the rational working of actual religions.

5. The Myth of the Sense of the Whole

The strategy of privatising differences and maximizing common ground fails not only for its neglect of the dynamics of faith and its narrow and abstract understanding of rationality and reason. It also follows a misleading paradigm in explaining the cultural role of religion. Persons and peoples, William Dean has argued, need a »sense of the whole«, i.e., »a sense that binds together and gives relevance to the parts of a person's internal and external worlds«[63]. Without such a sense of the whole, particular communities and societies are said to lose their social cohesiveness. If historical religions do not provide this sense, or provide it only insufficiently, it is the task of »religious critics« to design a rational religious alternative by exploring the spiritual culture that »inform[s] and mold[s] a society's deepest purposes«[64] and by rationally reconstructing it »in order to morally improve the whole«[65].

However, the very idea of a »sense of the whole« which is meant to overcome the cultural and religious fragmentation of our societies, is a perfect example of this fragmentation. If such a sense exists at all, it exists only in the plural. The quest for a sense of the whole reflects the increasing uneasiness with our modern society and culture perceived as imbued with individualism. But individualism is an offspring of individualization that, as one of the most decisive traits of secularisa-

---

[60] Ibid., 114.
[61] Ibid., 113.
[62] Ibid., 105.
[63] W. Dean, *The Religious Critic in American Culture*, New York 1994, IX.
[64] Ibid., XIV.
[65] Ibid., 146.

tion, is widely seen to imply the privatisation of religion and to render religion, whether of the traditional type or secular manifestations of civil religion, publicly and politically irrelevant. Even those who agree that social consensus is a prerequisite for a stable society differ widely as to how comprehensive and widely shared such a consensus has to be, whether it must include a common sense of the whole as the main source of social cohesion, and whether it can do so in the form of a religion in our secularised societies. But whatever answers may be given, if individualization is a fundamental trait of our culture, it is misleading to hope for a single common sense of the whole that binds together and gives relevance to all our individual lives in the same or a similar way. Fragmentation is not only characteristic of our societies, but also of the sense of the whole, which some propose as the cure of our social ills.

We live in a shrinking world in which different peoples, traditions, and cultures are increasingly brought together into common space. However, contrary to what some may have expected, the globalisation of the world has not produced a common sense of the whole but rather »a twofold dialectic« as A. Min has pointed out; »the dialectic of *differentiation*, in which we are made increasingly aware of differences in nationality, culture, religion, ethnicity, gender, class, language; and the dialectic of *interdependence*, in which we are compelled to find a way of living together despite our differences.«[66] The dynamics of differentiation and the fact of interdependence cannot be played off against each other. We have no alternative to living together – *with* our differences, not by ignoring or denying them. The challenge is to transform the »antithetical dialectic of simultaneous differentiation and interdependence« into a life of solidarity, but the solidarity needed is a »solidarity of others, the mutual solidarity of those who are different«,[67] not one that is based on common convictions, norms and values or a common sense of the whole.

This is not to deny that we all live against a background of what we take for granted and what goes without saying. But we do not and need not share our habits of viewing and interpreting the world in every detail or most respects. Indeed, we cannot share it completely because, in a very important respect, it remains inaccessible even to us. We can never wholly illumine, completely explore, or consistently ex-

---

[66] A. Min, *The Solidarity of Others in a Divided World. A Postmodern Theology after Postmodernism,* New York 2004, 1.
[67] Ibid.

press in all its details the background meaning of our life and culture that governs our ways of living. It is a complex, historically grown body of social meaning, which comprises layers upon layers of, in many respects, inconsistent beliefs, attitudes, hopes, and desires. As historical beings we cannot transcend this complex body of meaning and analyse it from without (at least not in principle and in every respect), but only critically examine it from within. Our entire individual acts of living draw their meaning from such a comprehensive social background of meaning, which is the creative source of the dynamic unity of our culture. Every living culture exists with an open horizon of meaning; it is continually integrating a changing variety of beliefs, traditions, and world-views; and it seeks to establish a (relative) unity by excluding, negating, or isolating some views and not others, by privileging particular views instead of others, or by balancing different views against each other. Thus every culture is pregnant with other cultures, and every given state of culture is in transition to a variety of possible other states.

What is the role of religion in this dynamic cultural process? Answers differ widely. Liberals who see religions primarily as sources of conflict and as potential threats to social cohesion insist on a merely private role of religious beliefs: in the public realm citizens should be committed to relying not on inaccessible religious convictions but on common, non-religious sources of guidance. Communitarians, on the other hand, who diagnose the decline of social commonalities as the cause of many social ills, look to the revitalization of religion to provide the sense of the whole, which people need to unite in a more cohesive society. Without ›a unified view of the world derived from a consciously integrated and meaningful attitude toward life‹[68], they think societies are unfit to overcome the disintegrating forces of cultural and religious diversity. And they look upon churches as paradigms for local communities that transmit shared values and common goals and nurture the sensitivity of their members for supraindividual obligations, duties, and goals. Thus both liberals and communitarians agree in reacting to the growing individualism and pluralism of our societies by seeking to *privatize difference* and *maximize common ground*. But they draw different conclusions from this agreement with respect to religion. Whereas the one seeks to privatize religion, the other seeks

---

[68] Cf. M. Weber, *Wirtschaft und Gesellschaft. Grundriss der verstehenden Soziologie*, Tübingen [5]1972, 275.

to strengthen its public role as providing the comprehensive background without which no common life can be cultivated in a society.

However, communities do not depend on a common sense of the whole, and religion does not provide it. To expect this role of religion is to seek a wrong solution to a misconceived problem. Communities that are religiously and culturally diverse do not need a common sense of the whole but rather legal, political, and juridical institutions that do not depend for their functioning on any particular view of life. The communitarian view, therefore, cannot mean a return to pre-modern societies with uniform religions nor a revival of the modern attempt to create a rational religion common to all, which has only furthered the departure from all religion by many. Commonalities whether religious or not are never neutral, free of all interests and accessible to everyone in the same way. They are bound up with particular perspectives in which they are identified, described, lived and defended, and the rules that regulate access to them reflect these local perspectives. There is never just one sense of the whole, whether religious or non-religious, and the sense is rarely exactly the same for different persons. Dewey's claim that »within the flickering inconsequential acts of separate selves dwells a sense of the whole which claims and dignifies them«[69], is wrong if taken to suggest a *common* sense of the whole which all individuals share. It is, if anything, a *different* sense of the whole that »dignifies« the acts of each individual, and neither logic nor the needs of social life allow us to conclude from the fact (if it is one) that everybody has some sense of the whole that there is a sense of the whole which all have in common. A *common* (to say nothing of *the same*) sense of the whole for different individuals even within a relatively homogeneous society is the exception, not the rule: All we can usually find are patches of overlapping consensus due to common interests, common needs, or a common history. And this is all we need. The social consensus needed to produce a stable and well-ordered society is neither monolithic nor homogeneous nor free of tradition nor all-encompassing. This consensus is a complex network of overlapping differences, similarities, and commonalities, which are continuously being merged in an ongoing tradition and are rational only insofar as they can be defended in terms of a commitment to respect persons and to make one's own opinions accessible to the criticism of others.

---

[69] J. Dewey, *Human Nature and Conduct, Middle Works vol. 14*, Carbondale/Edwardsville 1983, 227.

All this is also true of religions. They do not express a common sense of the whole in different ways but different senses of different wholes. In our societies there exist a variety of comprehensive perspectives of fragmented religions, a plurality of religious and non-religious perspectives, and a plurality of senses of the whole. Just as religions cannot be privatized in all respects, so they cannot be generalized to provide *the* common sense of the whole. On the contrary, as John Rawls has convincingly argued, the diversity of comprehensive (religious and non-religious) views is a »permanent feature of the public culture of democracy«[70]. But then the primary task in dealing with religious diversity is not to identify what is (or should be) common to all but to clarify distinctive differences among religions in order to make these accessible to public debate, criticism, change and correction. »*Clarification of defensible difference, not identification of ›common ground‹ may be what is required to gain the co-operation of disparate religious interests in achieving pragmatically defined goals*«, as John Clayton has put it.[71] This approach would require philosophers to engage critically with the particularities of given historical religions. For what is needed in coping with the dangers of religious diversity is not a rational religion that replaces particular historical religions but an attempt *to rationalize historical religions from within* by clarifying their defensible differences in public debate. What is defensible cannot be decided in advance but will only show in the actual process of making both these differences and their grounds publicly accessible and debatable: Some of these may turn out to be unacceptable to all or most of us for a variety of reasons. Some may be acceptable to some but not be live options for others. And some may turn out to be of much wider interest and relevance than we had expected. Clarifying defensible differences in public debate, therefore, is a means of improving both one's own religious tradition and one's understanding of others. And knowing in which respect one is different, and why, and how others react to it, and why, is a prerequisite for peacefully co-existing in religiously and culturally diverse societies. What we need are not common religious convictions but agreement on public procedures of debate, defence, contest, and decision-making that enable people with different interests, moral codes, and views of the good life to live together without using physical force or mental mobbing to sort out their differences.

---

[70] J. Rawls, ›The Domain of the Political and Overlapping Consensus‹, *New York University Law Review* 64, 1989, 233-255, 234.
[71] Clayton, ›Common Ground and Defensible Difference‹, 105.

Our societies comprise an increasing number of citizens who lack a common religious background and history, who participate in a growing variety of religious practices or in none. This fact by itself is no reason to worry about imminent culture wars or global clashes of civilizations. But to contain the potentially destructive effects of religious and a-religious diversity, we must learn to appreciate, not merely what we hold in common, but what makes us differ, and perhaps irreconcilably so.

Tolerance is the cement of our societies. But the crucial respect is for persons, not beliefs, codes, or practices. We must find out what constitutes the irrevocable otherness of the other, i.e., his or her religious or a-religious identity, and in the last resort, this otherness is to be found, not in what we share, but in what distinguishes us. It is precisely because tolerance is respect for persons and not for views that the condescending tolerance of the 18th century has been replaced in liberal democracies by fundamental *rights*, the rights of religious liberty, of freedom of speech and opinion, of the free exercise of religion. We have a *right* to be different, and the right to exercise these fundamental rights of liberty must not be made dependent on accepting a common view of life or sense of the whole in a given society.

The promising route to take in dealing with religious diversity, therefore, is to make publicly accessible what lies at the heart of religious convictions and traditions and to construct rules and rights[72] to deal with problems provoked by those differences without expecting these rules to lead to global consensus or a common view of life. After all, common convictions are no guarantee against conflict. On the contrary, even where there is a lot in common (such as in the Christian churches), it is often precisely what is shared in common which is the basis of conflict. Here as elsewhere it is not *what is believed* but *the way it is believed* which decides on the rationality of these beliefs and the defensibility of the corresponding moral codes and ways of life. But there is no valid reason why all rational beliefs and defensible views should have to be part of the same more encompassing whole. The fact that everybody loves somebody does not imply that there is someone whom everyone loves or that the person I love must be loved by all, or for reasons acceptable to all others, if my love is to be defensible. And as with love, so it is with religious belief. Different religious beliefs may be reasonable for different persons for different reasons

---

[72] »Human rights are historical constructions, not natural kinds«, as John Clayton rightly points out (ibid., 123).

without being part of some larger whole. This admission is not to give in to relativism. Just as there are no beliefs that are not beliefs of some-one, so there are no reasons that are not reasons for someone. But there are well-grounded beliefs that are false (scientific beliefs), there are ill-grounded beliefs that are true, and there are incompatible beliefs that are well-grounded for different persons, although one of them must, or all of them may, be false. Yet the problem is not merely one of the compatibility or incompatibility of beliefs. Religious beliefs are inti-mately bound up with ways of life and practices, and just as one cannot love everyone at once in the same way, so a person cannot se-riously engage in a plurality of religious activities at the same time. What is at stake here is not the logical incompatibility of opposing re-ligious beliefs, but the factual impossibility of living more than one life at once. We have to choose, we cannot choose not to choose, we cannot be made to choose all in the same way, and in most cases, we do not and cannot know in advance whether what we chose, or find ourselves to have chosen, will turn out to be right.

6. Wholes and Horizons

This is why we must depart from the model employed by William Dean and others to explain the cultural role of religion. Religions, as interpretative frameworks, are tied up with particular ways of life and practice. They are not merely systems of belief, but practical attitudes towards life that are best understood, not in terms of *parts and wholes,* but of *perspectives and horizons.* To perceive or to place something in a horizon is quite different from integrating it as a part into a whole. What does this change of metaphor amount to?

The existence of a whole such as this house may include its roof and its walls as its parts, as Husserl has argued.[73] But this type of analysis which conceives a whole as a large object made up of smaller objects as its parts is of little use when talking about cognitive phenomena such as experiences or social phenomena such as religions. Experi-ences are not objects, and religions are neither wholes that include be-liefs as their isolable parts, nor are they themselves self-subsistent parts of larger wholes such as societies or cultures. The same object may be-long to different wholes, albeit under different descriptions. But all de-scriptions are relative to perspectives, and perspectives are not objective

---

[73] E. Husserl, *Logical Investigations,* transl. by J. N. Findlay, 2 vol., London 1970, vol. 2, 458.

wholes but cognitive frames in which we identify objects and construct wholes. When we perceive an object in a perceptual horizon,
we do not integrate it into a whole but place it in a perspective which
allows us to determine the object in a particular way and to continue
this process of determination in an open series of acts. The object does
not thereby become a part of this horizon, and the same is true when
we describe social entities such as religions. Neither our account of the
whole in question nor our description of its parts is independent of the
perspective in which we describe it, and perspectives are not only relative to points of view, but have horizons which determine what we
can see and say of an object.

Now although a horizon limits a perspective, it is not for this reason
a limited horizon. Just because a horizon limits a perspective, it allows
us to determine what we see in a particular way. But this does not
make it a limited horizon. On the contrary, it allows us to continue
the process of determination in an open-ended series of acts of determination. Horizons can be changed, enlarged, or narrowed down and
thus change our view of the phenomenon in question. But a horizon
is not a whole, and phenomena in a horizon are not parts of a whole.
The external relations of an object, such as a house to its surroundings,
can be »bracketed«, to use phenomenological jargon, and the same is
true of the part-whole-relation of, say, the roof to the house if we
want to concentrate on the roof only. But we cannot bracket the horizon of a phenomenon without losing it altogether. Phenomena are *necessarily phenomena-in-a-horizon*, and experiences essentially *experiences-
in-a-horizon*: one cannot have the one without the other. Horizons,
however, are intrinsic to activities, practices, or ways of life. They are
not independent entities but are constitutive of particular life-worlds,
and hence can be identified and described only relative to the standpoint, perspective, and life-world to which they belong.

Apply all this to religions and one can see why religions can never
give us just one common sense of the whole. To expect this of religions is to expect something impossible of them. But we are only misled to do so by consensus thinkers who believe that social consensus is
needed to produce a stable society, and that ultimately only religion
can provide a genuine foundation for stability. Of course, these thinkers are not blind to the plurality of world-views, conceptions of the
good, and conflicts of interests that exist in modern societies. But, in
their approach, plurality has to be kept within certain bounds; diversity, as a potential threat to social cohesion, has to be managed carefully;

and religion can be used to achieve cohesion if the conflicts of religious sects are replaced by a rational religion common to all.

But this strategy turns religion into an ideology that not only fails as a cure, but also seeks to cure something which is not an illness. Social consensus, as Niklas Luhmann and others have shown[74], is not needed to achieve and maintain order and stability in a society.[75] And the Christian faith, in some of its most important strands, at any rate, has always been a critical and sometimes even destructive force that questioned given social consensus in the light of the greater justice, freedom, and love hoped for in the eschatological kingdom of God. Thus for both sociological and religious reasons we should not look for a *sense of the whole* with its implicit striving for the general and common but foster a *sense of the presence of God* that critically grounds diversity and helps to see difference as something which social consensus must, in important respects, safeguard rather than overcome.

All this, no doubt, raises new problems some of which I shall address in the following chapters. But to design a rational religion that is meant to provide a common sense of the whole for our societies is to offer a wrong solution to a false problem. The stability of culturally and religiously diverse societies does not depend on a common ideology but on legal, political, and juridical institutions that function independently of any particular religion, world-view, or ideology. And the dangers of religious diversity are not overcome by a rational Esperanto-religion but by sorting out the acceptable from the unacceptable within each religious tradition in public debate.

This requires public debate to concentrate on the specific particularities of religions traditions in order not to discuss mere chimeras of its own inventing. In order to understand and critically discuss religious views, convictions, and their implications we have to start from within

---

[74] Cf. Rescher, *Pluralism*, and J. S. Mill, *On Liberty*, London 1859, who criticised the insisting on social consensus to be a major cause of collective mediocrity and a serious impediment of the development of free and autonomous life of individuals.

[75] This is to deny that *if* consensus can be achieved on some fundamental matters, that will contribute to social coherence and stability. Even if agreement on essentials is not necessary to maintain a stable society, it may be desirable. Besides, it is one thing to argue from the example of societies with a fairly homogeneous background and history, quite another to speak about societies such as the USA which are very diverse. But in either case what is needed is a workable political and juridical system, which allows people with different comprehensive views to co-exist peacefully and to solve social, political, and economical problems in peaceful and legally acceptable ways.

the religious practice and perspective which we seek to scrutinize. For without paying close attention to the historicity and particularity of religious life, views and convictions, public debates about religions will miss their point.

7. The Sense of the Presence of God

The practice and tradition that will be explored in the following is the *Christian faith*, and my focus will be on *its sense of the presence of God*.

It should be clear from what has been said so far that there is no Christian faith in the singular. It is a living faith, and every living faith is not only one among many other faiths, religions, world-views or life practices but also exists only as a plurality of views, understandings and interpretations of itself and its world embedded in specific practices. As a living faith the practices, beliefs, forms and institutions of the Christian faith vary considerably with the contexts and cultures in which it is lived, and they take on a different character with the emphasis they give to specific aspects in distinguishing themselves from other practices, beliefs, forms and institutions in a given culture. Just as Christian faith is only one in a plurality of faiths,[76] so it exists only as a plurality of ›interpretations‹ embedded in practices that differ considerably from place to place and through time and history.[77] Thus to unfold the Christian faith in a Christian perspective in order to make its views and convictions accessible to public debate necessarily means to unfold a particular view of the Christian faith in a Christian perspective under-

---

[76] It should be noted that talking of faiths in the plural and describing Christian faith as one faith among many is using the term in a descriptive sense and not in the normative sense in which ›faith‹ is ›faith in God‹, and ›God‹ no other than the ›God disclosed in and through Christ‹. In this normative or (Christian) theological sense faith in God is unique in that it is faith in the one and only God who is the ›object‹ of faith just because he is trusted to be the sole ›ground and creator‹ of faith: Christians put their faith in God because God is the one who makes them put their faith in God who is the one who …; and they have tentatively worked this out in the doctrine of the trinity which conceives God to be the one in whom we can only have faith because God discloses himself to us as God (in Christ) and makes us see and accept this disclosure to be trustworthy and true (through the Spirit) so that we can live our life *in faith*, i. e. by trusting God's infinite loving interest in each and everyone of us. But if faith in God is understood in this way, then this allows for no plurality if ›God‹ is not to be pluralized into gods none of which is the one and only God who is worthy of worship.

[77] Cf. I. U. Dalferth, *Evangelische Theologie als Interpretationspraxis. Eine systematische Orientierung*, Leipzig 2004, 53ff.77ff.

stood in a particular way – hopefully a possible one, but hardly the only possible one, and hopefully one that is convincing, or at least less unconvincing than others. But just as I shall argue from within a Christian perspective in exploring the Christian sense of the presence of God, so I shall argue within my perspective on the Christian perspective. If I fail to convince, then shortcomings of my view of the Christian faith are not to be mistaken for shortcomings of the Christian faith. There is always room and, indeed, need for better arguments.

It should also be clear from the outset that *the Christian sense of the presence of God* on which I shall focus also does not come in the singular but only in the plural, and this for a variety of reasons. As a *sense of* the presence of God or, more vaguely, as a sense of divine presence, it is the sense of individual persons and particular religious communities and it shows in the specific ways in which they orient and live their lives. And as a sense of the presence of *God* it is tied to particular religious traditions and practices in which the divine is understood as *God,* and God is understood and worshiped in particular ways. Even where it is claimed that this sense is common to all human beings in one way or other, this claim is made from within a particular religious practice and tradition and it can be understood, assessed and evaluated in its force only by taking the perspective and convictions of this practice and tradition into account. The sense of the presence of God is always a *specific* sense of divine presence or, in the so-called monotheistic religions, a *Jewish* or *Christian* or *Moslem* sense of the presence of God; and since each of these religious traditions is itself pluriform, even the *Christian* sense of the presence of God comes in more than one way. Just as there is not *the* sense of the presence of God, so there is not *the* Christian sense of the presence of God.

However, in all its varieties the Christian sense of the presence of God *individualizes*, i.e. transforms particular human beings into individual persons. When it dawns upon me that I live in the present, and can become present to my present, because God becomes present to me, I begin to realise my infinite dignity and uniqueness of being singled out by God. God becomes present *to me* as *my God* or *God for me* and places me as his singled-out creature in the presence of my creator. This marks me off from my physical, communal and personal environments but also relates me to them as one who is meant to live his life in this world in the presence of God. To God's becoming present I owe (1) my presence in this world (my existence rather than non-existence), i.e. the fact of being and the possibility of becoming present to others; (2) my life in this present (my life as a persons rather than something else), i.e. the possibility of relating to the present, the past and the future as a self; and (3) the occasion of becoming present in and to my present (living my life as present in the present), i.e. the possibility of not just being present to someone but, by becoming present to my being present to someone, experience my presence open to the presence of the other.[78]

This heightened or intensified sense of presence also occurs with the Christian sense of the presence of God. I become aware of God's presence by becoming aware of how God becomes present to my presence. I cannot do so without realising how the divine Other breaks into my life and fundamentally changes its direction and orientation by opening it up for possibilities which I didn't see or expect before. Thus my sense of the presence of God discloses the infinite importance given to my contingent individual human life *coram deo* for no reason whatsoever. This not only places me in a new perspective which opens up a new understanding of my life, myself and everything else but in doing so requires me to live differently and to sort out the acceptable from the unacceptable in the light of the presence of God in all areas of my life.

So the sense of the presence of God does not just leave everything as it is or accept just any diversity or difference as something to be welcomed. On the contrary, it originates with a very specific change in a life and it manifests itself in very specific changes of a life: The *Christian sense of the presence of God* is a *sense of the change of direction of a life in and through the presence of God*. It is the becoming aware of how God becomes present to a life by opening it up for the possible and the new in unexpected and unforeseeable ways. This awareness places a person in a new perspective in which everything is seen and judged in the light of the presence of God, including one's own seeing and judging it.

The sense of the presence of God, therefore, does not directly disclose a divine reality (as the Calvinist *sensus divinitatis* is sometimes mistakenly understood) but rather displaces or dislocates persons from their given ways of life and relates them in a new way to reality, to themselves, to others and to God by disclosing their whole life to be a

---

[78] It is one thing to be co-present with someone in the externalist sense of being together with him or her in the same situation, another to be open to the presence of the other in an internalist sense of being attentive to the presence of the other as a person. Cf. G. Marcel, *Geheimnis des Seins*, Wien 1952, 263ff.

life lived in the presence of God. In this way the sense of the presence of God is not an additional sense alongside our other senses but a becoming aware of a change of one's life in all its dimensions from a mode of life in which God's presence is ignored (non-faith) to a mode of life which no longer can continue to do so (faith). It is a sense that dislocates and reorients human lives in ways that are specific to each life in which they occur. It is always first and foremost *my* sense of the presence of God because it changes the direction of *my* life in a particular way. Whether and in which way it does or can become a common sense always remains to be seen.

II Real Presence

1. What we cannot choose

Christians once set out to spread the sense of the presence of God throughout the world. In our generation and in our part of the world they have noticeably failed. The prevailing climate of thought and of feeling in European culture is a vivid sense of the absence of God, and in one way or other, we all share in this.

Of course, we still speak of God. But too often we speak only to ourselves, and much of what we offer as grounds and evidence for our beliefs carries little conviction beyond our own circles. Yet God, if God is, bears no confinement. God is not the tribal deity of the Christians or of any other group or tradition. Belief in God is a public belief, not a sectarian creed. It cannot be true if there is no God to believe in, and it cannot be true for anybody if it is not – in principle and qualified in the appropriate way – true for everybody. If God is, as Christians believe God to be, then we are all involved with God, whether we know and accept it or not; and if we all live our lives in the real presence of God, as Christians believe we do, we should better not ignore this fundamental fact of our existence.

But is it a fact? Is there more to God than the words made about God? Words are signs, and signs do not transport presences. But without the experience of real presence belief in God can, in the final analysis, neither be attained nor be sustained. Belief in God involves a realist attitude to reality, and this is at odds with a widespread sentiment of post-modern romanticism. In a world in which the growing industry of illusions rapidly dissolves the stable stock of common primary experiences in terms of which we define and construe what we take to be real, it becomes virtually impossible meaningfully to distinguish between God and our views and imaginative constructions of God.

Besides, after a century of unheard of atrocities and horrors and a consequent disenchantment with the powers of reason and rationality, many have abandoned belief in God. Where the term ›God‹ is still used, it lingers on in their routines of discourse and inhabits their vocabulary as a vacant metaphor, a mere phantom of grammar, as Nietzsche diagnosed it so pointedly long ago. Yet even where ›God‹ is still taken to signify something, it is not something whose truth is independent of our opinions about it. Indeed, we have been so successful in blurring the distinction between *God* and our *views of God* that many think it quite natural to turn to the psychiatrist rather than to the theologian when they need expert advice on problems with God.

Theology has had its share in these developments. It generally agrees with the current methodological dogma that not God, but only the religious phenomena of human existence and history can be studied in a way that is rationally defensible and academically respectable. What goes beyond this is a matter of private convictions, individual desires and, perhaps, social needs, something to be explored by social scientists or William Dean's religious critics, but not by theologians.

But if Christian faith is right, this is wrong. There is nothing to refer to, or to talk about or to study, unless there is God; there is no use of language or any other religious or non-religious activity or experience unless God is present; and there is no proper subject matter for theology unless God's presence is and can be known. The business of theology is not to explain what makes people believe what they do but what makes their believing right or sensible; and whatever psychological or social function believing in God may fulfil, it is only right if there is a God to believe in, and only sensible if what is believed about God can be true. There is truth at stake when we explore the sense of God's presence, and the possibility of learning, or of seriously missing, a fundamental fact about reality. For whether we believe it or not – indeed, whether we have good reason to believe it or not – God exists or does not, is present to us or is not, is our creator or is not, is close to us or is not.

It is quite true that there is not just one true description of reality but a plethora of competitive and sometimes contradictory views and descriptions. But it does not follow that there is no reality to be described, or that what we describe is merely a product of our descriptions, or that we totally lack strategies to discriminate the real from the unreal, at least not in those areas of our life that are really important to us. Even the eclecticism of the signifying process is not devoid of establishing contingent orders on which we can rely, and even the unpredictability of chaos can be teased into revealing patterns which are not of our making. If God is real, something similar should also be expected here: There is truth that can be missed, and reality that is not of our making, whatever our needs, wishes and desires may be.

All this is not to deny that what we think about God in many ways depends on prior thought and tradition. We are all born into a world not of our inventing. But we differ from other creatures in that we cannot live in it without inventing it. Most of the basic co-ordinates within which we move and decide have not been drawn by us. This is not merely true of most of our physical surroundings but also of the societies in which we live and of the languages which we have learned and whose grammar dominates our speaking and thinking. We are born into a world not of our making. But we cannot live in it without making it. We are – in a phrase dear to Austin Farrer – ›made to make ourselves‹.

This is not something we can choose to do or not to do. We cannot choose not to choose. We cannot avoid making ourselves. We cannot choose not to create our world. Everything we do may have been done otherwise. But often *we* could not have done otherwise. We are bound to do something, and what we do is done under conditions, which leave not everything possible a real option for us. We have to choose from what is chosen for us, we have to select from the selected. A double contingency is governing our lives, and our thought.

However, *as long as we live, we cannot choose not to choose. We cannot choose, and not choose in the present. And if God is, we cannot choose in the present and not choose in the presence of God*: This, in a nutshell, is my argument. It is a trivial truth that we cannot live now without living in the present; and it is also true, though perhaps not trivial, that if God is, then we cannot live in the present without living in the presence of God. We need not to be conscious of either in order to live. But just as the first guides our life in that it tells us, e.g., that we should better not spend our energy, time and money on trying to act in the past and win the Napoleonic wars today, the second guides, or should guide, our lives in stopping us from trying to achieve complete control about our lives and conditions of living: We cannot choose our parents, we cannot control all the unintended consequences of our good (to say nothing of our bad) actions; and we cannot escape the fact, if it is a fact, that we live our lives in the presence of God.

It may be objected that whereas we can be directly and even infallibly aware of living in the present, this is not so with respect to our living in the presence of God. However, we do not have to be aware of living in the present in order for this to be the case. But as soon as we pay attention to the temporal aspects of our living, we cannot fail to find out that we posses the property of living in the present. Similarly, we do not have to be aware of living in the presence of God for this to be the case. But if God is and if it is not in principle impossible for us to become aware of this, then we should in principle be capable of

finding out that we posses the property of living in the presence of
God by paying attention to the theological aspects of our living.

In either case it is not a matter of inference. We do not infer that we
live in the present rather than in the past or future from specific features of our life but we couldn't live, experience or infer anything at all
if we wouldn't live in the present. Similarly, believers do not infer
God's presence from particular aspects of their lives but look on their
lives in all their aspects as lives lived in the presence of God. God's
presence is not a contingent fact in their life but in Collingwood's
sense[1] the absolute presupposition of their life. If God were not
present, we wouldn't live without God but not live at all; and if this is
true, it is true independent of whether we believe, deny, or ignore it.
The truth of God's presence does not depend on whether it is believed, denied, or ignored, but if it is true, believing, denying or ignoring it are only possible because it is true.

2. Becoming a Believer

This is not to deny that it makes a difference to a life whether I believe, deny, or ignore living in the presence of God. On the contrary, it
makes a fundamental difference. Believers differ from non-believers
not by disagreeing about a contingent fact but in the whole mode and
orientation of their lives. To become a believer is not to accept a further fact, or enlarge one's set of beliefs by adding some beliefs about
God which one had previously ignored or denied, but to place everything, including oneself, in a new perspective. It is a change of life
from a life in which God's presence is ignorantly or wilfully ignored to
a life that pays attention to and becomes informed by living in the
presence of God. It is not a particular aspect but the whole mode of
life that changes, and this affects everything we believe and do, feel and
experience, remember and hope.

Since the change at stake is a change not *in* our life but *of* our life
that affects the mode of everything which we are and do by placing us
in a new perspective and horizon of orientation, we cannot effect this
change by anything we do in our given perspective and mode of life.
Just as we cannot bring ourselves into existence by effecting a transition from possibility to actuality since we cannot do anything before
we actually exist, so we cannot change from a God-ignoring to a God-

---

[1] R.G. Collingwood, *An Essay on Metaphysics*, Oxford 1940, 31.

sensitive mode of life by anything we do as unbelievers. The analogy has often been noted. Becoming a believer is to be changed into a new mode of existence without being able to perform or effect this change by oneself as Kierkegaard's Climacus points out.[2] What changes is the *how* not the *what* of a human life; the *how* modifies the *that* (existence) not the *what* (essence) of human beings; and the two modes of existence at stake in the change from unbelief to belief are the *mode of sin* and the *mode of faith,* the mode of living in which we ignore God's presence (life of sinners) and the mode of living in which we become informed by and are made aware of God's presence (life of justified sinners).

The point being made is best understood against the background of Kant's insight that existence is a »logical« but not »a real predicate«.[3] That is to say, ›exists‹ occurs grammatically as a predicate in subject-predicate sentences of the type ›a exists‹ but it is not a real predicate that determines what a is. ›a is F‹ and ›a is F *and exists*‹ do not differ in that the second proposition states a further determining attribute of a but claims the predicate F to have an application, i.e. states that there exists an a such that a is F. The logical predicate ›exists‹ does not *determine* a (or our concept or ›thought‹ of a, as Kant puts it) but *posits a in reality*, i. e. (in Kant's view) in the totality of what can be experienced or (more generally) in the world in which we live and act. Thus if Peter is a sailor (F) then to say ›Peter is F *and exists*‹ is to state no further determination of Peter but to claim that this sailor actually exists in reality. But, according to Climacus, ›Peter is a (Christian) believer‹ is a token not of ›Peter is F‹ but of ›Peter exists‹: It does not tell us *what* Peter is (›Peter is F‹) nor simply *that* Peter exists (›Peter exists‹) but *how Peter exists* in reality, namely in such a way that he lives his human life as it should be lived *coram deo* (›Peter exists as a believer‹). Whereas propositions of the type ›a is F‹ must be coherent in order to signify something possible, propositions of the type ›a exists‹ claim that ›a‹ is not only a possible but an actual entity so that ›a is F‹ is not only a possible truth but actually true or false. They refer not merely to a coherent and com-possible set of predicates but to a transition from possibility to actuality. This change from non-existence to existence cannot be added as another determining predicate to the set of predicates that are claimed to be instantiated by a without reiterating the problem: If ›a

---

[2] Cf. I.U. Dalferth, ›Becoming a Christian according to the *Postscript*. Kierkegaard's Christian Hermeneutics of Existence‹ (forthcoming).

[3] *KrV,* AA II, 69ff (my translation).

exists‹ is understood as a token of ›a is F‹, then it is always meaningful
to ask whether a actually exists, i. e. whether ›a exists‹ is true.

The same is true of ›Peter is a believer‹: If it is understood in the
sense of ›a is F‹, it always makes sense to ask whether it is true, and it
can only be true or false if the predicate ›being a believer‹ is compatible
with all the other predicates truly applied to Peter. If, on the other
hand, it is understood as a token of ›Peter exists‹, it can only be true if
the change from not being to being a believer is not a case of enlarging
the set of predicates that determine Peter by a further one (i.e. ›is a believer‹) but of positing Peter and of claiming the whole set of Peter's
predicates to be instantiated in a particular way in reality. ›Peter is a believer‹ then refers to a becoming that cannot be an activity of Peter
since it is that which makes Peter actual in the first place.

Becoming a believer, therefore, is not a matter of acquiring a new
attribute or determination but of changing to a new mode of existence; and just as I cannot make myself exist *coram mundo* by my own
decision, so I cannot bring about my way of existing as believer *coram
deo* by my own decision. In everything I decide or do my existence is
presupposed, and in everything I decide or do as a believer, my existing as a believer is presupposed. Just as the change from ›Peter does not
exist‹ to ›Peter exists‹ cannot be effected by Peter, so the change from
›Peter is not a believer‹ to ›Peter is a believer‹ cannot either. These
changes make Peter but they are not of Peter's making.

There is, however, an important difference between the two kinds of
change in that the latter but not the former presupposes Peter's existence: Only if you exist, you can become a believer. But no one who
exists must become a believer, and no one who exists can become a
believer by anything he or she can do by himself or herself. Coming
into existence and changing my mode of existence *coram deo* are not
my own decisions or doings; but existing in time is a process that proceeds through my choices and decisions. As far as *my existence* is concerned, which is continuously actualised in time through choice and
decision, it is never without my deciding and doing (for otherwise I
wouldn't be *existing*); but as far as *the mode* of my existence is concerned, my way of existing can only be continued but not changed by
anything I decide and do for whatever I do is done in the mode in
which I actually exist and live. But if everything I do is done in my actual mode of existence, then it cannot be changed by anything I do
but, if at all, only by what is done to me.

Thus in order to become a believer one has to exist, and since for
human beings to exist is to live by choice and decision, nobody can

become a believer independent of his or her choosing and deciding. On the other hand, no choosing or deciding can make you a believer since becoming a believer is a case of change akin to the change from non-existence to existence rather than to that of acquiring a new attribute or determination. My existence and my mode of existing as a believer are not of my own making. Nothing of what I decide, choose or do makes me a believer. But even though I cannot become a believer by deciding to become one, I cannot become a believer without existing and living a life of choice and decision. And if what Christians believe is true, both what I do and become by what I do, and what I become by what is done to me, infallibly entails the presence of God.

However, if God's presence is entailed by any present fact, then it is entailed by every present fact. It is not a sequence of observed facts, or something that can be inferred from some but not all present facts. Yet it has observable consequences because it determines the beliefs, attitudes and actions to which Christians are committed. It would be incoherent, for example, to live a Christian life if I were to deny that there really is a God in whose presence I live; or that we are totally unable to apprehend this divine presence; or that God can in no way be known as he really is; or that God exists but unfortunately is not present. All this must be wrong if Christian faith is to be true whatever the experiential evidence for or against may be. For Christian faith is *faith in God*, faith in God is *faith in a living God*, and for God to be living God must be *present* and *active*.

But then – to draw out some implications of the Christian grammar of ›God‹ – it is *impossible for God to be and not to be present*, and *impossible to be present and not come to be present*: Divine presence is *divine activity here and now*. Thus if God *is* present, then God *becomes present*: God's presence is the presence of God's arrival or advent, the coming-into-present here and now.[4] But if God becomes present here and now, God comes-into-present *to someone*, and if God becomes present to us, we will be, in one way or other, ›affected‹ by it – either in the sense of being *effected* by God becoming present to us, that is, by coming into existence or by being created, or in the sense of being *affected* by it,

⁴ Cf. L.M. Chauvet, ›The Broken Bread as Theological Figure of Eucharistic Presence‹, in: L. Boeve/L. Leijssen (eds.), *Sacramental Presence in a Postmodern Context*, Leuven 2001, 236-262, 258. The idea of God's advent as God's coming or breaking into our life has been the guiding principle and insight of E. Jüngel's doctrine of God. Cf. *God as Mystery of the World. On the Foundation of the Theology of the Crucified One in the Dispute Between Theism and Atheism*, trans. by D.L. Guder, Edinburgh 1983.

that is, by being given the chance – contrary to all odds and to what seems to be possible or probable for us – to exist in a particular way or to be changed and change from a mode of life that ignores God's presence to a mode of life that is aware of it.[5]

The two cases are importantly different. Since we cannot become aware of anything unless we are, we can become aware of God's creative presence only by either tentatively exploring what seems to be presupposed by the contingent fact of our existence or by becoming aware of it in the coming into existence of others. This is why belief in God's presence based on our being ›*effected*‹ (or made) by it is always explorative, i.e. tentative, recursive and hypothetical. On the other hand, we cannot become aware of how God *affects others* because whatever change we observe does not show that it is due to God (unless we believe on independent grounds that whatever change occurs, it wouldn't without God being present). And we do not become aware of how God *affects us* unless we experience this as the change of our mode of existing from living a life of unfaith (sinner) to living a life of faith (justified sinner). This change could not have been brought about by anyone else but ourselves (it must be *my* change of my mode of living in the presence of God), and at the same time it is impossible for us to bring it about ourselves (whatever changes I bring about in my life they *enact* my mode of living but do not *change it*). Therefore whoever experiences such a change will experience it as a break-in of an unforeseeable and inaccessible possibility, and will *thank God* for the chance of being opened up in this way to becoming what we must become but cannot become ourselves in order to leave our life of unfaith and live a life of faith. This is why the experience of the change from unfaith (sin) to faith regularly is expressed in the form of paradox: ›Not I but you‹; ›Not what I have done but what you have done for me‹; ›Not what I could have become myself but what you made and enabled me to become‹.

---

[5] In neither of these two senses can God's presence to our presence be construed as the presence of a cause that makes its effects more probable than they would have been otherwise. Rather we *are opened up to possibilities* not accessible to us before and from within our own causal history, and *we are changed* or transformed into the new mode of a life of faith *by changing*, i. e. by allowing the possibilities opened up to us to shape our life in becoming those whom they make us become. It is the ›advent‹ of these possibilities in our life which transforms it by providing a trace of the ›Christmas‹ at which we shall arrive by letting our life be redirected by this trace of who we shall become when we become what it makes us become: creatures of God's love who live for ever in the presence of this love.

For Christians, therefore, the *sense of God's presence* is inseparable from a life lived in a *mode of thanksgiving,* just as the *sense of God's absence* is lived and experienced in a *mode of lament*: God's presence or absence are not something that one may or may not experience (believe, know) without much impact on the rest of one's life. Either this experience changes *everything* in a life, or it is not an experience of God at all – and this is true of the experience of God's absence as much as of God's presence. Just as there is no sense of the presence of God without giving thanks for it, so there is no sense of the absence of God without bewailing it. Neither sense is just a particular experience or belief among and alongside others that could be understood in the same way as other particular experiences and beliefs. It may be expressed in particular acts, e.g. when the thanksgiving or the lament is explicitly addressed to God. But the sense expressed there is not merely that of a particular experience but informs the whole way of life and shows in the very mode in which a life is lived. If anything is tinged by God's presence, everything is, and the same is true of God's absence. Therefore only someone who cannot help but thank God, i. e. a believer (justified sinner), becomes aware of having been an unbeliever (sinner); only a believer becomes aware of the presence of God as that which made and enabled him or her to change from unfaith to faith; and only if this shows in a life of thanksgiving for God's presence, and of lament about God's absence, he or she lives as a believer.

This is why experience of God's salvific presence is open only to believers while at the same time nobody is in principle excluded from becoming a believer. Believers cannot become aware of it without becoming aware of being sinners who have been saved from their God-ignoring life of unfaith by being opened for a life of faith. They know that as sinners they were neither willing nor able to change from a life of sin to a life of faith. They know that this change altered not only something in their lives but the whole direction, orientation, and mode of their lives. For this reason they also know that it was and could not have been due to anything they did or could have done by themselves. What they have become, and were enabled to become, would have been impossible without God becoming present to their lives in a way that disclosed to them the nature of his presence (redeeming love) and the truth about their lives (saved sinners): They are, through God's grace, saved sinners who are set free to live a life of faith by turning away from their own history of un-faith in loving God and their neighbours. They know from their own experience that this transformation, opening-up and re-orientation of a life is exclusively due to the way in which God becomes present to a sinner by breaking into his or her life and making his present felt in the workings of his love. And since this change from a life of unfaith to a life of faith is solely due to God, Christians believe that nobody is in principle excluded from it.

But then it cannot in principle be impossible for us to apprehend that we live in the presence of God. For while we can live in the presence of God but ignore it, we cannot live a life of faith in the presence of God and ignore it. What is possible and indeed actual in a life of unfaith (to ignore that one lives in the presence of God) is impossible in a life of faith. But since the believer is a sinner who becomes a believer by God becoming present to his or her life in a specific way, *ignoring God's presence* and *not being able to ignore* it are to be found in one and the same life: Believers know that they are what they are (viz. *saved*) only because of God's presence, but they also know that they become what they become (viz. saved *sinners*) only because they ignore God's presence. Therefore it is the life of faith in which both the ignorance and the awareness of God's presence can best be studied.

This is why the sense of God's presence and of God's absence is to be unfolded from within the Christian life of faith. Only here can this sense be studied, and only by unfolding its perspective can we come to understand why and in which sense Christians believe in God's presence even though they experience God's absence as much as anyone else. For the Christian faith, for *God to be* is *to be present* whereas for *God not to be present* is *not* for God *not to be*: God's absence is not so much a denial and refutation but an indication and reminder of God's presence, whatever contemporary thought and experience may hold. Many today ignore or deny God's presence and existence[6] by taking

---

[6] It is common to talk of ›God's existence‹. But whatever we mean by ›existence‹, there is no ›existence‹ that is unequivocally common to the creator and the created, and no good reason to construe analogies between their different ›ways of existing‹. If the term is to be used at all, it is ›God's existence‹ rather than ›existence‹ that is at stake here. ›God's existence‹ is a basic notion that cannot be broken down into the terms ›existence‹ in conjunction with ›God‹ without loosing its point and distorting everything. In a religious perspective ›God's existence‹ signifies that without which there wouldn't and couldn't be any existence of anything whatsoever. And in a Christian perspective ›God's existence‹ is not to be understood in the Kantian or analytic sense of claiming the concept of God to be instantiated but rather as pointing out that by ›God‹ Christians refer to the one to whom they and all other things owe their existence: The genetive of ›God's existence‹ is a *genetivus auctoris,* and existence for Christians is something not simply taken for granted but valued as a gift for which they are grateful – grateful to God. Whenever I speak of God's existence in this inquiry it is to be understood in this sense.

for granted that experience shows that God is absent, or that God's presence is not experienced, or that there is no God whose presence could be experienced, and they have no difficulty in adducing facts of experience in support of their views. Believers do not need to deny these facts but to understand them in a different light and draw different conclusions from them. So the debate is not (or not normally and necessarily) one about facts but about perspectives and horizons of understanding and interpretation. It is here that believers differ from much contemporary thought and experience, and in order to focus this difference more clearly we must unfold the Christian faith in God's presence against the backdrop of the widespread ignorance and denial of it in contemporary culture. This is why I begin with *Steiner's Wager on God*.

3. Steiner's Wager on God

In his provocative book *Real Presences*[7] George Steiner has argued against the prevailing outlook of our time »that any coherent understanding of what language is and how language performs, that any coherent account of the capacity of human speech to communicate meaning and feeling is, in the final analysis, underwritten by the assumption of God's presence«.[8] Against Nietzsche and his postmodern followers Steiner insists »that ›God‹ *is*, not because our grammar is outworn; but that grammar lives and generates worlds because there is the wager on God«.[9] He is far from denying that language and literature is a constant creation of alternative worlds. On the contrary, it is the distinctive feature of human existence that we have spoken ourselves free of total organic constraint[10]: »we are at liberty to say anything, to say what we will about anything, about everything and about nothing«.[11]

Yet precisely this is the problem. How can we be sure that what we think and say, or what we hear or read others think and say, is really true or does refer to anything real? How can we trust that there are

---

[7] G. Steiner, *Real Presences*, Chicago 1989. See also Steiner's seminal Leslie Stephen Memorial Lecture ›Real Presences‹, delivered in the University of Cambridge in 1985 and published in G. Steiner, *No Passion Spent: Essays 1978-1996*, London 1996, 20-39. The lecture is discussed by P. Phillips, ›George Steiner's Wager on Transcendence‹, *The Heythrop Journal* 39 (1998), 158-169.

[8] Steiner, *Real Presences*, 3.

[9] Ibid., 4.

[10] G. Steiner, *After Babel. Aspects of Language and Translation*, London 1975, 234.

[11] Steiner, *Real Presences*, 53.

»any significant relations between word and world«[12], that there is more in what we say than what is said? There is no intrinsic limit to what we can say in language. »But the unboundedness of discursive potentiality has its negative side. The unarrested infinity of conceivable propositions and statements entails the logic of nullity and of nihilism«.[13] This is why we need a »covenant between word and object, the presumption that being is, to a workable degree, ›sayable‹«.[14]

According to Steiner this has traditionally been guaranteed by (a »semantic trust«[15] in) God's real presence. There is truth in what we say only if our words refer to the world, and a correspondence between ›word‹ and ›world‹ is ultimately guaranteed only by »a wager on transcendence«[16], a wager on the real presence of God. In modernity, however, this »covenant of reference«[17] has been broken. The rupture originated in the poetic revolutions in France and Russia in the late nineteenth century, in particular in »Mallarmé's disjunction of language from external reference and in Rimbaud's deconstruction of the first person singular.«[18]

Mallarmé's poetical »insistence that non-reference constitutes the true genius and purity of language, entail[s] a central supposition of ›real absence‹« which has led modern culture to a barely disguised »ontological nihilism«.[19] Words refer only to other words, not to anything ›out there‹. Indeed, the view that language coheres in any way with an external reality is not only illusory, but deeply misleading. »The word *rose* has neither stem nor leaf nor thorn. It is neither pink nor red nor yellow. It exudes no odour. It is *per se*, a wholly arbitrary phonetic marker, an empty sign. Nothing whatever in its (minimal) sonority, in its graphic appearance, in its phonemic components, etymological history or grammatical functions, has any correspondence whatever to what we believe or imagine to be the object of its purely conventional reference.«[20] Words are just words and signify nothing but other words, and not any determined reality beyond themselves.

If we want to object to this, as I think we must, it is no way out to point to the user of words, the human subject. This route is blocked by

---

[12] Ibid., 86f.
[13] Ibid., 57.
[14] Ibid., 90.
[15] Ibid., 92ff.
[16] Ibid., 214.
[17] Ibid., 96.
[18] Ibid., 94f.
[19] Ibid., 96.
[20] Ibid., 95.

Rimbaud's deconstruction of the first person singular. His notorious ›Je est an autre‹ denies any stable I and instead affirms many selves. However, »Where ›I‹ is not ›I‹ but a Magellanic cloud of momentary energies always in process of fission, there can be no authorship in any single, stable sense.«[21] And where there is no I, there is no We, and hence no »possibility for receiving or maintaining a ›meaning‹ that is capable of being ›shared‹.«[22] The dissolution of the self allows no recourse to a »common humanity«[23] or to a shared meaning accessible to all.

Thus not only is language reduced to a mere internal game of words (Mallarmé) but its users are also dissolved in a cloud of momentary acts of meaning unable to point beyond themselves to a determined reality, a shared referent or a mutually accessible common meaning (Rimbaud).

However, far from being the ultimate triumph of poetic imagination over the constraints of empirical reality, this is the definitive collapse and destruction of aesthetic experience, as Steiner points out. »There is language, there is art, because there is ›the other‹«[24], ›the other‹ *to whom* we speak, and ›the other‹ *about which* we speak. »It is out of the fact of confrontation, of affront in the literal sense of the term, that we communicate in words, that we externalise shapes and colours, that we emit organised sounds in the forms of music.«[25] Aesthetic experience, indeed all experience, is encounter and response[26], and both (can) disclose more than they say, that is, (can) open us up for a ›real presence‹, for *being* beyond any *saying*. »There is an experience of the transcendent in language«[27], and the same is true of music, art and other creative forms of culture.

This is a far cry from describing artistic production and reception as a free-floating process of unbounded imagination. There is a logic of creativity at work that must not be ignored: We encounter ›the other‹;

---

[21] Ibid., 100. Cf. Steiner, *No Passion Spent*, 22.

[22] Th.M. Kelly, ›Experience, Language and Sacramental Theology. George Steiner and Karl Rahner on the Postmodern Critique‹, in: L. Boeve/J.C. Ries (eds.), *The Presence of Transcendence. Thinking ›Sacrament‹ in a Postmodern Age*, Leuven 2001, 61-78, 63.

[23] Steiner, *Real Presences*, 102.

[24] Ibid., 137.

[25] Ibid., 138.

[26] Cf. Kelly, ›Experience, Language and Sacramental Theology‹, 66.

[27] Ibid.

we embody the recollection of this encounter in language, music, and art; and we communicate it ›to others‹ because this expressive and communicate process discloses and leads to a deeper understanding of our ›self‹ vis-à-vis »the irreducible weight of otherness … in the texture of and phenomenality of the material world«[28] – this, according to Steiner, is the real process and rationale of aesthetic imagination and communication. Language, literature, art, and music ›talk‹ *to us* and tell us something *about us*. They disclose who we are by transcending what we are, by opening our eyes and minds for the possible. We need not accept what they disclose. We are free to say no. But whether we reject or accept it, we choose from the chosen, we decide under conditions of a double contingency. Not only could *we* have *not* been and could have decided otherwise, but also *the work of art* could have *not* been, or could not have disclosed anything. There is freedom at stake, both in the subject and in the work of art. It can fail to disclose anything to me, and what it discloses can be rejected by me. But it is precisely this possibility of failure and rejection that gives meaning to my decision, and presence to the force of a work of art.[29]

It is mere »nihilistic sophistry«[30], therefore, to denounce the »intelligibility« of our cultural creations as »either wholly arbitrary or self-erasing«.[31] This mistaken view is, for Steiner, modernity's primrose path to »ontological nihilism«[32] where anything goes and nothing counts as it is born out by our present culture. Today we live in a world of secondary gossip and the pseudo-realities produced by the media. We have lost touch with the primary, the true, the real, that without which there is no literature, no music, no art – and, we may add, no religion.

This, in its barest outline, is Steiner's argument. He castigates the »dominance of the secondary and parasitic«[33] in literature, music and the arts; he attributes this to the one-sided and »irresponsible« approach to language as a mere endless interplay of signs; and he claims that without God's real presence language will, in the final analysis, be meaningless and unable to refer to reality: Only God's presence »makes credible the assertion that there ›is something *in* what we say‹«.[34]

---

[28] Steiner, *Real Presences*, 140.
[29] Cf. Kelly, ›Experience, Language and Sacramental Theology‹, 66.
[30] Ibid., 163.
[31] Steiner, *Real Presences*, 163.
[32] Ibid., 96.
[33] Ibid., 7.
[34] Ibid., 121.

The claim is strong but not very well established. Steiner not only fails to show how God's presence does or can secure our semantic trust in the referential capacities of language but even if this were established, he fails to show that other ways to explain the fact of meaningful discourse are impossible or at least less likely true. He rightly insists that there is ›being‹ at stake when we use language, and that what we say communicates more than the mere fact of saying it. But while it is true that literature, music and art, if they succeed, communicate ›real presences‹, it is not true that our trust in the ›transcendent in language‹, music or art can only, or indeed at all, be based on God's real presence. Before we jump to theological conclusions we should try more carefully to give semantic answers to semantic questions, aesthetic answers to aesthetic questions, and literary answers to literary questions and not confuse the issues by insisting on theological answers to non-theological questions.

This is not to say that there isn't a ›wager on God‹. But this wager doesn't help to answer any specific problems *within* the perspective in which we live and relate to our world but rather suggests a *specific theological perspective on us and on the worlds that we create in our world*. It is a wager in which a comprehensive change from a non-theological to a theological perspective is at stake, not merely a theological solution to a non-theological problem within our given perspectives. What is required is a change of our view of life, not merely a change within our view of life.

Steiner not only makes a stronger claim than he needs to make in order to answer the questions which he raises, but he also fails to show how what he proposes could help to answer them. Besides, in order to make his case he presents the cultural conesquences of the literary movements in France and Russia in a rhetorically effective but much oversimplified way, paying little attention to the fact that their symbolism was aimed at correcting the realism of the dominating literary traditions of the time. But these shortcomings notwithstanding he addresses a fundamental *misère* of our present-day culture. The current over-fascination with the potentials of unbounded discourse has fostered a widespread departure from a realist attitude to reality that has begun to undermine one of the major achievements of enlightened humanity: the critical divorce of truth from power. Since the days when Socrates insisted vis-à-vis the Sophists that knowing the truth is different from being talked into a belief the distinction between truth and power has been one of the driving forces of Western civilisation. It is fundamental to science, philosophy and theology as well as to moral-

ity, politics and the policy of democratic societies. Where claims to
truth are taken to be nothing but rhetorical moves to win an argument; where in the absence of truth-generating methods that come
with a guarantee questions of truth are lightly dismissed (since nobody
is said to be able to know for certain what is true anyway); there, truth
becomes parasitic on what those in power believe, or, in our societies,
on what majorities prefer; and then all that really counts is the power
to use language and the media to dominate public opinion and to win
majorities for whatever issue. No doubt, truth is not independent of
what we say but relative to a given language. But not everything we
say is true, and hence we must distinguish *within* language between
what is true and what isn't, and this is impossible unless what we say is
informed by something beyond our saying. By ignoring this and by
stripping language of its referential powers we are in danger of selling
out truth to economic power, the vacillations of public opinion, and
the forces of the market. We have even begun to look at religions in
this way: as a market of ›meaning of life‹ products from which we may
choose according to individual tastes and needs, but not in terms of
truth and falsity.

So the disease, which Steiner diagnoses, is real. But what about the
cure he proposes? Recourse to God's real presence does not even begin to explain how language can be used meaningfully. But perhaps
that isn't Steiner's point. Perhaps he seeks to uncover a necessary presupposition of any possible explanation of our linguistic or any other
capacities and activities: »any coherent account of the capacity of human speech to communicate meaning and feeling is, in the final analysis, underwritten by the assumption of God's presence«.[35] But what exactly does this assumption involve? This we are not told. Steiner leaves
us at a loss as to what he means by *presence*, or *real presence*, or *God*. His
claim is clear: Without God's real presence, no true art, music, literature, or language, no meaning, no experience, and no rationality. But
in order to make sense of his claim and evaluate its force we need to
know what he means by *God's real presence*.

4. Real Presence as Hidden Presence

There are at least three ways to understand the phrase ›God's real presence‹ if we analyse it against the backdrop of actual communicative
moves in religious life. It may be used there to summarise objections

---

[35] Ibid., 3.

to denials (1) of God's existence (›No, these are not just words about God, but God *really is*‹), or (2) of God's presence (›Yes, God is *really present* and has not left his people‹), or (3) of the disclosure of God's true nature (›Indeed, God is present here *as God really is*‹). So the phrase can be used to mean

(1) *God really is*

(2) *God really is present*

(3) *God is present as God really is.*

Steiner concentrates on the second understanding, which implies the first, but there is nothing in his argument to take account of the third. However, it is the third understanding, which is central to theological debates about God's real presence in the sacraments – debates, which are strangely neglected by Steiner. Although he alludes again and again to the sacraments he never stops to consider the problem or to discuss the arguments. For him all that counts is, that there is, and must be, a God who is present. It is never really clear what he means by ›God‹, and when a decade or so later he seeks to clarify it, he can only state his confusion: »How can ›the totally Other‹ act on us, let alone give any signal of its utterly inaccessible existence?«[36] So what is clear is only that his postulate is not that God really is, but that God really is present.

But isn't that a spurious distinction? Does it make sense to distinguish between God's existence and God's presence? Even those who deny that God exists rarely deny that *if* God exists, God is present. To believe in God and to deny God's presence appears to be incoherent. Not because everything that is somehow is present, as Heidegger claimed the Western tradition to have thought since the days of the Pre-Socratics. But because *God* cannot exist unless he is present: Presence is a fundamental trait not of existence but of God: *to be God is to be present.*

However, if this is true, it is not evident. The history of religions is full of absent deities and of gods who are not present, at least not always and everywhere. The Greek gods lived on the Olympus and came down at pleasure to mingle in human affairs. Jahwe only occasionally descended on the Sinai and had to be argued into accompanying his people by Moses (Ex 33,1-6). Baal was in no way to be moved to end his absence and come and help his supporters. Persephone absented herself from the world of the living for six months each year and disappeared into the Hades. Osiris was killed and buried and only

---

[36] G. Steiner, *Errata. An Examined Life*, New Haven/London 1997, 186.

returned to life when his son Horus brought him back. The neoplatonist Hen is beyond all being and in principal inaccessible to anyone. And nobody knows the father except the son and those to whom he has chosen to reveal it.

Examples could easily be multiplied. Just because the deity, as a rule, is not present, it often needs complicated ways to get into his or her presence: One has to go on long pilgrimages to holy places, climb on mountains, withdraw into deserts, build altars and temples, offer sacrifices, perform rituals and undergo extensive preparations before one can hope to be worthy of being admitted into the presence of the deity. The very fact of religions, cults, temples and rituals shows that the gods are not present. For if they were we would live in cities without temples and churches as the seer of the revelation of John described the heavenly Jerusalem.

Thus the very fact of religions bears witness to the absence of God but at the same time also to the human longing for God's presence. For to live in God's presence is the fullness of life hoped for, the salvation from the evils, ambiguities and atrocities of this life. This, at least, is central to the soteriological visions of Judaism, Islam and Christianity. The history of Israel has been a permanent struggle for life in the presence of God, a suffering from the experience of God's absence, and a longing for his definitive and real presence. When Jesus announced the advent of the kingdom of God he did not proclaim a new doctrine but summarised and actualised the faith of his people. His message was that the time of God's absence had come to an end and that the long waited for presence of God was about to begin here and now, in his own teaching and healing and, according to Christian faith, in his suffering, death and resurrection: Christ not only proclaimed the presence of God, he manifested this presence in person. This is why Christians have insisted not only on an indissoluble link between God and presence, but on a christological interpretation of this link: For God to be is to be present; but *what it means* for God to be present is definitively shown in the life and death of Jesus Christ.

However, doesn't Christ's suffering and death intensify the sense of the absence of God rather than disclose God's presence? Christ died with a cry of dereliction, and in this, surely, he was one of us. On its own the cross signifies a human tragedy but not the hidden divinity of God; and this is not undone by the resurrection: It is for ever the crucified one who is risen but his rising reveals *God* to be hidden in the cross.

This fundamentally transforms the situation. Without revoking to the least the human suffering and tragedy of the cross, it opens up another and completely different perspective on it, the perspective of faith. The cross now comes to be seen as the place where Christ's suffering and death disclose God's apparent absence to be God's hidden presence. Indeed, it is only against this background of God's presence hidden *sub contrario* in the cross that Christians are capable and entitled to understand the lack of any experience of God, that is, the experience of God's non-presence in a world of evil, suffering and death, to manifest God's absence rather than God's non-existence.

The sense of the absence of God never stands on its own. It is not simply a sense that there isn't a God, as the absence of definite proof indicates the lack or non-existence of a proof. Rather the sense of the absence of God is tied to – at least the possibility of – God's presence just as the sense of God's presence is always contrasted to – at least the possibility of – God's absence. Otherwise there wouldn't be much point in claiming that God is present rather than absent, and one couldn't even begin meaningfully to distinguish between the experience of God's absence, the fact that God is not experienced, and the claim based on this fact that there is no God to be experienced.

The dialectical contrast and tension between the sense of God's presence and of God's absence characterise Christ's experience as much as that of Christians. This is why Christians can be true neither to Christ's experience nor to their own if they insist on God's presence without a heightened sense of his absence. But neither would they be entitled to understand the widespread non-experience of God to indicate God's absence rather than God's non-existence. There is no experience of God's presence in this life that is not tinged by his absence. But just because Christians look upon their own lives as lives lived in the presence of God, they suffer from God's absence and hope for a life in which God's presence can be enjoyed free of all the ambiguities of this life.

It is precisely the difference between what faith knows to be true and what experience shows to be the case in this world, between God's presence which Christians confess and God's absence which they experience which defines their attitude to life and has been a driving force behind their moral and social engagement: Much of what the Western world has come to value as life worthy of human being is due to Christian sensitivity to the many aspects of reality that contradict God's presence (including the reality of the Christian churches and the unspeakable harm done by Christians to others and to each other in the course of history). Just because they suffer from God's absence, Christians have again and again drawn attention to

problems, which former generations had not even noticed, and identified evils that need changing before God's presence can become more
fully recognised.

For Christians, therefore, God's presence is a hidden presence in this
life. For many others the »density of God's absence, the edge of presence in that absence«, is still »charged with the pressures of a nearness
out of reach, of a remembrance torn at the edges«.[37] But there are also
those for whom there is no experience of God's absence but simply
nothing to be experienced. For them questions of the presence or absence of God have lost all actuality. Perhaps educated opinion has, to a
greater or lesser degree, entered upon this new world already, and if
general sentiment follows, we shall have definitely moved into a new
age.[38] But if God really is present, public opinion is in danger of falling
prey to a tremendous illusion. Christians, in any case, hold fast to
God's presence and for this reason can never rest content with the
present state of the world. They suffer from God's absence *just because*
they feel and believe his presence, and this is why they take the widespread sense of the absence of God to manifest the hidden presence of
God rather than God's non-existence.

However, all this needs a more probing analysis of what it means to
say that God is present, that presence can be mediated by absence, and
that God is hidden present rather than non-existent. So let us briefly
recall some aspects of the philosophical analysis of presence (something
strangely neglected by Steiner), and then look at some aspects of the
theological debate about Christ's real presence in the sacraments (again
something that Steiner completely ignores). I shall concentrate on the
analytical rather than phenomenological contributions because they
can help us to see more clearly what is at stake in the theological debates about real presence in the sacraments.

5. Presence in Analytical Theories of Time

The debate about time in 20th century analytical philosophy is mostly
a debate about *theories of time.* This debate usually takes as its starting-
point McTaggart's distinction between the A-theory and B-theory of
time[39], that is to say, between so-called ›tensed‹ theories of time build

[37] Steiner, *Real Presences*, 229f.
[38] Cf. ibid., 230.
[39] J. E. McTaggart, ›The Unreality of Time‹, *Mind* 17, 1908, 457-474; *The Nature of Existence*, Cambridge 1927, vol. II, chap. 33. Cf. M. Dummett, ›A Defense

on the distinctions between *past*, *present*, and *future*, and ›tenseless‹ theories that start from the ordering of events according to their being *before*, *after*, or *simultaneous* with each other.[40] The issue between them is whether past, present and future are objective. For A-theorists there are objective facts about past, present and future that are not derived from facts about before, after, or simultaneity.[41] For B-theorists, on the other hand, facts about past, present and future only hold because of facts about before, after, and simultaneity.[42]

Each of these positions comes in different versions.[43] A-theorists often hold (what sometimes is called) a *presentist*, a *growing block*, or a *moving spotlight* view. *Presentism* is the view that the present is the only time that exists: the past exists no more and the future not yet. The *growing block view*, on the other hand, holds that the present and the past exist so that reality is to be conceived as growing[44], whereas the

---

of McTaggart's Proof of the Unreality of Time‹, *Philosophical Review* 69, 1960, 497-507; D.H. Mellor, *Real Time*, Cambridge 1981, 92ff.

[40] This is often, but somewhat misleadingly, equated with ›dynamic‹ and ›static‹ theories of time. The former understand change as a change of (accidental) properties of an entity: If a cup of coffee is hot at t_1 and cold at t_2, where $t_1 < t_2$, then it has undergone change. The latter understands change as an entity having a particular property at one but not at another time of its extension through the four-dimensional space-time continuum (the three spatial and the temporal dimension): A cup of coffee is hot at one place of its four-dimensional extension through space-time, and cold at another, and this change in location in the space-time continuum is all there is to what we, for psychological reasons, perceive as change. Cf. P. van Inwagen, ›Four-Dimensional Objects‹, *Nous* 24, 1990, 245-255; Th. Sider, *Four Dimensionalism. An Ontology of Persistence and Time*, Oxford 2001. But ›tenseless‹ theories need not be understood in this ›static‹ sense but can be conceived as dynamic causal processes in which earlier events cause later events. Cf. R. Swinburne, *Space and Time*, ²1981; *The Christian God*, Oxford 1994, chap. 4; D.H. Mellor, *The Facts of Causation*, New York 1995; M. Tooley, *Time, Tense and Causation*, Oxford 1997, chaps. 6 and 7.

[41] Cf. Q. Smith, *Language and Time*, Oxford 1993; W.L. Craig, *The Tensed Theory of Time. A Critical Examination*, Dordrecht 2000; *God, Time and Eternity. The Coherence of Theism II: Eternity*, Dordrecht 2000; *Time and Eternity. Exploring God's Relationship to Time*, Wheaton, Illinois 2001.

[42] W.L. Craig, *The Tenseless Theory of Time. A Critical Examination*, Dordrecht 2000.

[43] I follow the brief summary of J. Pierce, ›Review of *God and Time: Four Views*‹, ed. G. E. Ganssle; contributors: W. L. Craig, P. Helm, A. Padgett, and N. Wolterstorff, Downer's Grove, Illinois 2001, *Faith and Philosophy* 20, 2003, 504-509.

[44] This is the view defended by G.J. DeWeese, *God and the Nature of Time*, Burlington, Vermont 2004, 15-89.

moving spotlight view thinks that »all times exist but the present is like a spotlight moving across the whole block of times«.[45]

The three versions raise different sorts of problems. According to presentism, the difference between past, present and future is ontological in that only the presence exists whereas the other times do not. This is good news for some free will theorists for whom it is an advantage that the future is not part of what exists although they may have more difficulty with the fact that the same is true of the past. But this implies truth-value gaps with respect to propositions about the future (and the past), which many philosophers find difficult to accept. According to the growing block view, on the other hand, the past is just as real as the present so that the difference between past and present cannot be ontological. This is even more so with the moving spotlight view according to which past, present and future all exist.[46] It comes as little surprise to find that presentism is the view held by most A-theorists.

B-theorists have mainly two objections against it. The first is the *truthmaker problem.* »If every truth has a truthmaker, and there are truths even about past [and future] events, then something in the present needs to ground that truth.«[47] But what in the present grounds the truth about Caesar's crossing of the Rubicon, or what in the present grounds the truth about my future death? Various answers are given, but »the main solutions proposed to date are not fully satisfying even to many presentists.«[48]

The other objection is from *physics.* Presentism, as commonly conceived, is inconsistent with relativity theory. »Presentism entails that things simultaneously with what I'm now doing have a privileged ontological status. The problem is that what is simultaneous with what I'm now doing is relative to one's frame of reference«[49], and this directly conflicts with the ontological point of presentism according to which what is present »is wholly objective. As a result, almost all meta-

---

[45] Pierce, ›Review of *God and Time*‹, 505. For a dynamic view of time in a world where past, present and future exist on an ontological par cf. G.N. Schlesinger, *Timely Topics,* New York 1994, 70-77.

[46] This does not necessarily mean to hold the view that there exists only one future. Cf. St. McCall, *A Model of the Universe. Space-Time, Probability, and Decision,* Oxford 1994 who holds that possible futures are just as real as the past or the present.

[47] Pierce, Review of *God and Time,* 506.

[48] Ibid.

[49] Ibid.

physicians and philosophers of physics hold the static theory«, i.e. a B-theory view of time.[50]

However, the question is not merely whether (a version of) the A-theory or the B-theory is ontologically more adequate but whether ontological adequacy is the decisive respect in terms of which one should compare and judge theories of time. Before we discuss the pros and cons of theories, we should pay attention to the point(s) of our use of temporal terms in general, and of their use in religious or Christian discourse and practice in particular. For it is not at all clear that metaphysical or physical *theories* of time grasp or even help us to understand what Christians say and mean when they speak of, or rely on, God's presence. Indeed, it is most unlikely that they do, given the problems that they seek to solve. To hold, without qualifications, that »Metaphysics precedes linguistics, not vice versa«[51], is to overlook the important fact that ›hermeneutics precedes metaphysics‹ if we want to make sense of the Christian sense of the presence of God rather than replace it by theoretical constructions and substitute something else for it. Metaphysical theories can help us to sharpen our view of theological problems. They do not provide their answers.

6. Being Present

In ordinary discourse and everyday religious practice we use temporal terms in a variety of ways. For us *presence* is a temporal term or, more precisely, a term of our scheme of orientation in time. We distinguish *past*, *present* and *future*, and we apply these distinctions to everything that is in time: things, persons, thoughts, events, actions, facts etc. These are said to be *in time* because they can be located in the sequence of events which results from ordering events in terms of their temporal relations with other events – the relations of being simultaneous with some events, and earlier or later than others (McTaggart's B-series). Thus last Christmas was earlier than my writing this in January but later than the birth of Christ, which it celebrated, and every other event falls into a similar order. For every event takes time, and no event occurs in isolation. Events are durations, they have temporal parts, and they differ from things in that they do not change themselves in time but fall into a series or succession of events in which their position is fixed relative to other events simultaneous with them,

---

[50] Ibid.
[51] DeWeese, *God and the Nature of Time,* 68.

or earlier and later than them. There is not just one way of locating an event within such a series: I write this on Thursday, but also in January, in 2004, in the 21st century or in the third Christian millennium. And neither is there just one such temporal ordering of events: What is simultaneous with a given event depends, at least in part, on the frame of reference that we choose. But once chosen, there is nothing arbitrary about the temporal relations between the events in the series, and hence they are fixed independently of what we might think or believe about them.

All this is part of the conceptual background of the notion of presence but does not explain it. It is only when we take our stand at a definite place *within* some such series (*now*) that we can apply the distinctions between past, present and future to events, things, thoughts or whatever. The function of these distinctions is not to specify further the dating-scheme by which we order events. Rather they express our temporal perspective on these events from a definite place within that series. That is to say, they do not help us to *locate something else in time* but to *locate ourselves in time*, and either is necessary for us in order to be able to live and orient ourselves in reality. Thus I cannot locate myself in time without participating in the B-series of events in which I seek to orient myself; I cannot orient myself in this series without working out its temporal order in my perspective (i. e. relate to these events with respect to what is past, present, and future) and placing or locating myself in this order (i. e. locate myself in the present); I cannot locate myself in the present without thereby employing the whole scheme or pattern of temporal orientation *present, past* and *future* in temporally relating to the events of the B-series in question; and I cannot employ this scheme of temporal orientation and locate myself in terms of it without learning to distinguish between that to which I am temporally related (i. e. that which changes its temporal position relative to me in that it was once future, is now present and will soon be past) and that to which I have real but not temporal relations so that whenever I am present it is present (as some think is the case with numbers[52] or, in a different way, with God). For while I have real relations to everything to which I am temporally and causally related (B-series events), not only that to which I am causally related is real, i. e.

---

[52] W. Kneale, ›Time and Eternity in Theology‹, *Proceedings of the Aristotelian Society* 61, 1960-61, 98 takes numbers to be atemporal entities, S. T. Davis, *Logic and the Nature of God*, Grand Rapids, Michigan 1983, 17 takes them to be eternal but not atemporal.

such that it is not merely a function of my relating to it but independent of my relating to it accessible to others as well.[53]

However, temporal orientation is not the sole function of the notion of presence. Originally presence was used as a spatial, not a temporal term. It signified a specific mode of co-existence, a special way of the being together of one thing with another. Thus in the 18th century we find presence defined as »a state in which a person by his [or her] own substance, without any intermediate moral causes and indeed without the help of any instruments or tools, can act in a place«.[54] Persons are *agents*, that is, they can take the initiative in performing actions; and they are *present* when the action is initiated in the very situation in which it is performed. For example, falling off the roof is an event that happens to someone; jumping of the roof is an act; but it is an act that cannot be performed unless the agent herself is present. Presence, in short, is a property not of particular actions but of the *performing* of actions, and this necessarily implies the presence of the agent.

This is why the notion of *presence* does not name a specific temporal moment such as the indexical *now*. In medieval thought *a* now (*nunc*) was any instant of time and as such distinguished from *the* now, i.e. the *present* instant. *Now* represented simply a moment of time, not necessarily the present one. The present now is the now present *to someone*, and this relativity is decisive. Presence cries out for a recipient, for whatever is present, is it *to someone*. This is not to say that to be present is to be present to consciousness, i.e. that only that of which I am aware is present. On the contrary, most of what is present I am not aware of, partly because of the crudeness of my perceptual capacities, and partly because what is present to me depends at least in part on a more or less arbitrary choice of a frame of reference in terms of which we decide and describe what is simultaneous with me.

Thus *to be present* in no way implies *to be known to be present*: The presence of something or someone is neither an epistemic nor a subjective fact but true or false, as the case may be, quite independently of what I know or experience. But neither is the property of being present a real quality or defining determination of anything that is present. Nothing is present, past or future in itself but only *in relation to* something else in whose perspective it is past, present or future. For

[53] Cf. I.U. Dalferth, *Existenz Gottes und christlicher Glaube. Skizzen zu einer eschatologischen Ontologie,* München 1984, 33–41.

[54] J.Chr. Adelung, *Versuch eines vollständigen grammatisch-kritischen Wörterbuchs der hochdeutschen Mundart,* vol. 2, Leipzig 1755, 483 (my translation).

such a perspective to obtain the entity whose perspective it is must either *exist in time* or *exist in a real relation to things that exist in time*. If it doesn't *exist*, nothing can be related to it; if it doesn't exist *in time* such as fictional entities or numbers it doesn't have any real perspectives on anything; and if it doesn't exist *in time* and *yet is real and has real relations to things in time* as is the case with God it cannot and need not differentiate between past, present and future in its perspectives on others but everything in time will be present to it as it occurs. Thus the French Revolution is past relative to us; it is neither past nor present nor future relative to the number 4 or to Pegasus; and it was present to God as it occurred, it is now present to God as something that for us has occurred, and when Descartes was present it was present to God as something which for Descartes had not yet occurred.[55] Thus whereas only some temporal entities can be present to us, all non-temporal entities are necessarily present to us, i.e. simultaneous with all our perspectives, and all temporal and non-temporal entities are present to God as they occur in our or any other perspective.

7. Presence and Self-Presence

The property of being present, therefore, is not a temporal property of a thing but of the relation of a temporal thing such as us to that at which we are present or which is present to us. But what sort of relation is this? If I am present at the meeting when the news is announced I am contemporary with this event. But my being present is not a further event in the series of events that make up the meeting but the *way or mode* in which I take part in it. The relation ›being

---

[55] There is no sense in ascribing memory to God, and no need to do so. A memory can only fulfil its function of orienting a life by being selective, i.e. by remembering some things or aspects of things (past or present) while forgetting others. A memory that *per impossibile* included everything that can be known from all possible angles would be indistinguishable from the very reality that is remembered – just as a map of a city that included all possible information about the city would be indistinguishable from the city itself and thus fail to orient anyone. But the difference between God and us is not that God remembers everything that we do *and* what we have forgotten *and* what we never knew. The difference is rather that God is not tied to a particular perspective in relating to his creation. God does not have a (selective or total) memory but the capacity to know every temporal truth from each perspective to which God is present. This is not to say that God has a single, absolute, privileged perspective on everything but rather that God embraces the perspectives of everything to whose presence he is present, i.e. knows everything temporal in an infinite multitude of ways.

present at‹ locates me in such a way relative to this event that I can orient myself by applying the term *present* to the *now* of this event, the
term *past* to everything that was earlier than it and is no more present,
and the term *future* to everything that is later than it and not yet
present. The terms *present, past,* and *future* are not used to state any further events in the series or specific properties of the events in question
but characterise how I temporally relate to them by being located at a
specific place in the series. They do not specify further events, or further properties of events, but my temporal relations to these events.

That is to say, I am not only part of a series of events (B–series) but
also able to relate to it from within it (A–relations), and this ability lies
at the heart of our experiencing and acting. It presupposes a capacity
of distancing or differentiating ourselves from our place in the series of
events to which we belong (i. e. a minimal self[56]) for only then can we
relate to it and are not merely part of it; and this capacity must be such
that it allows us to adjust our relating to the change of events in the series to which we belong (i. e. it must be a temporal self). For in relating to the events of the series to which we belong we relate differently
to what is simultaneous with our relating or earlier or later than it, and
as our world is an unending flux of events, we have continuously to
adjust our relating to the permanent change of situation – including
ourselves: We not only relate to events but can also relate to our relating to events and thus form our biographies by building up the perspectival continuities of our life.[57] While there is no presence without a
self being present, the presence of a self is not a self-presence, i. e. a self
being present to itself, but that without which self-presence wouldn't
be possible. A present self only becomes a self-presence when it relates
not only in A-relations to events but to its relating to events in this
way. It then not only experiences and acts in a 1ˢᵗ-person perspective
but relates to his experiencing and acting in this perspective, and while
the first requires a self continuously to adjust to changing events in
time which are present, past or future for it, the latter always takes

---

[56] The capacity of distancing or distinguishing itself from its place in time is
necessary for being a *self* but not sufficient for a self to be a *subject*. To distinguish
selves from non-selves is one thing, to allow for developments of a self and for a
range of selfhood another.

[57] A.R. Damasio, *The Feeling of What Happens. Body and Emotion in the Making of
Consciousness*, New York 1999, 16f.127 calls this the ›autobiographical self‹. He
distinguishes it, among other things, from the ›proto-self‹ which is his name for
any »coherent collection of neural patterns which map, moment by moment, the
state of the physical structure of the organism in its many dimensions« (154).

place in the present an hence gives continuity to the self in its changing temporal relations to events.

Thus we, our experiences and actions and many other things and events contemporary with us were once future, will soon be past, and are now present. For to call something *future* is to say that it is later than now, *past* that it is earlier than now, and *present* that it is now present, i.e. simultaneous with now. But while our A-relations (being present, past, future) to events in the B-series change with the ongoing (causal) change of events, our *relating* to these events and hence also our *relating to our relating* to these events always takes place in the present: Whereas I am not always present at a concert but only while it occurs and as long as I take part in it, I am always present, and trivially so, in my relating to this or any other event. Whatever I experience or do I experience or do in the present[58]: I cannot fail to be present because it is me who experiences or acts, and it is me rather than anyone else because it takes place *here and now*, i. e. in the present.

This is the invariant aspect of all my experiencing and acting: It takes place *in the present*. This is not to say that *the self* is the invariant dimension of first-personal givenness in the multitude of changing experiences.[59] What is invariant is my *place in the scheme of orientation in time* where I experience and act, i. e. *the present*, not the self that experiences or acts in the present. But then the decisive characteristic of the 1st-person perspective is not an invariant ›sense of the self‹ that I, rather than anyone else, is experiencing or acting, but rather an invariant ›sense of presence‹ that my experiencing or acting takes place *here and now*. Because everything I experience and do takes place *here and now*, it is *me* who experiences or acts and not someone else. Indeed, this question simply doesn't arise in my 1st-person perspective because the indexicals ›I‹, ›here‹ and ›now‹ can only be used interchangeably so that whoever is present here and now is the one who experiences and acts, and whoever experiences and acts here and now is the one whose 1st-person perspective (›I‹) is at stake. Whereas the ›sense of presence‹ accentuates the invariant presentness of my experiencing and acting to

---

[58] The proof is simple. Whatever we say is true if what we say is in fact the case, and false if it is not. ›I have a headache‹ is true if and only if I have a headache at the very time I say so. But I say it in the present, and hence it is only true if I have the headache also in the present. And as for headaches, so for all experiences: whenever I am having them, they unfailingly posses the property of being present. Cf. Mellor, *Real Time*, chap. 3.

[59] This is the view defended by D. Zahavi in his forthcoming book *Subjectivity and Selfhood. Investigating the First-Person Perspective*, esp. chap. 5.

be decisive for understanding the 1ˢᵗ-person perspective, the ›sense of the self‹ claims a special self-presence or self-awareness to be a necessary feature of my experiencing and acting in this perspective. The former understands 1ˢᵗ-person perspectives to be a function of the *temporal place* where I experience and act, the latter turns it into a structure of the *self* that experiences or acts at this place. In short, not ›Necessarily: Whenever I experience, I experience *in the present*‹ is taken to be the decisive truth about the 1ˢᵗ-person perspective but ›Necessarily: Whenever I experience, *I am present to myself* in experiencing‹.

However, while I cannot fail to experience in the present whatever I experience, and while it is true that whenever I experience something it is me who experiences it, I can experience something without thereby experiencing myself. It is one thing to say that it is *me* who experiences, another that I *experience me* (i. e. my self as *idem* or my sameness that can be re-identified over time in a 3ʳᵈ-person perspective) or that I *experience myself* (i. e. my self as *ipse* or my self-hood that is accessible only in a 1ˢᵗ-person perspective).[60] ›I experience something‹ does entail ›I experience *in the present*‹ but not ›I experience *myself* in the present‹. For either ›myself‹ and ›in the present‹ are (very misleadingly) taken to be interchangeable phrases for localising the experience in question here and now, or ›I experience *myself* in the present‹ adds something substantial to ›I experience *in the present*‹ and this needs further argument. Self-experience is not an intrinsic feature or dimension of my or any experience, at least not if it is taken to mean ›the self is experienced‹ rather than ›the self is experiencing‹. In the latter sense it is trivially true for the reasons given that my experiencing something entails that it is me who experiences it. But this does imply that in experiencing something I experience myself. ›I experience a bird singing‹ states an experiential phenomenon in a 1ˢᵗ-person perspective but does not express a special 1ˢᵗ-person mineness or »built-in self-reference« of the phenomenon that is an intrinsic feature of the experience in question.[61] It simply states that it is me who

---

[60] Cf. P. Ricœur, *Soi-même comme un autre*, Paris 1990, who distinguishes between identity as *mêmeté* (sameness) and as *ipséité* (selfhood) in his attempt to analyse the identity of the narritive self.

[61] J. Parnas/P. Bovet/D. Zahavi, ›Schizophrenic Autism: Clinical Phenomenology and Pathogenetic Implications‹, *World Psychiatry* 1, October 2002, 131-136, 133: »We may speak of a pre-reflective self-awareness whenever we are *directly,* non-inferentially or non-reflectively conscious of our own ongoing thoughts, perceptions, feelings, or pains; these appear in a *first-personal mode of presentation* that immediately reveals them as our own, i.e., it entails a built-in self-reference. In other words, when the experience is given in a first-personal mode of presen-

has this experience, i. e. that it takes place *here and now* where I am, and this is not to say that I experience me (in a 3rd-person perspective) or myself (in a 1st-person perspective) as having it.

Similarly, if I am present at an event, then I am not for this reason also present to my being present at the event, or present to myself as being present at it. It is, no doubt, *me* who is present, and I am indeed present *myself* rather than someone else. But *being present myself* is not to be confused with *being present to myself,* and *my being present at an event* not with *my being present at my being present at the event*: It is a trivial truth that I cannot be present at anything without *me* being present at it. But it is neither true nor trivial that whenever I am present at something I am also ›present at me‹ or ›to myself‹: I am not something *at which,* or someone *to whom,* I am present but the one *who is present.* And it is not the case that I can only be present at something or to someone if I am also prior or intrinsic to it *present to myself.* In a purely formal way we can of course reiterate the A-relation (›being present at/to‹) by applying it to an A-relation (›being present at/to‹). But this is an empty operation of signs that doesn't correspond to a specific move in a cognitive practice or in the phenomenal givenness of an experience, and if it did it would merely restate the problem: Even if it were true that *I am present at my being present* there would still be the difference between that *at which* I am present (›my being present at‹) and the one *who is present* at it (me). So higher order iterations of A-relations collapse into the first order problem: It is *me* who is present, and this is not to say that I am present *at me* or *to myself.*

So there is a problem with the claim, made in different ways in the phenomenological tradition, that I can only be present at something *because* I am present to myself. *Being present to oneself* is taken to be the condition of the possibility, or a necessary feature or ingredient, of being present at something else (including oneself as a cognitive object). If this is not to reiterate the problem (I can be present to myself only because I am present to myself because …), it is, as in M. Henry, the postulate of a *basic self-presence* prior to or necessarily given with any presence of someone at something or to someone: »Ce qui constitue l'essence de l'ipséité, de l'egoïté … c'est l'intériorité de la présence immédiate à soi-même«.[62]

---

tation (to me), it is, at least tacitly, given as *my* experience and therefore counts as *a basic selfmanifestation.*«

[62] M. Henry, *Philosophie et phénoménologie du corps: essai sur l'ontologie biranienne,* Paris 1965, 52. Cf. J.G. Hart, ›Michel Henry's Phenomenological Theology of Life: A Husserlian Reading of *C'est moi, la vérité*‹, Husserl Studies 15, 1999, 183-230.

One of the reasons phenomenologists give for this is that I can become explicitly or thematically aware of being present at (say) singing a song; that becoming aware of this is becoming aware that *I* sing the song; and that I couldn't become aware of this unless it were true prior to my becoming aware of it: thematic self-awareness presupposes unthematic self-awareness which is »a non–reflective, tacit sensibility (›operative intentionality‹), procuring a background texture or organization to the field of experience, and so constituting our primary *presence to the world*, upon which the explicit intentionality configures its perceptual or cognitive disclosures« (e.g., hearing *this particular song*).[63]

But this is problematic for a number of reasons. To become aware of being present at singing a song is to become aware *that* I am singing, not (at least not normally) that *I* am singing. I may focus my awareness on *me* in reply to the question ›Who is singing?‹, but this is not a question I could sensibly ask myself, at least not in normal circumstances. If I hear someone singing and wonder who it is, and then find out that it is me who is singing, I have a serious problem. If I am singing, I may in a Cartesian mood doubt whether this is real or whether I am dreaming. But even in a dream I cannot sing and wonder who is singing. For whether in a dream or in reality I cannot become aware of *what* I am doing without being aware that it is *me* who is doing it. There are not two separate acts of awareness, one of *singing* and another of *me* singing, which have mysteriously to be joined in order to become aware that I am singing. Rather to become aware of this is to become aware not of a *singing* in search of a subject whose singing it is, but of *my singing*, and to become aware of this is to become aware that I am *singing* and *not* that *I* am singing. There are problems in a 3rd-person perspective (›Whose singing is this?‹), which simply do not arise in a 1st-person perspective, and it is misleading to analyse in a 3rd-person perspective my singing in the 1st-person perspective. Moreover, the postulate of an unthematic self-awareness presupposed by my thematic self-awareness seems to be little else than a reading back of the structure of a later reality into an earlier possibility. It is true that I can only truly become aware of being present at an event if I was present at it before I became aware of it. But if I become aware of it I become aware that I am *present at the event*, not that I am *present to myself* in being present at the event: I am the one *who* is present, not the one *to whom* I am present. Similarly, when I become aware of this, I am the one *who* is aware of being present, and not the one *to whom* I am

---

[63] Parnas/Bovet/Zahavi, ›Schizophrenic Autism: Clinical Phenomenology and Pathogenetic Implications‹, 133.

present when I become aware of it. In short, the postulate of a primordial self-awareness seems to rest on a confusion of *being present myself* with *being present to myself*, and of a mistaken inference from the (trivial) fact that *I cannot be present at an event without being present myself* to the wrong idea that *I cannot be present at an event without being present to myself*.

However, while it is not true that whenever I am present at an event I am also present to myself but simply present at it myself, it is true that I am present whenever it *becomes present to me that I am present at* an event. This differs from the case just discussed in that it is a B-series event of a special sort, viz. a cognitive event, in which I *become aware* of being present at an event. But ›It becomes present to me that I am present at an event‹ is not to be confused with either ›I am present at my being present at an event‹ or ›I am present to myself when I am present at an event‹: I am not an event at which I am present but the one who is present at events. But for this to be true I need not be aware of it, neither thematically nor unthematically if this is to mean »our primary *presence to the world*«[64] and not merely the possibility of becoming aware of this.[65] I do not have to be aware of being present at a meeting of spies in order to be present at it. If I become aware of it, then this is a different event from my participating in the meeting. It is an event in which something dawns on me of which I wasn't aware before but which couldn't be true and be known to be true, if I wouldn't have been present at the meeting.

8. The Mode of Presence

To get this clearer, let us look more closely into the capacity of what I have called ›a minimal temporal self‹ without which the use of the A-series distinctions and hence orientation in time wouldn't be possible. The capacity shows in the ability to distinguish the *place* of an event from the *event* that occurs at this place, for to make this distinction is

---

[64] Ibid.

[65] In this case we must beware of another confusion: The *possibility of becoming aware of this song* cannot to be construed analogously to the *possibility of becoming aware of something*. If it is possible for us to become aware of something and if *the singing of songs* is something that falls within the range of what we can become aware of, then there is no need, and indeed no point, to postulate an unthematic awareness for each thematic awareness. All that is needed is that *we can become aware of something* and that *songs are something of which we can become aware*, but not that there is a *special possibility that we can become aware of songs*.

possible only from a position that is different both from the place and the event in question. To draw a distinction (any distinction) not only means to differentiate something into two aspects but necessarily assumes a point of view from which the distinction is drawn: To differentiate A and B is to distinguish them in some respect or other, and this respect depends on the point of view of the one who differentiates A and B. Just as there is no unity that is not the result of a unifying process with respect to something, so there is no difference that is not the result of a process of differentiation with respect to something. But both processes necessarily assume a point of view or a ›third‹ position from which and in terms of which the respect in question is conceived, that is to say, *for which* the unity or the difference is constituted or *by which* it is united or differentiated. Thus to *distinguish A and B* is to distinguish them not only *with respect to C* but also *for (some) X*, and it is this, which characterises the ›self‹ in the minimal sense required here: A self is that *for which* a distinction is drawn, a difference is made, a contrast is constituted, and which thereby *becomes enabled to distinguish itself* from that from which it is differentiated and to which it is contrasted.

In this sense, ›a minimal temporal self‹ is the capacity of differentiating oneself from the events of which one is made up and to whom one belongs in time (B-series) and of temporally relating to them (A-relations), and this capacity is constituted by becoming that *for which* something becomes something *other* by being distinguished *from it* through being related as *something other* to it. So the ›self‹ is not just there as a primal given but is itself the result of a process in which it becomes differentiated from its environment by becoming *that for which* something else becomes *an other* and which thereby is differentiated *from* and contrasted *to* others. This process of differentiation between ›self‹ and ›non-self‹ or ›other‹ cannot (logically cannot) occur as an interaction between ›self‹ and ›other‹ because this would assume the very difference which is to be constituted.[66] It rather becomes possible only in a more complex situation in which a ›third party‹ differentiates between ›self‹ and ›other‹ by relating differently to both of them.

This active interference of a ›third party‹ (not necessarily the same for everyone, and for no one continuously the same) opens up and sustains a process in which selves (can) develop as selves in interaction

---

[66] This seems to be a further (misguided) reason for postulating a primordial self-awareness prior or intrinsic to all explicit self-awareness that is constituted by interactions with others.

with other selves (›others‹) and other non-selves (›other‹) in unfolding
and living their relations to others, to other non-selves and to themselves. For they only exist in and through these relations; they can only
exist in this way by permanently *becoming* selves in living these relations
in a continuous receiving from and giving to that to which they are related; and they cannot do this without continuously being faced with
the task of integrating their relations to others, to other and to themselves by actively relating to them; in doing so they become what
Kierkegaard has called ›subjects‹ who build up their individual identity
through the discontinuities and continuities of their lives in existing as
relations that relate to their relations; and since these relations only exist in relating, i. e. in being enacted, selves not only are *selves* only by
continuously *becoming* selves, they also are *subjects* only if and insofar as
they *become* subjects in the course of their lives.

In short, only in a *situation of communication with other selves* can a ›self‹
become that *for which* something else becomes an ›other‹ by being differentiated *by others from* the ›other‹. There are no selves in the world
independent of the communication between selves[67]: Only because
there is communication, there are selves, and not the other way round.
In this sense a minimal ›self‹ never occurs on its own but only in a context of communication in which it is *spoken to* and not merely spoken
about.[68] For by being *spoken to* it is differentiated as a ›self‹ from that

---

[67] Not only in the sense underlined by Ch. Taylor, *Sources of the Self. The Making
of Modern Identity*, Cambridge, Massachusetts 1989, 35: »There is no way we could
be induced into personhood except by being initiated into language«. The process
starts much earlier in life, and is not restricted to linguistic communication. As
empirical studies in developmental psychology have shown in recent decades, the
ability to discriminate between self and non-self can be traced back much further
than Piaget and others have assumed (J. Piaget/B. Inhelder, *The Psychology of the
Child*, New York 1969; M.S. Mahler/F. Pine/A. Bergman, *The Psychological Birth of
the Human Infants: Symbiosis and Individuation*, New York 1975). Psychologists now
»propose that already from birth infants have a primitive core ability to differentiate between self and non-self, and that infants are attuned to their environment
from the outset« (Parnas/Bovet/Zahavi, ›Schizophrenic Autism: Clinical Phenomenology and Pathogenetic Implications‹, 134; cf. P. Rochat, *The Infant's World*,
Cambridge 2001). It does not follow that human beings are never without a minimal or core self (D. Zahavi), but rather that the ontogenesis of the self starts much
earlier, certainly long before babies are born, and not independent of the interaction of mother and unborn child.

[68] Not merely in a verbal or linguistic way, of course, though this is by no means
excluded, but in all the ways in which they become the addressees and recipients
of communicative activities (feelings, touch, gestures, sound etc.) directed at them
or integrating them into the presence of an ongoing communicative event.

which is *spoken about,* and while every ›self‹ spoken to is also something which can be spoken about, not everything is such that it can be
spoken to and thereby *become differentiated* as a ›self‹ from an ›other‹. You
can speak as long as you wish to a tree but it never becomes a ›self‹.
This only occurs where through being spoken to a being is provoked
and enabled to *interact and communicate with* other ›selves‹, i. e. develop
the capacity of *distinguishing itself* as ›self‹ from ›other selves‹ and from
the ›other‹. Whether our speaking to x provokes x to become a ›self‹
remains always to be seen though we know from experience that there
is a better chance for this to occur with human beings than with stones
or trees. But unless there is a process in which *that for which* something
becomes an other becomes *that which distinguishes itself* from other(s)
there will not be a ›self‹. This process involves (first) that something is
distinguished *by others* as a potential ›self‹ from other(s) by communicating with it, and (second) that this potential ›self‹ becomes actual by
learning to distinguishing *itself* from other(s) in communicating with
others. Since this process takes place as a specific becoming in time, it
is a B-series of events in which through communication and interaction with other selves the A-series capacity of a ›self‹ is constituted. For
this capacity consists in the ability to distinguish oneself from the
events to which one belongs in differentiating the *place* where one is
(*now*) from the *events* at the place and in relating temporally to the
events at the place where one is as *being present at them* and to other
events at other places as either *being past* or *being future* as the case may
be. So a ›self‹ is precisely one that not only is part of a B-series of
events but also capable of haven A-series relations to it. It lives in time
by relating to time, and it relates to time by *being present at* some events,
and *earlier* or *later* than others.

We have to distinguish, therefore, between *being part of an event* and
being present at it. If I am at a concert, I am present at it. But while the
concert does not depend on my being present at it but would just as
well have taken place without me, and whereas I could not have been
at the concert but instead have read a book, I could not have been at
the concert and not been present at it. For me, and for every other
self, participating in an event necessarily means being present at it. I
cannot fail to be present when I participate in an event, and the reason
for this cannot be in the *event* (as if it were true of some events but not
of others) but only in *my participating* in it. Everything can be part of a
series of events, and everything that exists in time is part of at least one
such series. This is also true of selves but they are also *present at* the
event in which they participate because the event in question is

present *to them*. For, generally, to be present at an event is for the event
to be present to the one who is present at it. But this is not a case of simultaneity because it does not relate two distinct events in time. It
rather involves a *difference* of myself from the event in which I participate for otherwise I couldn't relate to this event as present or to other
events as past or as future. This difference does not differentiate and relate two (separate) events in the same or in two different B-series. This
wouldn't solve the problem of my being present at the event but merely reiterate it with respect to two events at which I am now (allegedly)
present. The difference in question cannot be the occurrence of another event or separate or distance me from my participating in the event
but must be inscribed in my very participating in it. *My way of participating in the event is by being present at it*: Presence is my mode of participation in temporal events. And as for me, so for every self: We participate in events by being present at them.

But then we cannot be present at an event without participating in
it, and we are only present at events in which we participate. Presence
entails participation. Without participating in a B-series of events we
cannot be present at it, i.e. have A-series relations to it. Selves (existing
selves) share with things and events that they are part of B-series of
events, but they differ from things and events because they are present
at the events in which they participate. It follows that even if they fail
to relate as selves to them, they can still be part of the series just as other things and events are. For a self to exist as a self is both *to participate
in* a series of events and *to be present at* it. Before I become a self there is
already a series of events to which that belongs which will be me
when I have become a self. Similarly I may cease to live as a self but
continue to exist when I loose the capacity of temporally relating to
the series in which I participate by being present at it, and yet continue to participate in it. We cannot participate in meals without being
present at them. But we may still participate in meals, though not as
selves, even when we have lost the capacity of being present at them.

Being present at an event, therefore, is different from participating in
it in that the former but not the latter involves the capacity of having
A-series relations to the B-series events to which we belong. Can we
say more precisely what this involves? If I am present at an event, the
event is present to me. But the relation ›being present at/to‹ is not a
property of the event but of my temporal relation to the event. However, what about me enable events to be present to me? The answer
cannot be found in any further event that might be discovered by
more refined scientific means for this would merely require us to iter-

ate the question. If there is an answer, it must lie in the intrinsic structure of my being present at an event. Now to be present at a meeting is my temporal mode of participating in it: it is the way in which I as a self participate in this event. But as a self I can relate not only to this event but also to my mode of participating in it, that is, I can become aware of being present at the meeting when my being present at it becomes present to me. But whereas *my being present at an event* is not a B-series event but my temporal A-series relation to these events, the *becoming present to me of my being present at an event* is a B-series event in which I relate not to an event but to my A-series presence at an event. If *my being present at an event becomes present to me*, then this doesn't iterate *my being present at an event*, but rather changes the situation. It is not an iteration of an A-series presence (›being present at‹) at an A-series presence at a B-series event (i.e. a change in the character or intensity of the *mode* in which I am present at it), but rather a new B-series event (›becoming present to‹) that continues the series in a new direction in the wake of the A-series present at the B-series event that it continues. That is to say, if *it becomes present to me that I am present at a meeting*, then I do not merely become aware of an intrinsic and unthematic feature of my presence at the meeting that now becomes explicit and thematic but take part in a real *change of situation* by another B-series event: I *participate* in a meeting by being present at it, and I *become aware* of this when my being present at it becomes present to me. What we have here is not so much an iteration of an A-series relation (›being present at being present at‹), that is, a making explicit of a character trait of my mode of presence that has been there all the time, but rather a bifurcation of the B-series events into those, which make up the meeting and my participating in it (non-cognitive events), and those, which make up my awareness of my being present at it (cognitive events), and it is precisely the occurrence of cognitive events that differentiates non-cognitive from cognitive events.[69] Thus I participate in

---

[69] This shows in the terminology we use: We talk of ›non-cognitive‹ events because the distinction is (and only can be) drawn from the point of view of cognitive events: Only where we become aware of something we can distinguish between *what* we become aware of (events) and *that* we become aware of it (cognitive event). And since cognitive events are events of which we can also become aware or, rather, better aware, it is only both *relative to* cognitive events and *in the realm of* cognitive events that higher order cognitive forms such as *reflection* or *memory* become possible. In this sense all our dealings with the world are cognitively impregnated. Just as the distinction between ›non-cognitive‹ and ›cognitive‹ events is cognitive, so are the various ways in which we – according to our explorative interests, practical needs or theoretical requirements – divide up ›non-cognitive‹ events into ›physical‹ and ›historical‹, ›natural‹ and ›cultural‹, ›mental‹

a meeting (B-series event), and as a self I do so in the mode of being present at it (A-series relation). However, when I become aware of this, I do not iterate the A-series relation (›being present at my being present at‹), that is, leave everything at the B-series level of events as it is but relate to it by *being present at being present* (rather than simply by being present) at it. Rather I am involved in a *real change of situation* by, on the one hand, continuing the meeting (B-series event) and, on the other, becoming aware of it (cognitive B-series event).

It is important to note that cognitive events are B-series events and not merely a-temporal cognitive relations to or symbolic representations of such events. They *change* the situation and do not simply symbolically ›register‹ it. This is why becoming aware of something *interferes* with what we become aware of and not merely ›represents‹ it in a symbolic mode. Moreover, since we are present at all events that are present to us, the bifurcation of a series of events into events and cognitive events entails that we are not only present at a meeting (event) but also at our becoming aware of being present at the it (cognitive event). But whereas I can be present at a meeting of spies without being aware of it, I cannot be present at my becoming aware of being present at it without being aware of it: becoming aware of being present *is* being present at becoming aware of it. This is what distinguishes cognitive events from others: I cannot be present at them without being aware of it. However, to be aware of being present at the meeting does not entail me to be aware *of myself* in being present at it. Self-awareness is at best a possibility but not that without which I cannot be present at an event or become aware of being present at it.

What I cannot fail to be aware of is that I am aware of being present at the meeting. It is impossible to be present at my becoming aware of being present at the meeting without being aware of becoming aware of it: This is precisely what becoming aware of being present at the meeting consists in. For, in general, awareness of presence is not an awareness *of presence* but rather an awareness *in the present of what is present*: ›Presence‹ is not that of which I become aware, but the place in time in which I become aware of whatever it is.[70] But then being

---

and ›social‹ etc. events. There are e.g. no ›natural‹ events independent of our ways of distinguishing ›natural‹ from ›cultural‹ or ›political‹ or whatever other ›non-natural‹ events. These distinctions too are cognitive and not given with the events as such.

[70] Phenomenologists who assume an original primal self-presence in affection, feeling, sensing, suffering etc. rightly stress that »we must resist the temptation to treat these as that *of* which we are conscious« (Hart, ›Michel Henry's Phenomenological Theology of Life‹,186).

aware of my becoming aware is nothing else than becoming aware of *what is present* and, in a reflective mood, that I am aware of it *in the present*. But the problem whether it is *me* who is present, simply doesn't arise in my becoming aware of my being present at something. It is only in a retrospective reflective mood that I can raise this question, and only by knowing its answer beforehand. Thus what I become aware of when I become aware of being present at the meeting is that I am *present at the meeting*, not that it is *me* who is present at the meeting. To focus on this aspect of my awareness is a distinct reflective act that is enabled by cognitive events (my awareness of being present at the meeting), that is a cognitive event itself (reflection is a cognitive activity), and that is directed at an aspect of cognitive events (that is *my* awareness). I couldn't reflect on the fact that it is *me* who is present at the meeting without being aware of being present at it. I cannot reflect on it without performing a cognitive act that changes the situation (cognitive B–series event). And I perform this act precisely by focussing my awareness not on the fact that I am *present at the meeting* but that *it is me* who is present at it.

However, to focus on this does not make explicit a pre-reflective sense of *mineness,* which the reflective act shows to be an intrinsic but unthematic feature of all my cognitive acts. It simply draws attention to the *1ˢᵗ-person perspective* in which all cognitive and non-cognitive events take place at which I am present: As a self I participate in a meeting by being present at it. I become aware of this in cognitive events in which it becomes present to me that I am present at the meeting. That is to say, I become aware that I relate in A-relations both to the event of participating in the meeting and to the cognitive event of becoming aware of it because being present at them is my mode of participating in them. Relating in this way to these events locates them relative to me in my 1ˢᵗ-person perspective: *For me* they are *present* events and not past or future ones. But their being *present to me* does not require, on my side, any special ›sense of mineness‹ without which they couldn't be present to me. They are *present to me* just because they are located *in the same presence* in which I am located, i. e. in the presence in which I am present at them and they are present to me. All that is needed is *our co-presence* in the same perspective, not a special sense of self or mineness on my part for this perspective. *Co-presence* is the decisive point of the givenness of phenomena in a 1ˢᵗ-person perspective, not a sense of mineness that is allegedly made explicit in reflection.

What reflection brings out when it focuses on *me* who becomes aware rather than on what I become aware of is the fact that I and that which is present to me are located in the same presence, i. e. are *co-present*. It looks at my 1st-person perspective in a 3rd-person perspective and distinguishes between *me* and *my awareness or experience* in a way in which I cannot distinguish in my 1st-person perspective. And it is misleading to read back as an implicit or unthematic reality in the 1st-person perspective what is a cognitive or reflective distinction in the 3rd-person perspective of reflection.

So there is no need to postulate an (unthematic) self-presence prior to all presences at events because there is no need to stop an infinite regress of presences at presences at presences … Just as *my being present at an event* is not an event (of a B-series) but a temporal relation (of the A-series) to events, so *the becoming present to me of my being present at an event* is not an iteration of an A-series relation but a different B-series event. We only have to be careful not to confuse B-series events with A-series relations, or vice versa, when we describe and analyse the situation of being present at an event.

Besides, just as we can become aware of participating in a meal, so we can become aware of our mode of participation, i. e. of our being present at the meal. Both cases of becoming are B-series events and they differ from (say) eating the meal in that they do not continue the bodily activities that make up the meal but are cognitive activities that signify (aspects) of the meal or of our mode of participating in it. *Becoming aware* of something is a B-series event, not an A-series relation, albeit of a special sort: It is a cognitive or semiotic event which occasions a bifurcation of the B-series in events signified and events that signify, and since a sign »is something which stands to somebody for something in some respect or capacity«[71], I can become aware of something only if I participate both in the series of events of which I become aware and in the series of events in which I become aware of it. For just as every event is earlier and later than others, so every sign-event is before and after some other sign-event. Signs belong to sign-processes, which they continue or which they open up, and these processes are structured as triadic relations of (in Peirce' words) ›representamen‹, ›interpretant‹ and ›object‹. In short, events that form B-series can be of different sorts, and cognitive events are one sort that can only occur where sign-processes of the relevant kind take place.

---

[71] Ch.S. Peirce, *Collected Papers of Charles Sanders Peirce II*, hg. v. Ch. Hartshorne/P. Weiss, Cambridge, Massachusetts 1932, 228.

Now while it is true that only selves can become aware of something, i.e. become part of a series of cognitive events, it is not true that they can do so only because of their (primitive or pre-reflexive) self-awareness prior to all actual cognitive events of becoming aware of something. The capacity of becoming aware of something does not presuppose a core self-awareness that becomes aware of something but communication with other selves in and through which the self becomes constituted, aware of others, and (more or less) aware of itself. The whole process wouldn't even begin if it were not embedded in actual communication with others. But in such a communicative context the processes of becoming a self involve semiotic processes which, by repeatedly turning on themselves, differentiate the becoming of a self into e.g. the (complexly interrelated) processes of the *embodied self* and of the *cognitive self*, and the becoming of the cognitive self again into the becoming aware of that of which one becomes aware (›object-awareness‹), of the becoming aware of it (›process of awareness‹), and of the one who becomes aware of it (›self-awareness‹): Awareness of something, (reflexive) awareness of awareness, and self-awareness coemerge in actual cognitive (sign-)processes (B-series events) – that are embedded in the processes of the embodied self which in turn are embedded in the natural (physical) and communicative processes in and through which they emerge – in which the difference between that which becomes present to me, its becoming present to me, and me to whom it becomes present is established and successively deepened and sharpened. Thus only selves who can be present at events can also become aware of being present at events. They do not have to be aware of it in order to be present at them, but neither can they become aware of it unless they are present at them. I may be present at a concert without being aware of being present at it because I am so absorbed in what I hear and see and feel and experience. I do not have to be aware of being present at it in order for this to be the case. But unless I am present at it, I cannot become aware of it. And I become aware of it only by participating not only in the series of events that make up the concert but also in the series of cognitive events that signify those events to me as events at which I am present.

In short, if I am present at an event, then I can become aware of being present at it. This entails participating in it, but this is not enough: I must participate in it in the mode of a self in order to be present at it and be able to become aware of it. The capacity of being present at an event entails the capacity of becoming aware of being present at it. Selves are not only able to relate in A-series relations to B-series

events, but also to become aware of this, that is to say, to participate in
the bifurcation of the B-series in events and semiotic (cognitive etc.)
events. Only selves can be present at an event, and only selves can become aware of being present at it. But just as participating in events
does not depend on being present at them (i. e. on participating in
them as a self) so being present at them does not depend on being
aware of it (i. e. of being a – even minimal – conscious self).

So just as it is one thing *to be part of* a temporal series of events, and
another *to be present at* it, so it is one thing *to be present at it* and another
to become aware of being present at it. We have, therefore, to distinguish
different modes of temporal participation: the causal or *physical mode* of
being part of a series of events that are before, after and simultaneous
with each other; the personal or *subjective mode* of being present as a
self at events in such a series; the *conscious mode* of being aware of being
present at an event. The subjective mode presupposes the physical
mode, but not vice versa (and together they make up the mode of the
embodied self); and the conscious mode presupposes the subjective
mode, but not vice versa (and together they make up the mode of the
cognitive self). We do not cease to be selves by not (no more or not yet)
being conscious selves, and we do not cease to exist by ceasing to live
as selves. But only if we exist as selves we can become aware and conscious of living in the presence, and only if we exist in physical series
of events we can live as selves. Therefore it is one thing to exist in time,
another to live in time, and a third to be aware of living in time. And
while we may not be aware of orienting ourselves in time by distinguishing present from past and future events, we can only consciously
orient ourselves in time if and insofar as we become aware of it.

The property of being present, therefore, is not a cognitive but a
temporal property, and it is a temporal property not of a thing but of
our relation from our place in time to ›things‹, i. e. to everything that
is real and not merely a correlate of our relating to it. That is to say,
presence is not a common property shared by some entities but a
property of the relation of temporal selves to something at which or to
someone to whom they are present. Thus a lecture is present while it
occurs, and it is present to those who are present while it occurs. But
whereas we exist in space and time, neither everything that is related
to us nor everything to which something temporal is related must exist
in space and time.

Being present is the mode in which selves in time (B-series) are related
(A-relation) to things or events in which they participate: We are
present at them, and those at which we are present are present to us.

Being present at an event is therefore our way of having A-series relations to B-series events. *Being present to* us, on the other hand, is the
way in which something is related to us who are selves in time, i.e.
who are present at an event. But not everything present to us is an
event in time or made up of such events. Presence – and this is to be
explored next – is also the mode in which temporal selves such as we
are related to God who is non-temporal (at least in some respects) but
real and becomes present to us in the various ways in which he comes
to participate in our lives: God is present to our presence by becoming
present to it. In short, when we call something present we do not locate it in time but locate it relative to us and our present activities and
experiences in time. *We* are in time but not necessarily that to which
we relate as being present to us. Whether it is a temporal entity itself is
a further question. For not all entities to which we are related are temporal, and not all relations of something to us change with time.

9. God's Presence

It is this, which allows us to apply the notion of presence meaningfully
to God without locating God in time.[72] Just as it doesn't make sense to
locate God to the right or to the left of me, so it doesn't make sense to
describe God to be later or earlier than me: God cannot be located in
space and time. But we can locate God relative to us who exist in
space and time, and everything that occurs in space and time can be
located relative to God. But we exist both in time (B-series) and as
selves in being present at events in time (A-relations). Therefore to locate God relative to us is to locate God relative to our being part of
events in time (B-series) and to our being present at events in time
(selves in A-relations). That is to say, God is co-present with everything
as it occurs and with *every presence* at that which occurs. The first is God's
co-presence with the *occurring* of events (in the B-series), the second
God's co-presence with the *presence* of selves at events (in A-relations).
These are not two sets of entities with which God is co-present but
rather two ways or modes of God's presence: God is *present with* everything *as it occurs*, and God is *present to every presence*, i.e. to every self *that
is present at what occurs*. In short – and this is how I shall use the terms –

---

[72] What follows are not arguments for God's existence or presence, but explorations into the concept of God: How is God to be conceived, if faith in God's
presence is to make sense in the light of contemporary views of time and the
widespread lack of experience of God's presence?

just as God is *present with* the occurring of events (B-series) so God is *present to* the presence at events (A-relations), i. e. to those to whom some events are present, and others past or future.

This does not entail that God is temporal. To speak of God's presence is not to speak of a temporal relation between things or events and God but of God's relation to temporal things and events as they occur, and to selves as they are present to what occurs. However, this divine co-presence cannot be a temporal state of affairs. Not everything is and can be present or occur at the same time. Either you go to a lecture or you eat lunch, listen to a concert or counsel a student. None of these activities is impossible *per se*, but they cannot be done all at the same time by the same agent and hence cannot occur all at once. Not everything possible is compossible as Leibniz put it. If today is Thursday it cannot be Wednesday and hence *not everything possible can occur or be present at the same time.*

Moreover, every event takes time. A lecture starts and, hopefully, ends, and the same is true of concerts, meals and revolutions. They all can only be present while they last. Before they begin, they are future. And when they have ended, they are past. They occur at different times and have different durations, and not all of these are contemporaneous with us so that we could be present at them, because our lives have a beginning and an end and do not last forever. Hence *not even everything compossible can be present* to us *at the same time.*

It may be objected that all this is true only of events, not of things. The world of events can never be completely present because it is by definition a world of temporally ordered events. Add to this the conviction that we can only know what is present, and you can see why pre-modern philosophy has postulated an unchanging world behind the flux of events that is completely present and hence can truly be known. For suppose we live in a world of classical physics in which there is an absolute distinction between what things are and what they do or what happens to them.[73] Then there could be a world of things present to us even if nothing whatsoever happens. For only events take time; if at a given instant there are no events – and mathematical instants are by definition such that nothing happens at them –, there are still things or bodies; and if we define ›nature‹ as the total assembly of bodies at a given instant, then it can be completely present and, in principle, completely known to us.

---

[73] Cf. Collingwood, *An Essay on Metaphysics*, 266f.

But this not only fails because we do not exist at mathematical instants. It also fails if we drop the distinction between events that happen and the bodies to which they happen, as modern physics does. At any instant at which there are no events there are no bodies. But then there »is no nature at an instant. Nature is not body as distinct from event; it is body, no doubt, but body itself is only a complex of events; and since events take time, it takes time for nature to exist«.[74] This is to say that reality as such is temporal, or that time is real: There is a real order of events in terms of their being earlier and later than some others; and this order is due to the causal processes that structure reality. But a temporal universe can never be temporally present at once to anybody, not even to God. Hence God's presence with everything cannot itself be a temporal relation: God is not simultaneously present with everything but *God is present with everything as it occurs* and *with every presence at that which occurs.*

It follows that God is not a cause of what happens but that without which there would be neither cause nor effect. A cause makes its effects more probable than in the circumstances they would have otherwise been. But take God away and there are no circumstances, and hence no causes or effects, left for anything to be more or less probable. God's presence does not contribute to the probability of an event, but is that without which there wouldn't be anything to be probable at all. That is to say, God's presence is the presence of what Austin Farrer has called the *cosmological relation.*[75] It posits – without any intermediary causes and hence not as cause in temporal distance from its effects but in a direct and immediate act[76] – a temporal universe, i.e. a plurality of

---

[74] Ibid., 267.

[75] A. Farrer, *Finite and Infinite. A Philosophical Essay,* Glasgow 1943, 27, passim.

[76] To call this a ›metaphysical cause‹ in contrast to ›physical causes‹ is a problematic way of restating the fact that it is *not* a cause but something different, namely that without which there wouldn't be causes and effects. If ›metaphysical cause‹ is taken to be a descriptive term referring to a special kind of cause rather than a limiting notion that underlines that something is *not* a cause, then distinguishing between ›metaphysical‹ and ›physical causes‹ is a primrose path to distinguishing between *metaphysical* (ontological) and *physical* (empirical or measured) time, as A.G. Padgett, *God, Eternity and the Nature of Time,* New York 1992 does, and to conclude that whereas we exist in empirical time God exists in metaphysical time. This only restates the problem of relating divine activity and created activity but does not solve it. This clearly shows in the result of Padgett's argument. God's time is not only said to be in principle different from empirical or measured time but also related to it. This relation cannot be temporal in the empirical sense because this would subject God's time to the structures of empirical time. It rather must be what Padgett calls a ›Zero Time Relation‹: »Two events are Zero Time

events which (logically) cannot occur at one and the same time but none of which can occur without entailing the presence of God; it places us in this temporal universe; and it thus makes it necessary for us to orient ourselves in time by distinguishing between present, past and future.

That is to say, because we exist in a temporal universe, we cannot live, experience or act without participating in causal and temporal processes of events. But in order to be able to act successfully we must know what is and what is not at our disposal, what can and what cannot be influenced by what we do. Thus we ascribe the property of *being present* to that, which is simultaneous with our acting; the property of *being past* to that which we cannot influence any more; and the property of *being future* to that which we can influence. Past is what I cannot affect, future is what I can affect, the present is the here and now of my acting. We are temporal recipients of what is present, i.e. we are placed within a temporal framework of earlier and later relations and we order our world in our temporal perspectives of past/present/future from our particular point of view within that framework. That is why presence is not a quality or property which we infer from anything. It is an aspect of our acting and experiencing, not something we infer but something of which we are directly and infallibly aware. We do not experience what is present but *whatever we experience we experience in the present.*

However, if God is, then just as unfailingly as I live in the presence, I live in the presence of God: No presence (occurrence) without the presence of God. If for God to be is to be present, and if without God's presence there wouldn't be anyone to experience anything nor

---

Related if and only if no duration occurs between them.« (ibid., 21) But this negative definition only restates that the relation between God's time and empirical time is not temporal in the sense of empirical time but doesn't explain what it is. But Padgett not only assumes (a) a metaphysical difference between God's time and empirical time and (b) a Zero Time Relation between them but also (c) that there is no congruence between God's time and empirical time (cf. A. Padgett, ›Can History Measure Eternity? A Reply to William Craig‹, *Religious Studies* 27, 1991, 333-335; cf. W.L. Craig, ›God and Real Time‹, *Religious Studies* 26, 1990, 335-347) and yet that the ›now‹ of God's time must correspond to the ›now‹ of empirical time if the Zero Time Relation between the two time structures is to obtain. But this is confused and the inconsistency shows that Padgett's elaborate argument does not really lead beyond Farrer's statement of the ›cosmological relation‹ that claims, on the one hand, *that* there is a relation between creative and created agency but is, on the other, unable to *describe* this relation in positive terms by specifying the ›causal joint‹ between them.

anything to be experienced by anyone, then God is present whenever I experience or act. And as for me, so for everyone: *Whoever experiences, experiences in the presence of God; whoever acts, acts in the presence of God; and whatever occurs, occurs in the presence of God.* To speak of God's presence is to characterise God's relation to us from within time but not to place God in time (God is not thereby located in the series of events). If God is to be co-present with the occurrence of every event as well as with every presence of selves at what occurs, then God cannot be an event himself, not even an event of endless duration. He must be wholly present whenever something occurs or is present to anybody.

It follows that we cannot specify our relation to God in terms of our temporal perspectives on the world: God is neither past nor future, but eternally (not sempiternally and with infinite duration) present with us. For if God is present with anything at all, God is present with everything that occurs and to every presence at what occurs; and if anything lives in the presence of God, then everything that exists now exists in the presence of God. In short, God's presence is such that nothing is actual or possible without God being present. However, not all is and can be present at one and the same time: Today is Thursday and not Wednesday, and at present I am writing a book in Zurich and am not flying to San Francisco. If I were I could rely on God being present, just as I can rely on God being present here and now. For God is present with everything that is present, i.e. with everything as it occurs and to every presence at what occurs.

This does not entail the incoherent view that God is *simultaneously* present at »what I did yesterday, what I am doing today, and what I will do tomorrow« as Swinburne and Kenny have argued, for then »yesterday would be the same day as today and as tomorrow – which is clearly nonsense«.[77] Rather it means that divine omnipresence is *God's co-presence with every occurrence of an event* (B-series) and *to every presence at the occurrence of an event* (A-series), or – to put it the other way round – every occurrence and every presence entails the presence of God.

This view avoids the charge of incoherence brought by philosophers like Swinburne or Kenny. While some things are present to us, and other things present to others, all things that are present to anybody are present to God. This is not to hold the incoherent view that there is a divine presence, which joins together everything as being absolutely simultaneous. God is not at the same time present to Thursday and Wednesday but whenever it is Thursday, or Wednesday or any oth-

[77] R. Swinburne, *The Coherence of Theism*, Oxford ²1993, 228.

er day God is present to it. It follows that God is not present to past events (which have come to an end) or to future possibilities (which have not yet come to be).[78] The terms ›past‹ and ›future‹ are not used here as determinations of events relative to God but relative to someone present in time, and while God is present not to what is past or future, he is present to every presence. So whenever something is present, or past, or future to anything or anybody, then God is present to that to whom or to which something is present, or past, or future. If God's omnipresence is God's co-presence to all that occurs as it occurs then if God is present with my writing this paper here and now, God is also present with the fact that the beginning of my writing is now past (but God is not now present with that beginning: there God *was* present), and God is present with the fact that the end of my writing this paper is future (but God is not now present with the end of my writing it: there God *will be* present).

It is not the case, therefore, that »God is just plain simultaneous with everything in creation«.[79] This would result in the incoherent view criticized by Swinburne, Kenny, and others. To avoid it, B. Leftow has suggested that everything in time is also in eternity, and whereas God is simultaneous with everything created in eternity, he is not simultaneous with it in time.[80] This solves the problem of God's simultaneity with all creation, but at a high price: It ›dualises‹ creation into its temporal and eternal aspects; it conceives time and eternity as two quasi-independent ontological schemes or patterns of temporal existence and eternal being in which things can be located, exist (in time) or be (in eternity); and it restricts the relationship of God and creation to relations in eternity: Everything created is in time *and* in eternity. But whereas God is present with everything different from God in eternity, God is not present with it in time.[81] In time temporal things are with-

---

[78] God is present to *possibilities* but not to *future* possibilities or to *past* facts.

[79] Pierce, Review of *God and Time*, 507.

[80] B. Leftow, *Time and Eternity*, Ithaca, New York 1991, in particular chaps. 10-16.

[81] Contrary to those who argue »that if God is present with us, He must be present with us in time«, Leftow suggests »that God may be present with us because we are present with Him in eternity« (ibid., 245). God is eternal and exists only in eternity, whereas we are temporal but also exist in eternity. This view assumes that »eternity is a date logically speaking« (ibid., 215; cf. chap. 4). But dates stand in relations to other dates, in particular in »relations of temporal contiguity« and »of temporal distance« (ibid., 215). This must also be true of eternity, understood as a date, and to mark its difference from other (temporal) dates, Leftow argues (1) that eternity is »the unique date which is temporally contiguous with

out God, related only to temporal things, only in eternity they are together with God. Everything that is in time is also, but differently, in eternity, whereas God is only in eternity but not in time.

However, if in eternity temporal things have no temporal relations but only analogous ones, then they are just *things* but not *temporal* things there. But you cannot differentiate temporal things into *what* they are (i.e. *things*) and *where* they are (i. e. *in time* or *in eternity*) in this way: Take their temporality away and what is left is not things without time but simply no things at all. Temporal things are either temporal in eternity as well or they are not things in time. In either case, the proposed solution to God's co-presence with them does not succeed. Either there is nothing with which God is present, or God is present with temporal things whether in time or in eternity.

There is no need, therefore, to multiply ontological modes of creation beyond necessity. Whether God relates to creation in time or in eternity, it is a relation to a temporal reality. But if God is co-present with all that is present without implying that everything is simultaneous with each other, it follows that God does not exist in time. And indeed God has neither temporal location nor temporal duration. There is for God no past and no future; it makes no sense to ask how long God has existed, or to divide up his life into periods of time because God, as Boethius put it, »is in the complete possession all at once of illimitable life«[82]. This is not all that has to be said about God's relation to creation, but it is part of it. God is *related to a temporal creation* because not all that is, was and will be exists at one and the same time. But God is *not temporally related to his creation*: He is neither earlier nor later than anything, nor simultaneous with events at different times nor extended in time with the totality of creation, i.e. of sempiternal duration. Rather God is present with all that is as it occurs. His presence is neither a cosmic Now that joins together all events as being absolutely simultaneous nor the sempiternal duration of an actual infinite but that

---

every date« and (2) that »the temporal distance from eternity to any other date is zero«: »eternity lies at a zero temporal distance from any date« (ibid., 215). But this boils down to saying that the ›distance‹ of eternity to temporal things is that there is no distance, and this is not a »well-formed and meaningful« way of talking about »their distance-relation«, but the very negation of such a relation: Eternity does not lie at a zero temporal relation from any date, but at no temporal relation at all.

[82] That is to say, God is *eternal*: »Aeternitas ... est interminabilis vitae tota simul et perfecta possessio«. Boethius, *Philosophiae consolationis*, V, 6, in: H.F. Stewart/ E.K. Rand (eds.), *Boethius: The Theological Tractates*, New York 1926, 400, II.9-11.

without which nothing could be simultaneous with, or later or earlier than anything else. But then God's presence is not a temporal relation with any of his creation at all but a relation that is time-less in the sense of time-free[83], namely the actuality of divine creativity in the presence of everything that is as it occurs.

This is not to say that God is the cause of everything, at least not in the sense in which we have come to understand causation. For us causes precede their effects (i.e. are earlier in time), there is a means-end relationship between them (if an effect is an end, its causes are means to it), and they explain their effects (i.e. raise their probability).[84] But not so with God: God is not earlier in time than creation; God is not one of the means by which something is effected in creation nor a means that could be used by anyone to effect creation; and God does not explain creation, or anything in creation: The fact of creation can neither be deduced from God nor can it be made more probable than possible alternatives by reference to God because, as Hartshorne has pointed out: »Apart from God not only would this world not be conceivable, but no world, and no state of reality, or even of unreality, could be understood«.[85] But if God is compatible with every conceivable world or state of the world, God's presence does not raise the probability of any of them and hence doesn't causally explain anything. God does not cause anything but rather enables that there can be causes and effects by investing situations with the possibilities and chances from which some become realised in causal processes while others aren't. God, in short, is the poet of the possible, not the maker of the actual.

This is only embarrassing for those who think that God's relation to his creation has to be explanatory in order to be real. But why should it? To deny that God is causally related to our world is not to say that the world is not related to God but that there is no conceivable world which would not be related to God: Any possible world entails God's existence. God does not cause anything to occur but his activity is a necessary or absolute presupposition (in Collingwood's sense[86]) for anything being caused to occur: Events are caused by other events, and they cause further events. But nothing occurs unless God is present to it: Without God there would be no cause for something to occur,

---

[83] P. Helm, *Eternal God. A Study of God Without Time*, Oxford 1988, 39.
[84] Cf. D.H. Mellor, *Matters of Metaphysics*, Cambridge 1991, 226.
[85] Ch. Hartshorne, *A Natural Theology for Our Time*, La Salle, Illinois 1967, 53.
[86] Collingwood, *An Essay on Metaphysics*, 31f.

there wouldn't be any possibilities that could be realised in the situation in question, and there would be no motive to actualise the one rather than the other. Thus writing this book could not have taken place without a great many things having taken place before, but neither they nor my writing (nor, indeed, any of their contingent alternatives) could have occurred without God being present. For God – as Austin Farrer put it – makes things being made, or makes them make themselves, and he is present to that making.

God's presence, therefore, is the presence of his divine activity. There is nothing which is not in the presence of God when it occurs because (a) God is intrinsically active, i.e. God's being is activity; (b) God is active everywhere, i.e. wherever something is actual, it is within the scope of God's activity; (c) God is never active at a distance, i.e. God's activity is co-present with all created activity as it occurs; and (d) God's immediate activity is accessible to us only as it is mediated through the situations with whose present God is present. It follows not only that God's presence can only be apprehended by us in the myriads of ways in which it is reflected in the situations with whose present God is present by paying attention to the possibilities played in one's way in those situations. It also follows that God is immediately co-present with all that is, including his own activity. For if God is (time-free) present with my writing here and now, he is also (time-free) present to his being present to my writing, and hence (time-free) present to himself, i.e. – if this relation is construed as awareness – self-aware of his presence. But the very fact that we can differentiate between the relations of *God's presence with created reality* and of *God's self-aware presence to this relation* implies that it is possible for us to think of God as distinct from any divine presence to creation.

And so it must be, if we want to move beyond the claim that *God really is present* to the more important theological claim that, to some presences at least, *God is present as God really is*. God's divine life is sovereign and free vis-à-vis created reality because God does not depend on it but is able freely to relate to it. If it were different, religious activities such as prayer would loose their point. But this, for the Christian, is not to say that the agency of God is enacted regardless of created agents but rather that God freely relates to them in ways that open up possibilities of life to them: God's activity is informed by his love for his creatures, and his love is not diminished by those who ignore him but determined to overcome their ignorance by love and to wait for their free response in love. God is the sovereign poet of the possible but he freely tunes the possibilities that he creates to the needs of his creation.

This not only requires us to differentiate God's relation to his creation into different modes. It also assumes that there is more to God than God's relation to creation: Unless God has a life of his own independent of creation but open to it, God cannot be present to creation, and it is the structure of this divine life which accounts for God's different relations to creation in being *really present* and in being *present as God really is*. It is the point of the doctrine of the trinity to work this out in terms of the distinctive relations of Father, Son and Spirit; and only a trinitarian conception of God will allow us to combine, without contradiction, that God is in principle beyond time, that God is supremely active, and that God permanently interacts with agents in time. But it is incoherent to be trinitarian with respect to God and not also with respect to everything else. Since the trinitarian structure of God's time-free co-presence to his own activity is at the same time the creative ground and salvific end of all there is and can be, we must also conceive God's co-presence to all the logically contingent things apart from God to be structured in terms of the internally differentiated trinitarian activity of God Father, Son and Spirit; and this entails that God's time-free co-presence with his creation is not the only mode of divine presence.

The property of being present to God, therefore, is not a property of things or events but of the *presence* of things or of the *occurrence* of events. It does not help us to describe or define anything but to locate its occurrence relative to its divine ground of being. For just as we locate ourselves and everything to which we are temporally related *in time* by using the tensed A-determinations *present, past* and *future*, so we locate our being located in time *in reality* by placing everything at which we are present and which is present to us *in the presence of God*.

So the picture that emerges when we try to work out how we in time orient ourselves in relation to God is a successive embedding operation: We and everything else that exists in time are part of the causal B-series of events that make up the universe by being *before, after,* or *simultaneous* with each other. As selves we orient ourselves in this temporal universe by relating from within our place in time to events and time in terms of the A-determinations *present, past* and *future*. And as creatures we orient ourselves in reality by locating both the B-series of events of which we are part and the presence in which we orient ourselves in A-relations with respect to what for us, is present, past or future in the presence of the creator. This requires us to distinguish between the ways in which God is *present with* the occurring of events (B-series), and the ways in which God is *present to* the presence of selves at events (A-relations). However, if God is what he is by doing what he does, that is to say, if God is *semper ubique actuosus* as the love which God is as faith knows, then there is no being of God that is not a becoming, and no being present of God that is not a becoming present. So just as God's being present with everything as it occurs is a becoming present of God which is occurring, so God's being present to every presence is a becoming present to every presence of every self. And just as the first way of God's presence is to be differentiated in terms of the distinct ways in which God becomes present with everything in his divine activity as Father, Son and Spirit, so the second is to be differentiated in terms of the distinct ways in which God the Father, Son and Spirit become present to the presence of selves in time. For to conceive God's presence in this dynamic way does not entail that God is everywhere or to everyone present in the same way. God is really but timelessly present whenever something is present, but not at every present God is fully present as he really is. There is not only a difference between *God's presence* and *God's absence*, but also between *God's becoming present* and *God's becoming present as God truly is*. This brings us finally to the theological or soteriological problem of *God's real presence*.

10. Real Presence as Salvific Presence

As every student of theology knows, the notion of *real presence* has played a key role in the controversies about the Lord's Supper between Zwingli and Luther.[87] They both believed that the mass was not a sac-

---

[87] It should be kept in mind that the whole debate was not just about the Lord's Supper, nor about the ›sacraments‹ as distinct from the ›word‹, but about the real presence of Christ (i.e. the self-giving and self-disclosing presence of the triune God) in the communication of the Gospel in word and sacrament. Nothing here allows playing off God's real presence in the sacraments to God's real presence in the Word. The Word (communicated in preaching, counselling or the care of souls) is as ›sacramental‹ as the sacraments are ›Word‹. This is not to deny the differences between preaching, baptism and the Lord's Supper but they are *not different with respect to God's real presence:* In each case the promise of the gospel is that in communicating it through Word and sacrament God really becomes present as God truly is by breaking into human lives, effecting their change from sin to faith, and renewing them to the communion of love with God and their neighbours. With respect to God's real presence, there is no special ›sacramental presence‹ that is different from God's real presence in the communication of the Word. But then there is no difference in principle between the ›Service of the Word‹ and the Lord's Supper or ›Eucharist‹. The celebration of the Word is no less ›sacramental‹

rifice, and that transubstantiation – the theory that in the Eucharist the substance of bread and wine are changed into the substance of the body and blood of Christ, while their accidents, their appearance, colour, taste and shape remained those of bread and wine – was an irrational doctrine, not to be warranted by Scripture. But whereas Luther insisted that both the biblical text and the Christian faith plainly demanded a belief in the real presence of the body and blood of Christ in the Lord's Supper, Zwingli treated it not so much as a means of grace but rather as a symbol or sign of the covenant between God and humanity, a memorial of Christ's atoning death and a thanksgiving for it. He understood the words ›This is my body‹ to mean ›This is a sign of my body‹, while Luther insisted on their literal reading and flatly rejected all attempts to interpret the *is* as meaning *is a sign of* because this would put the real presence of Christ at risk and wreck the Christian faith.

In support of his position Zwingli advanced, first, *hermeneutical arguments*: We normally understand what Jesus says in the Bible metaphorically, not literally. No one insists that ›I am the vine‹ or ›I am the way‹ has to be understood literally, and neither should ›This is my body‹. All it can mean is ›This is a sign of my body‹.

He supported this conclusion by a *metaphysical argument*. Since bread and wine are physical objects, they cannot be vehicles of spiritual gifts. These have to be received by the soul, not the body, and the proper channel of receiving the spiritual gift of Christ's redemption is faith, not bread and wine: only through faith does the divine gift pass into the faithful soul whereas the faithless receive nothing but bread and wine. This not only entails that we must have faith in order to receive the sacraments and that these are not instrumental to acquire faith, but also that all that is accessible to us is the divine gift, not the divine giver.

The reason is, as Zwingli argues in his major *christological argument*, that after the ascension the body of Christ is ›located‹ at the ›right hand of the Father‹. If the resurrection was truly a resurrection of the body, and if bodies can be present in only one place at a time, then the risen

---

than the Eucharist, and participating in the ›worship of the Word‹ a no less complete and intense involvement with the salvific presence of God's self-giving love than sharing in the bread and wine of the Lord's Supper. Unless this is clearly kept in focus the search for a specific ›sacramental presence‹ in the world becomes a mystifying movement and not the much needed theological clarification of the ways of God's real presence in the world today. Cf. Boeve/Leijssen, *Sacramental Presence in a Postmodern Context*; Boeve/Ries, *The Presence of Transcendence*.

body must be in heaven and cannot still be present here on earth, under the elements of bread and wine. Zwingli did not deny that Christ
is still active in our world. But his mode of operation is not bodily
presence, but spiritual activity, i.e. the activity of the Spirit who conveys to us what Christ has earned for us. Since Christ's body is now in
heaven, we can only refer to it by signs. But these signs are not to be
mistaken for the thing referred to. Bread and wine are signs not so
much of the present as of the absent Christ. They are efficacious or
grace-bearing signs only as special modes of the universal presence of
the divine Spirit.

Luther's response was his doctrine of the *ubiquity of the risen body of
Christ*.[88] He objected to Zwingli's arguments that the phrase ›sitting to
the right hand of the Father‹ does not signify a place (like ›a bird sitting
in a tree‹) but is a way of describing Christ's participation in God's divine presence, nature, power and wisdom after the resurrection. Just as
God is omnipresent, so is Christ, and since Christ exists in the hypostatic union of his divine and human natures, the divine attribute of
omnipresence also applies to his body.

The argument rests upon a novel interpretation of the ancient doctrine of the *communicatio idiomatum*. The fruit of the communion of natures in Christ, Luther argues, is a sharing by the human nature in the
attributes of the divine nature. Hence Christ's human nature (including his body) is present wherever the divine nature of the Logos is
present. To explain this Luther takes recourse to a scholastic distinction
of different modes of presence. Something can be present at a place *lo-
caliter* or *circumscriptive, diffinitive* or *repletive*.[89] The first is ›local or circumscribed presence‹, i.e. the presence of a thing that fills a space. This
is how we normally understand the present of something or someone.
The second is ›definitive presence‹, i.e. the presence where two substances can share one place without sharing the dimensions of the
place where they are. This is the presence which angels or spirits enjoy,
or in which Christ can be present in, with and under bread and wine
here and now and at the same time in other places.[90] The third is ›repletive presence‹ where a thing is »simultaneously present in all places
whole and entire, and fills all places, yet without being measured or
circumscribed by any place, in terms of the space which it occupies«.[91]

---

[88] M. Luther, ›Vom Abendmahl Christi. Bekenntnis‹ (1528), *WA* 26, 326–337.
[89] *WA* 26, 327.
[90] *WA* 26, 327–329.
[91] *WA* 26, 349.

This mode of presence is unique to God and Jesus Christ because of the hypostatic union of the divine and human nature in Christ. For »although we shall be where he is, according to the first or second mode as described above, we shall not be where he is according to the third mode, viz. the right hand of God as one person with God, according to which mode Christ exists wherever God is.«[92]

In this mode of presence both God and Jesus Christ are said to be *ubiquitous*.[93] Since it is the mode of the presence of God, ubiquity is a more authentic mode of presence than the circumscribed and definitive modes of presence. And since in this mode God is present everywhere and nowhere[94], God is beyond manipulation and cannot be captured in any way by anything different from God.[95] Moreover, it is the mode in which Christ is present as God is present: in the form of hiddenness.[96] That is to say, it is a presence tied to an absence, and it can only be apprehended by apprehending the present of the absent or the absence as sign of the present. This requires a special mode of apprehension which Luther calls *faith*. Faith apprehends Christ who is really present[97] but hidden in Word and Sacrament[98], and faith does so by apprehending the presence of Christ *sub contrario* hidden in the cross; in and with the word of the cross; and in, with, and under bread and wine. In faith we apprehend the presence of the hidden God in the dialectics of concealment and revelation because faith is the way of grasping God's presence under the contrary by first being grasped by God. This is why faith is the mode in which we can really apprehend

---

[92] *WA* 26, 349.

[93] Cf. A.G. Jorgenson, ›Luther on Ubiquity and a Theology of the Public‹, *International Journal of Systematic Theology* 6, 2004, 351-368.

[94] *WA* 23, 148-151.

[95] *WA* 33, 594-596.

[96] *WA* 26, 302-303.

[97] Christ is present in faith, as Luther insists: »in ipsa fide Christus adest« (*WA* 40, 228f). Cf. T. Mannermaa, *Der im Glauben gegenwärtige Christus: Rechtfertigung und Vergottung. Zum ökumenischen Dialog*, Arbeiten zur Geschichte und Theologie des Luthertums, Neue Folge, Band 8, Hannover 1989; R. Saarinen, *Gottes Wirken auf uns: Die transzendentale Deutung des Gegenwart-Christi-Motivs in der Lutherforschung*, Stuttgart 1989; ›The Presence of God in Luther's Theology‹, *Lutheran Quarterly* 3, 1994, 3ff. To contrast it with a mere epistemic or subjective experience of the believer in neo-Protestantism, Mannermaa has interpreted Christ's presence as ›real-ontic‹. But he is more aware than some of his followers that this is just a manner of speaking to make an important ›realist‹ point: that faith places us in the presence of God whose saving love is hidden but present in our life.

[98] *WA* 26, 329f.

God and apprehend God as God really is: self-giving love even in, with and under suffering and death. So for us faith is not only the key to grasp God's hidden presence in the cross of Christ but it discloses God's presence to us by the analogy of faith (*analogia fidei*) as the promise and the gift of his presence to us: As God is hidden present to Christ, so God is hidden present to us: as saving, self-giving love. Just as we cannot grasp it there without faith in God's word, so we cannot grasp it here without this faith. For in faith we participate in Christ, and Christ is the co-presence of divine and human ›natures‹, i.e. the presence of Almighty Love for us concealed under human suffering and death.

The nub of Luther's argument is his novel interpretation of the *communicatio idiomatum* according to which Christ's human nature directly shares in the attributes of the divine nature (*genus maiestaticum*). But – to ask only some of the most obvious questions – (1) why affirm a direct communion between the divine and human natures in Christ and not, as the Reformed theologians did, an indirect communion, a communion not of the natures between themselves but a communion of the natures through the person of the union? Because it presupposes an understanding of the human and divine natures, and hence of God and of human beings, that is untouched by the incarnation: The Reformed argument entails a merely theistic understanding of God, i.e. a view of God apart from Christ, a naturalist understanding of human nature, i.e. a view of human nature independent of any relation to God, and a non-Christian understanding of the Spirit, i.e. of a divine spirit without Christ. It is not by accident that the Reformed tradition has been particularly susceptible to the pitfalls of enlightenment theism and naturalism, whereas Lutheran theologians have insisted that a proper understanding of God's real nature must be based on God's incarnation in Christ. Any tenable account of the hypostatic union of the two natures in Christ must argue from the incarnation to the two natures and not from an abstract conception of deity and humanity to the incarnation.

But (2) why restrict the exchange of attributes to a communion of divine attributes to the human nature and not *vice versa* – a consequence accepted only much later in the kenotic theories of the past two centuries? The answer is not merely that it seemed to endanger the divinity of Christ but that it was true to Jesus's own emphasis and message as known from Scripture. Jesus proclaimed *God's presence with everyone*, not *his own special presence with God*: He did not extol himself but God, and he argued from God's presence to the reality of his people, including himself, not the other way round. This is what Lutheran teaching sought to safeguard.

(3) But then why restrict the argument to the risen Christ only? Since the hypostatic union provides the ground for it, should it not equally have been true of Jesus during his earthly ministry? To this the Lutherans responded by appealing to a »distinction between the ›state of humiliation‹ (in which the human nature voluntarily dispensed with the use of the attributes of divine majesty) and the ›state of exaltation‹ (in which such use was established)«.[99] But this implied different sorts of Christ's presence. Thus Luther distinguished between the *bodily presence* of Jesus from birth to crucifixion, his *spiritual presence* between resurrection and ascension, and his *divine presence* after his ascension into heaven. However, does distinguishing these different modes of Christ's presence help to solve the problem or is it merely a way of re-describing it?

To see what Luther is up to we must pay attention to the Augustinian background of his argument: The distinction between *signs* (*signa*) and *things* (*res*). According to Augustine reality is constituted of things of various sorts that can be denoted by signs. Signs are themselves things of a particular sort: denoting things (*res significantes*) and they denote other things (*res significata*). We understand signs if we allow them to direct our mind to that which they are used to signify; and we miss their meaning if we hang on to the signs and do not move on to their signification. Augustine marks this distinction with the terms *frui* (enjoy) and *uti* (use): »To enjoy a thing is to rest with satisfaction in it for its own sake. To use, on the other hand, is to employ whatever means are at one's disposal to obtain what one desires«.[100] Since in the created order all things are at the same time signs of other things, we must never enjoy any of them but only use them to direct us to that which alone is to be truly enjoyed: God, the *res vera*. In this sense, in Alanus ab Insulis famous words, »*Omnis mundi creatura, quasi liber et scriptura nobis est, et speculum.*«[101] It is a mirror of truth, not truth itself; and it must be used as a mirror, i.e. as reflecting something beyond itself, and not mistaken for that which it reflects. This is true of both the book of nature and the book of scripture: We must read them in such a way that

---

[99] B.L. McCormack, *For Us and Our Salvation: Incarnation and Atonement in the Reformed Tradition*, Princeton, New Jersey 1993, 5.

[100] A. Augustinus, *De Doctrina Christiana libri IV,* MPL 34, 16-121, 1.IV.4.

[101] Alanus ab Insulis, *De Incarnatione Christi. Rhythmus Peregans*, MPL 210, 577-580a, 579a.

we allow their different signs to refer us back to their common *res* and author: to God.

In the light of this theory we can distinguish a semantical, metaphysical, epistemological and soteriological sense of the notion of *real presence*[102]:

1. Something is really present when the *res* is present which a given sign signifies (*semantical sense*).

2. Since all things that we can denote are themselves signs that point to God, there is, in the final analysis, only one thing that really is really present: God (*metaphysical sense*).

3. However, what is really present in this unique sense cannot be present to our senses. Our senses grasp signs, not what they refer to, and if we content ourselves with what is given to our senses, we cannot move beyond a merely negative theology, i.e. experience God as absent. To discern the presence of God we must use our minds to reach beyond the flux of visible things to the invisible orders of unchangeable and permanent truths and, ultimately, to their divine source and ground (*epistemological sense*).

4. This is a difficult task which only the happy few can perform who have got the brains, time, money and leisure to do it. The great majority of us would be unable to become aware of God's presence if God had not instituted a particular *res* which truly and unfailingly refers everyone to God as he truly is because it cannot be used without being enjoyed, and not be enjoyed without being used: Jesus Christ, and the sacraments which re-present him as truly present (*soteriological sense*).

This is where Luther starts from: If salvation means to live in the eternal presence of God's love, and if God is present as he truly is only in Christ, then Christ must really be present in the Lord's Supper if it is to place us in the salvific presence of God. But Christ cannot really be present only in the mode of Spirit: he has to be present in both his divinity and humanity. Therefore Luther insists for soteriological reasons on the ubiquity not only of the Spirit but also of the body of Christ.

---

[102] In order to clarify the theological notion of ›real presence‹, it is not enough trace the history of the term. Cf. G. Ward, ›The Church as The Erotic Community‹, in: Boeve/Leijssen, *Sacramental Presence in a Postmodern Context*, 167-204, in particular 172-190; K. Hart, ›Response to Graham Ward‹, ibid., 205-211. One has to scrutinize and reconstruct the theological and hermeneutical issues at stake in the complex debate in the 16th century.

Luther's soteriological vision is right compared to that of Zwingli: God must really be present (and not merely be remembered[103]) as he really is, if we are to be saved. But Luther's argument is flawed because it conflates the semantic aspect of the presence of the *res* to which a sign, or a complex of signs, refers with the *corporeal* or *substantial* understanding of *res* common at the time: God's real presence does not entail the bodily presence of Christ. The doctrine of the two natures, his basic premise, is not a metaphysical description of the peculiar corporeality of the risen (or, derivatively, incarnate) Christ but a theological rule of faith to safeguard the reference to the real presence of God's true nature in Christ: We cannot refer to Christ as he truly is without thereby referring to God, and we cannot refer to God as he really is without referring to the life, death and resurrection of Jesus Christ. Similarly the point of Christ's resurrection is not that he was transformed into a ›spiritual‹ corporeality that miraculously can exist at different places at the same time but that he is eternally co-present to God, i.e. that God and Christ are for ever inseparable; and this is simply to say, with respect to God, that what Christ has disclosed about God's nature is eternally true of God: God is intrinsically active as pure, self-giving love, the love shown in Christ; and this divine love is continuously and invariably active in the manifold workings of the Spirit.

So why insist on Christ's real presence in the Lord's Supper? Because the Lord's Supper is not merely a memorial of events long since past or a sign of hope for events to come, rather the symbolism of the Lord's Supper recalls particular events of the past in order to disclose a present reality: God here presents himself to us through the Spirit as the love which Christ has shown to be his real nature. This love affects all aspects of our being, but we become aware of and respond to it only in faith. For just as God's love was present to Christ in all dimensions of his being, to his body and mind, to his life, suffering and death, so God is also present to us in all dimensions of our being; and just as Christ was drawn into total communion with God by the Spirit, so we are drawn into God's communion with Christ by the same Spirit. Therefore to insist on Christ's real presence in the Lord's Supper is to

---

[103] In the sense of *something past*, not of *something forgotten*: It is one thing to remember God's salvific activity as a past action or event, another to remember it as a present but forgotten or ignored reality. Zwingli based his arguments for the *memoria*-character of the Last Supper on the first view, Luther followed Augustine in defending the second.

insist that God really is present here, and presents himself to us, as he really is: as self-giving love.

If we look at God's presence in the Lord's Supper in this way it is clear that in the highly polemical debate between Luther and Zwingli each side defended a partial truth: Since to be present is to be present *to someone*, Zwingli insisted that we are only saved because Christ is present *to God*, while Luther insisted that we are only saved because Christ is present *to us*. It is easy to see why they had to talk at cross-purposes, and that the real issue, as always in Christology and soteriology, is one about *God*: Since salvation depends on *God being really and truly present to us*, both aspects must be kept together if we want to say that God here really presents himself to us as he really is: as self-giving love.

When and where this occurs we are not only present (in time) or relate to our present, past and future (by living in time) but become present to our present in a particular way: We relate to our present as the present of God's self-giving love. God is present to us *here and now* in our present, and God is present to us here and now *as self-giving love*, i.e. as the love to whom we owe that we are and how we can live our life as persons *coram deo*. For in becoming present to our present, God communicates the possibilities and creates the occasion for us not merely to be present but to become present in our present.

III Discerning God's Presence

For Jews, Christians, and Moslems alike God is not an inference, an absent entity of which we can detect only faint traces in our world. On the contrary, God is present reality, indeed the most present of all realities, and his presence is unrestricted: If God is what believers believe God to be, then God *is present*. But for God *to be* present is *to become* present; for God *to become present* is to become *present with* the becoming (occurring) of something in the present and *to* the presence of someone at the becoming of something in the present; and if God becomes present with anything at all, then God becomes present with all that is or occurs in the present. Whereas we are present at some times and places, and to some things or persons but not to others, God becomes present with all times and places where something occurs in the present, and to all and everyone to whom something is present. God, in short, is *present to presence* in *becoming present with it* and *to it*.[1] Hence either no one lives his or her life in the presence of God and the idea is baseless, absurd or meaningless, or everyone does because there is no presence without God's presence.

However, this neither entails that God is present at all times and places, nor that God is always present in the same way, nor that God is known to be present by everybody, nor that, if God is known, God's presence is known by everybody in the same way. Not everything present is known to be present, and not everything known to be present is known as it truly is. On the contrary, we know much of what is present to us only rather vaguely or not at all. If it were different, detectives, treasure-hunters and most scientists would be put out of work. It is often difficult to find out what is present and what exactly it is that is present.

Why is it difficult in the case of God? Answers differ widely. If there is no God, there simply isn't anything that could be discerned: A treasure that doesn't exist cannot be discovered; a book that never was

---

[1] When I speak of God *being* present in the following I mean it in this dynamic sense of *becoming present* with the becoming of what occurs in the present and to the presence of those who are present in the present.

written cannot be read; and a God who doesn't exist cannot be discerned. But even if God is, God may be such that God is or cannot be present. Or if God is present, God's presence may be such that it cannot be discerned. Or if it can be discerned, we may not be able to discern it. The first answer dissolves the problem by denying *God's existence*. The second questions whether the *concept of God* includes presence as one of its defining traits. The third is about the *concept of presence* and denies that ›being present‹ implies ›can be discerned‹. And the fourth is about *our epistemic capacities* and holds that *we* are incapable of discerning God's presence.

Now I have already argued that for God to be is to be present: a God who is not or cannot be present does not deserve to be called God. But God's presence can indeed not be discerned if there is no God who is present; or if God's presence is in principle such that it cannot be discerned; or if we are – in principle or in fact – unable to discern it. So we must look more closely into the arguments for these claims.

1. Can God's Non-Existence be (Dis)proved?

Few will deny that it is much easier not to discern God's presence than to discern it. This wouldn't come as a great surprise if there wasn't a God. No matter what we mean by ›discerning God's presence‹, the epistemic difficulty would be a mere chimera if there were no God who could be discerned. But this is not an obvious truth either. There have been many serious persons in the history of religion who have claimed to have encountered God or apprehended God's presence in one way or other. Their witness cannot be dismissed out of hand as obviously false or erroneous. They may be wrong because they have an inadequate conception of God; or misinterpret what they believe to have encountered; or mistake a psychological state for a perception of an objective reality etc. Yet to refute their claims conclusively one has to show either that there is no God to be encountered; or that, even if there were a God, he could not be encountered; or that God, even if he could be encountered, cannot be encountered by us. If God cannot be encountered by finite beings (because of what God is like, or because of what they are like), or if God's presence is such that it cannot be discerned in principle, claims to have apprehended God's presence must be wrong. And this is even more obviously so if God, in the sense assumed, does not exist. The first requires us to discuss the understanding of ›God‹ and ›God's presence‹[2], the second to prove that God doesn't exist, and whereas the former requires us to pay close attention to believers' use of ›God‹ and ›God's presence‹, the latter is notoriously difficult, if not impossible, since God is (taken to be) unique.

Believers use the term ›God‹ as a title term for *the one and only who is worthy of worship.* The term only has a proper application if there is a ›being‹ than which no worthier of worship can be conceived; and it is obvious that if there is such a ›being‹ at all, then there can be no more than one. However, precisely because the term ›God‹ is used to refer to a unique ›being‹ or ›individual‹[3], it is so difficult to show that there is no God, or that there is a God, for that matter. For unless we can show on conceptual grounds alone that such a being cannot possibly exist, it is always possible that there is a being answering to this unique status-description; and for different and only partly overlapping reasons Jews, Christians and Moslems believe that this is not only possible, but indeed the case.

Some have gone even further. They argue that it is quite enough to know that God possibly exists, because then God must exist. God, they say, is marked off from the world precisely because God, and God alone, either exists necessarily or is impossible; and since God is possible because the concept of God is not incoherent, it is impossible that God does not exist.

But why distinguish between God and world in terms of necessary vs. contingent existence? The difference between *necessary* and *contingent* can be recast in terms of the difference between *world* and *state of the world* by arguing that it is impossible for the world not to exist even though any given state of the world could have been otherwise. This would make the world necessary rather than contingent, but the term ›God‹, understood in this sense, would have lost its application.

Moreover, unless it can be shown on conceptual grounds alone that it is impossible for God not to exist, it is always possible that God may not exist, and contrary to what philosophers like Hartshorne have argued this cannot be shown by argument alone. Just as there is no con-

---

[2] Again it is the *concept* or *notion* of God that is at stake in what follows even where, for stylistic reasons, I talk of God rather than ›God‹.

[3] Just as in the case of ›existence‹ (see above chap. 2) the use of terms like ›being‹ and ›individual‹ in conjunction with God have to be taken with a pinch of salt. They signify the referent of an individualising reference but do not imply that being a ›being‹ or an ›individual‹ is something God shares with others. Rather God is the one to whom we owe our being, and our becoming individuals.

clusive proof of God's non-existence, so there is no conclusive argument that God exists and is present.

One reason is the structure of deductive a priori arguments. To arrive at true conclusions they must be formally valid, i.e. their premises must logically entail their conclusion, and their premises must be true. But whereas the truth of our premises is independent of what we believe, the premises that we accept as true are not. They depend on our background beliefs that are derived from our experience of the world and of ourselves in the world, including our experience, or non-experience, of God.[4] What we take for granted in our premises reflects our convictions and experience prior to all argumentation. Arguments are important to check the beliefs we hold about God, to explore their implications, and to correct them if necessary. But they are never primary or basic. In the end it is our pre-argumentative experience, not particular arguments taken in isolation, that convince us of God's existence and presence, or of its contrary.

Take Hartshorne, for instance, who rejects all arguments for God based on experience as »a logical scandal«[5]. He rests his argument for God not on the existence of anything in particular, not even the world as such, but on the more general ›Something exists‹; and he claims a necessary relationship not between God and this actual world but between God and one world or another: Not the existence of this world but »the existence of any world at all is what proves God«[6]. Nothing, so it seems, could be further removed from experience: God is not inferred from but entailed by everything that is because, as Hartshorne argues, if anything is possible, then God is necessary, and if God is not, then nothing is possible. But to assert God's non-existence is to affirm

---

[4] It is clear that whatever we mean by the ›experience of God‹, it must be something very different from the ›experience of the world‹. If the difference between God and world is essential to the notion of *the only one who is worthy of worship,* God must not be turned into a part or aspect of the world by being experienced. It is true that we do not experience ›the world‹ but *worldly things* (persons, state of affairs etc), that is to say, things that are or can be experienced in a *worldly way* (e.g. by our senses, through interaction with our physical or personal surroundings etc.); and the world is the totality of what can be experienced in such a *worldly way.* But if there is any substance to the idea of experiencing God, God differs from the world (thus understood) precisely in being *not* capable of being experienced in such a worldly way. The basic notion to be clarified, therefore, is the idea of *experiencing God,* not the concept of *experience* that is then applied differently to worldly things (the world) and to God.

[5] Ch. Hartshorne, *A Natural Theology for Our Time*, La Salle, Illinois 1967, 52.

[6] Ibid., 83.

one possibility (i.e. that God is not) while at the same time denying every possibility, which is self-contradictory; therefore God exists necessarily.

There is nothing wrong with the logic of this argument. But is it independent of all experience? Its force depends on our accepting that nothing is possible if God does not exist or, equivalently, that God's existence is either impossible or necessary. But why should we? Because, as Hartshorne argues, we cannot consistently understand God in terms of perfection, unsurpassibility or maximal greatness and assert that God does or may not exist. God is not a contingent being but either impossible or necessary.

However, this is not a self-evident truth. R. Swinburne for instance takes the non-existence of God to be logically quite compatible with the existence of the universe[7], and understands God to be an ultimate brute fact that explains the universe better and with a higher probability than any rival hypothesis. Others, like W.E. Hocking, were less confident and argued that »The world would be consistent without God; it would also be consistent with God: whichever hypothesis a man adopts will fit experience equally well; neither one, so far as accounting for visible facts is concerned, works better than the other«.[8] And there are also those for whom the ›visible facts‹ clearly point to non-theistic conclusions.

So the internal consistency (or inconsistency!) of a notion of God is not enough to produce a convincing argument for (or against) the existence of God: We can always reject (one of) the premises, if we do not agree with the conclusion. For instance, if we replace Hartshorne's premise ›It is possible that God exists‹ by ›It is possible that God does not exist‹, the same chain of reasoning results in an ontological argument for the necessary non-existence rather than for the necessary existence of God. In either case the truth of the conclusion depends on premises that are not self-evidently true. In order to decide between them the mere consistency of the notion of God is not enough. We need further arguments which cannot be purely conceptual but must be based on experience and, in the final analysis, will appeal either to our experience of God's presence or of his non-presence. Whereas those who believe (for whatever reasons) in the presence of God will opt for the possibility that God exists, those who believe (for whatever reasons) in the non-presence of God will opt for the possi-

---

[7] R. Swinburne, *The Existence of God*, Oxford 1979, 120.
[8] W.E. Hocking, *The Meaning of God in Human Experience*, 1912, 143.

bility that God does not exist. In either case we accept those premises as true that seem most likely in the light of our background knowledge that is not derived from argument alone but from our total interaction with our environment.

Thus the conviction of God's existence or non-existence is never based on argument alone because even ontological arguments give discursive form to prior convictions based on what we have learned from others (communication) or on our own apprehension of God's presence or non-presence (absence) in our daily dealings with the world or in special circumstances (experience). Both the believer and the unbeliever do not believe anything independent of the communicative processes with others in which they are involved. Both know that some or most of what they believe on the basis of communication is in need of correction and clarification. Both seek to check it, wherever possible, against their own experience. Both operate on the same basic principle that what they experience gives them good *prima facie* grounds to believe that what they experience is true. And since it is always possible to construct an argument for one's prior convictions, it comes as little surprise that there exists for every proof of God's existence that is convincing to some a proof of God's non-existence that is convincing to others.[9] Arguments are a means to test or explore beliefs but they are not a source of belief. If there is to be any knowledge of God at all, there must be some source of knowledge other than argumentation, e.g. reliable communication from trustworthy others and/or an experiential apprehension of God. And since we cannot know whether what is communicated to us is reliable (or more likely so than not) or whether those who communicate it to us are trustworthy (or more likely so than not) unless we are in a position to check it against our own experience, it has been claimed that »God, being a unique existent, must be apprehended if he is to be known at all«.[10] A posteriori apprehension, not a priori argument or mere second-hand belief is the way to discern God's presence.

However, experience cannot guarantee its own validity, and the credibility of experience-based claims depends on the evidence adduced. But whereas there is ample evidence that God is not apprehended as present, we cannot infer from this that God does not exist.

---

[9] For a more extensive discussion of arguments for and against God's existence cf. I.U. Dalferth, *Die Wirklichkeit des Möglichen. Hermeneutische Religionsphilosophie*, Tübingen 2003, 211-218.280-307.

[10] A. Farrer, *Finite and Infinite. A Philosophical Essay*, Glasgow 1943, 45.

Precisely because God is a unique existent, it is always possible that God is apprehended by others and may be apprehended by us, provided God can be apprehended at all and we are not in principle incapable of apprehending God. On the other hand, claims to have apprehended God's presence in or with our everyday experience, in special ›religious experiences‹[11], in revelation(s), or in trendy experiments of inducing a ›feeling of presence‹ by stimulating the appropriate areas of the brain[12], will hardly convince the sceptic. Given his or her background knowledge, other explanations of these alleged experiences are always possible and would seem for many to be more likely. So without being already persuaded of the existence of God in one way or another ontological arguments do not get off the ground.[13]

However, provided there is no proof that God cannot be apprehended, the fact that we lack a proof of God's existence need not worry the believer. In the end it is always our experience of the presence, or non-presence, of God that sustains our belief or disbelief in God and makes us lead, or keeps us from leading, a life of thanksgiving and lament. Moreover, there is no other or more convincing evidence for claims to have apprehended God's presence than the apprehending of God. This is not to say that (alleged) apprehensions of God are self-authenticating nor is it to appeal to a vicious circle. In the end we can test the reliability of an apprehension only in terms of other apprehensions; and hence have to rely on some apprehensions in order to test others. The difficulty is rather why God is apprehended only sometimes and by some and not always and by all. For even if the experience of the absence of God is nothing but the absence of experience of God, how is this possible if God is present to every presence?

To answer this we must ask more carefully whether *God* is such that his presence can be apprehended and whether *we* can apprehend it. And if both questions are to be answered in the affirmative, as I shall argue, *what* exactly do we apprehend when we apprehend God's presence and *how* do we apprehend it?

---

[11] Cf. C.F. Davis, *The Evidential Force of Religious Experience*, Oxford 1989, for an interesting attempt to present a cumulative argument.

[12] Cf. A. Newberg, E. d'Aquili, V. Rause, *Why God Won't Go Away. Brain Science and the Biology of Belief*, New York 2001.

[13] I.U. Dalferth, *Gott. Philosophisch-theologische Denkversuche*, Tübingen 1992, 218ff.

2. Can God be Discerned?

There is ample evidence that God's presence is not discerned. But what about the contrary: Can or could God's presence be discerned? A strong tradition in philosophical theology denies it. According to David Klemm, for example, »God is not a possible object of experience or cognition, but is always understood as the unity which breaks into the difference between self and world«.[14] He supports this view by arguing, in the tradition of negative theology, that God is »not-world«, »not-I« and »not-nothing«[15]: »No God we can name is God. Only God is God, and God is not-nothing«.[16]

But we must be careful that we do not first raise »a dust and then complain we cannot see« as Bishop Berkeley once remarked[17]. Just as the word ›nobody‹ is not a name of some being as the Messenger thought in Lewis Carroll's *Through the Looking-Glass*[18] but »a way of saying that there was *not* a being who walked either slower or faster than the Messenger«[19], so to call God ›not-nothing‹ is a way of saying that God is neither a thing nor not a thing, i.e. that God is not the sort of being which we could know, or could fail to know, as we know the things given to our senses. But all that follows from this is that God cannot be known and experienced *in this way*. That God is no »possible object of experience and cognition« at all would follow only if know–ledge based on sense experience of things were the only possible kind of knowledge.

This is the view of empiricist epistemologies but it is also often ascribed to Kant and to the transcendentalist tradition that he has sparked off, and although its epistemological underpinning has been criticised since the days of Jacoby and Hegel, it still exerts its misleading influence on contemporary philosophy and theology. But Kant's views were much more sophisticated. For him God was indeed not a possible ›object‹ of theoretical knowledge. In order to avoid the antinomies of the ›dialectics of reason‹ he critically restricts the cognitive capacities of reason to knowledge accessible to understanding and

---

[14] D. Klemm, ›The Autonomous Text, the Hermeneutical Self, and Divine Rhetoric‹, in: *Hermeneutics, the Bible and Literary Criticism*, ed. A. Loades and M. McLain, London 1992, 3-26, 5.

[15] Ibid., 18ff.

[16] Ibid., 22.

[17] G. Berkeley, *The Principles of Human Knowledge* (1710), ed. G.J. Warnock, Glasgow 1962, 46.

[18] L. Carroll, *Through the Looking-Glass*, 1887, 85f.

[19] D.H. Mellor, *Matters of Metaphysics*, Cambridge 1991, 1.

sense experience. This excluded the topics of 17th and 18th century
metaphysics – ontology (being), rational cosmology (world), psychology (soul) and theology (God) – from the sphere of theoretical knowledge. All theoretical knowledge is either mathematical or empirical,
i.e. consists in true analytical judgements (propositions) of the type ›A
is A‹ or of true synthetic judgements (propositions) of the type ›All a is
F‹ (empirical laws) or ›a is F‹ (empirical propositions) where ›a‹ is a singular term that refers to a referent *a* which can be located in time and
space and ›F‹ is a predicate or general term which ascribes a property *F*
to *a*. But ›God‹ is not a term of mathematics, nor is it a term that can
function in empirical laws which explain empirical phenomena or in
empirical statements that describe phenomena of experience. Since
›God‹ does not function in mathematical formulae God is not a ›formal‹ object of analytical knowledge; since the referent of ›God‹ cannot
be located in time and space, God is not a possible ›object‹ of empirical
knowledge; and since ›God‹ cannot function in empirical hypothesis
reference to God does not help to explain empirical phenomena. In
short, God is not a possible candidate for theoretical (analytical or synthetic) knowledge of what is true or false and hence neither something
to be explained by science nor explaining anything in science.

However, knowledge of truth (*verum*) is not the only kind of knowledge that is relevant to or important in human life. There is also practical knowledge of what is good (*bonum*), aesthetic knowledge of what is
beautiful (*pulchrum*), or functional knowledge of how something fulfils
a particular purpose (knowledge how; *finis*). And while God doesn't
fall within the scope of any of these kinds of knowledge – God is neither an ›object‹ nor a ›person‹ nor a ›value‹ nor an aesthetic principle
nor a means to an end nor a final end of any empirical process – what
we mean by ›God‹ is related to all of them: In the perspective of theoretical reason ›God‹ is not an object but an *idea*, the principle of the
unity of all true knowledge; in the perspective of practical reason
›God‹ is an *ideal*, the principle of the ultimate harmony of good will,
happiness and true knowledge; and in the perspective of judgemental
reason – and this is what Kant has failed to work out in sufficient detail
– ›God‹ is a dynamic, directing and unifying force both of the real and
epistemic processes in our world of nature and culture and the world
of the true, the good and the beautiful. So there is more to what we
mean by ›God‹ than can be spelled out in one perspective of reason
only. But in each of the three main perspectives of theoretical, practical and judgemental reason Kant is at pains of pointing out, on the one
hand, that what we mean by ›God‹ is not to be confused with any of

the phenomena in these perspectives nor with a way in which phenomena are dealt with in them but also, on the other, that what we
mean by ›God‹ is not divorced from but related to what is at stake in all
of them.

So Kant's critical warning is well-founded: What we refer to by
›God‹ in philosophy[20] is not to be mistaken for an object of empirical
knowledge nor for the standard of empirical truth but is the principle
of unity of all true knowledge about objects; ›God‹ is not to be confused with ›the good‹ or any other moral value but is the principle of
the hoped for harmony between morality and happiness; and ›God‹ is
not an aesthetic value nor a means to an end or the end of all means
but that which dynamically unifies the manifold processes of nature
and culture into a coherent reality. So ›knowing God‹ becomes something different in principle from having theoretical, practical (moral),
aesthetic or functional knowledge about anything that is different from
but necessarily related to God since neither what is known (the object)
nor who knows it (the subject) is possible without God.

Kant's critical distinctions need to be observed in theology as well if
discourse about God is not to become obscure and obfuscate the fundamental difference from other kinds of discourse: Faith in God is not
just another kind of belief (religious belief) alongside other beliefs but
different in principle. In order to heed this warning it is not enough to
argue in line with classical transcendentalism that God is not a possible
object of empirical knowledge because God is a transcendental reality.
This is the view endorsed by Robert M. Adams who holds »that because God, if he exists, is transcendentally real, he therefore cannot be
experienced and we cannot have certain knowledge of his existence«[21].
The problem is not one of certain knowledge. If this is what we are interested in, mathematical formulae seem to be much better candidates
than most facts of experience. Normally it is quite enough to *know*
and not necessary to be *certain* to know. We are able to know many
things, that is, we are capable of error and also capable of correcting it;
and in order to know in this way we do not need to have absolutely
certain knowledge. It is wrong therefore that whenever I know, I am

---

[20] Kant was careful to equate this not too directly with the use of ›God‹ in (biblical) theology. But he did hold in line with many Enlightenment thinkers in the
tradition of rational religion (cf. chap. 1) that the philosophical understanding of
God could and should serve as a critical standard for evaluating and, where necessary, correcting the use of ›God‹ in religious discourse and theology.

[21] R.M. Adams, *The Virtue of Faith and Other Essays in Philosophical Theology*, Oxford 1987, 6.

absolutely certain. Mostly I am not. And sometimes I am certain but do not know, e.g. when I am simply taking things for granted. Similarly with God: It is not *certain* knowledge but just *knowledge* of God's presence that is at stake; and the question is whether this is impossible because, as is alleged, God cannot be experienced.

Positions such as this are usually supported by arguments of the type *finitum non capax infiniti*. God is said to be, as it were, too ›big‹ to be experienced by us. For whatever we are able to experience, is not God; and if something is God, we cannot experience it. There are two major reasons offered for this: God's infinity and principle constraints on our capacity to experience.

First, God is said to be infinite and perfect, while we are finite and imperfect. But the finite cannot grasp the infinite, and the imperfect not the perfect. Hence we cannot discern or experience God. Second, we can only experience what we are capable of experiencing, and there are general a priori constraints on what we can experience. Thus ever since John Locke proclaimed experience to be the foundation of all knowledge and all true belief, both Empiricists and Kantians have held that we can only experience what is given to our senses, and that our senses can only be affected by physical objects in space and time; and since God is not a physical object but beyond space and time, God cannot be experienced, and hence not be known (in the strict sense of the word).

However, neither of these arguments is ultimately convincing if God *is* experienced or if God *could be* the cause of experience. For »[n]o matter what subject-related challenges sceptics produce and how possible their rival explanations are, since ›God moves in mysterious ways‹, it is always *possible* that he brought the experience about and was a real percept to the subject. One can only show conclusively that a religious experience was not veridical by showing that God does not exist.«[22] So let us look at those arguments in more detail.

3. Making a Difference

We can apprehend (and not merely think we apprehend) only what is not merely in our apprehending or because we apprehend it; and we can only discern something (and not merely think we do) if it makes a difference to us that is not merely the result of a self-affection by us. Whether we talk of physical objects or of alleged transcendental reali-

---

[22] Davis, *The Evidential Force of Religious Experience*, 193.

ties: *to be is to make a difference*, to make a difference is to make a difference *to something or someone*, and whatever makes a difference to someone capable of acquiring beliefs at all can, in principle, be apprehended. For to *apprehend something is to discern the difference it makes*. Whatever does not make a difference to me, I cannot discern. A shade of
green that does not make any difference to me, is nothing to me even
though others may delight in it. The striking colours of a van Gogh
painting are nothing to a colour-blind person. And many people cannot enjoy three-dimensional pictures because they cannot see in the
relevant way without (or even with) some visual aid. Not everything
real makes a difference to everybody. But if something does not make
any difference to anybody at all, it cannot be discerned and does not
exist. Therefore if God exists, it must make a difference, and this difference must be such that it can be discerned in principle, if God or
God's presence is to be discerned.

But isn't God an exception to this because God is infinite? This is
what Austin Farrer held: »God, being an unique existent, must be apprehended if He is to be known at all.«[23] This »apprehension is not a
sensation ... and the pretence of induction ... is spurious. For induction is *(a)* concerned with differences, and *(b)* never perfectly verified
by a number of instances, and *(c)* is concerned with a relation expressible by AND; and none of these qualities belongs to the believer's (alleged) awareness of God's activity.«[24] But God's presence cannot be inferred in such a way from particular instances of experience. If »we are
to know God at all, it is necessary to suppose some apprehension of
Him, as opposed to any mere inference.«[25] This »apprehension will be
of something unique«,[26] and hence cannot be achieved by comparing
God with or distinguishing it from others. Unless »we have a self-authenticating apprehension of God in and by Himself«[27], we have no
knowledge of God at all, and of this »apprehension there is no other
evidence but our apprehending«.[28]

However, even this apprehending must involve some appreciation of
difference. Otherwise we couldn't distinguish God from us, or apprehending God from apprehending ourselves. God's uniqueness becomes
utterly inexpressible if we understand God to be completely beyond

---

[23] Farrer, *Finite and Infinite*, 45.
[24] Ibid., 17.
[25] Ibid., 27.
[26] Ibid.
[27] Ibid., 12.
[28] Ibid., 103.

anything we can think or experience, name or describe. The result will be not a negative theology, but no theology whatsoever. On the other hand, it is no help either to claim a specific faculty for apprehending God, as the Calvinist *sensus divinitatis* tradition does[29], or a unique self-authenticating apprehension of the unique, as Farrer does by reference to the »cosmological relation« by which finite being is related to the infinite God.[30] The first postulates a special *sensus* to make an alleged perception of God possible, which seems to be impossible by reference to our other senses. But this is only to explain the problematic by postulating something even more problematic: Before we have reason to look for such an explanation, we need to establish that there is something to be explained. Farrer, on the other hand, leaves us with the problem of relating the unique cosmological apprehension of divine activity to our ordinary apprehensions of finite activities, and pleading ignorance, as Farrer does, with respect to the »causal joint« between divine activity and finite activities is at best a way of stating the problem but not a solution.

It may be objected that God's uniqueness is not to be thought of in this way at all. We do not need to apprehend God independently of everything else in order to apprehend God; and we do not have to apprehend the whole of God in order to apprehend him. When I happened to see the Queen in London some years ago all I really saw was her hand waving as she passed by in her car, but this doesn't preclude me from being justified in claiming that I have seen the Queen. And so with most other things. We apprehend something in the way in which it is related to us in our perspectives; we use signs to symbolise in our perspective what we apprehend in terms of this relation; and it is the sign and the symbol rather than the ›object‹ itself that we must be able to handle. Thus, it is argued, I must not grasp infinity in order to apprehend God. I must only be able to grasp God in the way God presents himself to me, i.e. discern and symbolise the difference God makes to me by the way God relates to my life or our lives.

Now it is true that we cannot discern anything without using signs and symbolising it, and since every symbolisation involves interpretation, our apprehensions are governed by a twofold contingency: We can only discern something in terms of the difference it makes to us, and we can only apprehend this difference in terms of the language (in the widest possible sense of the systems of signs) available to us in our

---

[29] Cf. A. Plantinga, *Warranted Christian Belief*, New York 2000, chaps. 7 and 8.
[30] Farrer, *Finite and Infinite*, 27, passim.

common interpretative practices. So what we apprehend of God, if we do at all, does not need to be identical with God. If God makes his presence felt to us, what we apprehend of him need not be such that we (can) identify it as (some aspect of) God and symbolise it accordingly.

4. A Presence Felt?

But does God make his presence felt to us? Does his presence make a difference to us at all? And if so, do and can we apprehend it as a difference that *God's* presence makes to us? Various answers have been given but the most prominent one is the *argument from revelation*. In this argument the term ›revelation‹ is used to refer to events in history of which it is claimed that there God is, or has been, apprehended *as* God. God makes his presence felt to us, it is argued, because in revelation God presents himself to our apprehension in such a way that we apprehend him *as God*, i. e. as the God he is for us so that we can meaningfully distinguish God from everything that is not God and that God is not.

Yet none of the events referred to is such that it is unanimously or unambiguously experienced as God's revelation. There are not events in history that are revelations and others that aren't. In Christian theology ›revelation‹ is not a descriptive term that could be used to classify events. It is a localising term used in theological reconstructions of confessional discourse to mark the position of believers (the recipients of revelation) relative to God (the source of revelation) whom they confess to be the one (the author of revelation) who has opened their eyes and lives for his presence by using something in their life (the medium or media of revelation) as a means to disclose the mode of his relation to them and to others (the content of revelation). And the particular point of the use of this term in Christian theology is that God is ascribed not only the role of the source of revelation (Father) but also that of its author (Spirit), media (Son, Gospel) and content (Love). In this way revelation is understood not merely as a cognitive event that discloses something about God but as the way in which God becomes present to someone as God. And since God's becoming present is a dynamic and creative act in which those to whom God becomes present are created by God becoming present to them, revelation is not merely something that happens to believers but rather the divine creation of believers: A person *becomes* a believer by being transformed from living a life of non-faith to living a life of faith through God's revelation being addressed to him or her, i.e. through God becoming present to him or her as God in such a way that everything done or not done in a situation that is determined by God becoming present as God becomes an explicit expression and manifestation of either faith or non-faith.

Thus revelation is always a revelation *to someone* in a specific situation. Where it occurs it determines a situation in such a way that whatever is done or not done in this situation becomes an expression either of faith (i.e. of apprehending and acknowledging God's presence) or of non-faith (i.e. of a failure to apprehend and acknowledge it): through revelation the difference between faith and non-faith is brought to the fore. It and its specific determination of a situation are perceived as such only by the recipients of the revelation who become transformed by it into believers, and what they perceive as God's revelation to them is not obvious and accessible as a revelation to others as well. Thus Christians cannot confess Christ's cross to be the revelation of God's creative love without being aware that this is revealed in the cross only *sub contrario* and accessible only in faith. Without the ›word of the cross‹, i. e. the proclamation of the cross as the definitive revelation of God's love for his creation, the cross does not manifest to be God's revelation; and without faith the ›word of the cross‹ is seen only as a human interpretation and not understood and accepted as a true communication of God's revelation of his love for us in the cross. So the word of the cross is decisive for understanding the cross as God's revelation (and not as something else) and for understanding God's revelation (as revelation of God's love and not something else). Not only are there many who do not experience the cross as God's revelation but even among those who confess that they do there is no unanimity how it should be understood. Every revelation involves interpretation of what is apprehended as revelation in terms of the language, culture and religion of its recipients, and hence every revelation is open to different lines of interpretations.

Besides, since nothing is apprehended as revelation by someone that is not so apprehended by others, reference to revelation can never settle the dispute about whether God makes or doesn't make his presence felt to us. For those who find themselves to be addressed by revelation it does, for others it doesn't. Revelation, by its very nature, is contingent, relative to recipients, and not only unconvincing but non-existent to those who are not its recipients. It makes those who become believers change from non-faith to faith, and it makes those who do not become believers manifest their non-faith explicitly.

So the argument from revelation settles the questions raised only for the recipients of revelation but not for others. To those not concerned there is nothing in the world to which the term refers. But for those concerned it marks a displacement from their former world and a placement in a new world altogether. What Christians call ›revelation‹ does not refer to anything that takes place as an event in the common world of human experience and action but to a change *in their relation* to what takes place in the world: Revelation marks not a change in the world but a change of heart in its recipients and hence a fundamental change of their attitude and relation to the world. Nothing must change for others but everything has changed for the recipients of revelation. History continued as if nothing had happened after Christ's death on the cross. But for Christians everything had changed because the world had been disclosed to be a different place altogether from what it seemed to have been before. It was not merely a change of detail in the picture, a further fact added or another event to be taken into account in history books but a whole new picture of the world that emerged. What Christians refer to as God's revelation does not add another fact to the world but opens up a new view of all the facts of the world, and this is impossible without fundamentally changing those whose view it is by inspiring their hearts, enlightening their minds and empowering their will to live in this new perspective on everything opened up to them by God's revelation. Revelation, in short, is not a fact in the world open for inspection to everyone but the God-given point of view from which believers see the whole world in a different light: Revelation is not one of the things they see but that which makes them see everything differently.

Thus if discerning God's presence is discerning how God makes his presence felt to us, and if what we discern is determined, on the one hand, by what becomes accessible of God and, on the other, by our mode of apprehension, then apprehending God is not something that could be construed and understood along the lines of apprehending something in the world or of ourselves. We do not *discern* God's presence if there is no difference in the way we experience our life between not discerning God's presence and discerning it. We do not discern God's *presence* if we do not discern our *whole life and world differently* in the light of God's presence. And we do not discern *God's* presence if this difference is not experienced as a the break-in of unforeseen possibilities and chances that transform a human life ignorant or despairing of God into a life of hope, trust and love by opening it up to the apprehension of the creative presence of God the creator with his

creation, the salvific presence of God the saviour with his God-ignoring and self-centred creation, and the perfecting presence of God with
his suffering creation.

However, if revelation is the apprehension of God who makes us apprehend God and our life in the presence of God in a new way, then
for this to occur God must be present both with what we apprehend
and to our apprehending: Only because God is already present with
our life we can apprehend his presence, and only because God becomes present to our apprehending in a specific way we can apprehend it. Without the first there couldn't be an apprehension *of God*,
and without the second there would be no *apprehension* of God. So
unless God becomes present to us in the way outlined by making a
specific difference to us in changing our hearts and perspective on
everything, there will be no revelation for us even though God may be
present. But if God becomes present in this way, it is no longer possible to view one's life as a life that is not lived in the presence of God.
In this sense Christians claim that although »God has never been seen
by any man« (1 John 4,12), he has made his true nature known to us
through Christ as the Spirit assures us so that we know him as divine
love which »dwells in us if we love one another« (ibid.). They can explain God's presence and love only by reference to the changes this
love works in their lives and in the way they live in the world. They
can only offer a complete new description of the world in which they
live, and not refer to any particular aspect in isolation.

5. Limits of What We Can Discern

So far I have argued that we cannot apprehend God unless there is a
God who can be apprehended; that we need not apprehend every aspect of God in order to apprehend God at all; but also and most importantly that to apprehend God's presence is to apprehend how one's
whole life becomes changed and transformed by God's presence. But
there is still the second question to be answered whether there are any
a priori constraints on what we can experience which make it impossible for us to discern God's presence.

Now it is true that the *uniqueness* of God, and the *uniqueness* of divine activity, pose serious problems here. Our cognitive capacities that
we have acquired in the course of evolution are designed to enable us
apprehend the particular and the general, not the singular and the
unique. We have learned to operate with patterns of perception and

conceptual structures that help us to reduce the complexities of our environment by concentrating on selected aspects; and we habitually select those aspects and configurations of aspects that re–occur in different situations and therefore help us to orient ourselves in changing contexts. Perception, Dawes Hicks has argued[31], is an act of discrimination, a selection from within the immense complexity of our environment; and different observers placed in the same environment will pick out different sets of qualities depending on their discriminating powers and conceptual background knowledge. That is we perceive particulars by identifying what we perceive (the *object* which stimulates us to apprehend immediately certain *qualities*) as an instance of some general type or sort, and we conceive generalities by concentrating on what is common to different particulars.

However, the cognitive strategies of selection, abstraction and classification which help us to orient ourselves in the complexities of everyday life are of little help when it comes to discerning God: What is needed here is not the capacity to reduce the complex to the simple, but to grasp the singular and the unique; and this is not done by way of selection, abstraction and classification but by the opposite strategy of contextualising the singular and of particularising the unique: We apprehend the singular indirectly through the context in which it occurs, and the unique through its effects in a particular situation, but can never conceptualise it *per se* and independent of the particularising context in which it makes its presence felt.

This is why discourse about the singular and the unique typically is not conceptual and propositional but metaphorical, symbolical, or narrative, full of images and stories that we cannot replace by concepts without loosing sight of the singular and the unique. So just because God is unique we can apprehend God only as God becomes present with our apprehending in particular situations in which we apprehend something. We never apprehend God in isolation or *per se* but only as God relates to us, and our imaginative constructions of God reflect how we apprehend this relation.

However, the objection that we are discussing does not have this sort of constraint in mind. It assumes that all experience is sense experience, and that is a different matter. For why should it? Or why should sense experience be restricted to those senses that are affected by physical objects?

---

[31] G.D. Hicks, *Critical Realism. Studies in the Philosophy of Mind and Nature*, London 1938.

It is one of the widely held convictions of contemporary philosophy and theology that all religious knowledge is symbolical because the »object of religion, is transcendent; it is not a phenomenon. But in order to express that object our imagination has nothing at its disposal but phenomenal images, and our understanding logical categories, which do not go beyond space and time. Religious knowledge is therefore obliged to express the invisible by the visible, the eternal by the temporal, spiritual realities by sensible images. It can speak only in parables«[32] and think only in metaphors.

The argument proceeds on the assumption that our only direct knowledge is of sensible reality; and ever since John Locke proclaimed sense experience to be the foundation of all knowledge and all true belief, philosophers and theologians have held that only by »starting from that knowledge, we can argue our way to the existence, eternity, omnipotence, omniscience and omnipresence of God«.[33] However, as Francis Bacon already pointed out, »a knowledge of God obtained in this way may suffice ›to convince atheism, but not inform religion‹«.[34] What is completely left out of the picture is the possibility of a divine presence, a present activity and communication of God with us that yields in a direct awareness of God. But those who have enjoyed a living religious experience have commonly understood it as an active intercourse between God and them; and they have expressed this not in terms of the experience of physical objects but of persons (selves, minds, spirits, hearts) in communication.

---

[32] A. Sabatier, *Esquisse d'une Philosophie de la Religion d'après la Psychologie et l'Histoire*, Paris ⁴1897, 390 (translation). However, the problem is not God's transcendence but God's *uniqueness*. What is unique can never adequately be described or conceived in general terms, i.e. in terms applicable to other (possible) instances or phenomena as well. The unique can only be referred to by signs continuously replacing other signs used to refer to it, that is to say, by not stopping to talk (think, communicate) about it, by continuously creating chains of signs which can only be secured against misnaming and missing the unique by being permanently qualified, modified, corrected, negated, replaced etc. by new and other signs in the attempt to name and refer to the unique. Whenever we stop replacing our terms by other terms in referring to the unique, it will be misunderstood to be one of the particulars identified or described by the terms used so far. But whatever God is, if God is unique, God is not a particular, and no chain of signs will ever be sufficient to name God unmistakeably, or describe God adequately. Cf. Dalferth, *Die Wirklichkeit des Möglichen*, 546f.

[33] Quoted in J. Baillie, *The Sense of the Presence of God*, Gifford Lectures, 1961-1962, New York 1962, 122.

[34] F. Bacon, *Of the Advancement of Learning*, Book II; quoted in Baillie, *The Sense of the Presence of God*, 123.

Human experience is not restricted to sense experience, nor sense experience to being causally affected by physical objects without taking into account the specific way in which these are experienced in the 1ˢᵗ-person perspective of those who experience it. A rainbow is not just drops of water refracting sunlight but the arc-shaped and multi-coloured phenomenon that appears to us in our perspective in a definite direction and yet at no definite distance from where we are. A sunset is not just the disappearing of the sun from sight because of the earth rotates about its axis on its way around the sun but the complex of feelings and emotions, impressions and thoughts, memories and expectations, sadness and happiness which it brings to mind. And the same is true of flowers, trees and mountains, cities and buildings, costal lines, misty mornings and starry skies which we experience, to say nothing of persons, friends, colleagues or family. Even physical objects are never just that which affects us causally, or which we mirror in physical and chemical ways in our corresponding brain-states, but something invested with meaning in our 1ˢᵗ-person perspectives that both resonates former experiences and makes us expect new and further experiences. If we restricted experience to being causally affected by physical objects we would simply ignore its most important aspect: that which our experiences *mean to us*, for it is this which make us live our life in this way rather than another in response to what we experience.

Besides, restricting experience to physical objects causally affecting us would exclude not only a great variety of (alleged) experiences from mystical and religious traditions but also experiences of my own emotional states and feelings and experiences of other persons or agents. Persons, as Kant was ready to admit, are not just physical objects of a certain type but require other ways of experiencing and apprehending. And the same holds true of God. »Why suppose that the possibilities of experiential givenness, for human beings or otherwise, are exhausted by the powers of *our* five senses?«[35] Christian theology has always insisted that *faith* is a way of coming to know God that cannot be reduced to sense experience. And others who agree that all experience is sense experience have postulated a special ›sense of God‹ or ›religious a priori‹ to account for religious experiences.

Thus to avoid begging the question against religious experiences of God it seems more appropriate to take experience in a generic sense

---

[35] W.P. Alston, *Perceiving God. The Epistemology of Religious Experience*, Ithaca, N.Y./London 1991, 17.

that is not confined to sense experience: Experience, in the broadest possible sense, is a process of acquiring beliefs which are provoked and informed by that to which they refer – *provoked* because *what* we experience *makes* us experience it, and it makes us *experience* it precisely in that we cannot avoid acquiring beliefs about it when we apprehend it; and *informed* because what we believe on the basis of experience is not simply due to our symbolising (i.e. a mere imaginative construction) but reflects our attempts at symbolising that which provokes our beliefs (i.e. is an imaginative reconstruction of a given reality in the context of a particular – common and contingent – epistemic practice). In short, neither *that* we acquire beliefs nor *the beliefs* that we acquire are a matter of our choice when we experience, whatever needs to be added about the choices that make up the specific *symbolisation* of our beliefs.

All this is part of the grammar of ›experience‹ as it is used here. It is an entirely empirical question what we can experience and how we experience it: »We have to learn from experience what we can be experientially aware of«[36] and even if there were strong empirical grounds against the possibility of having sense experience of God, this would not count against the possibility of experiencing God in a non-sensory fashion as Alston has argued.

Thus we must be careful not to confuse two questions. There are general constraints on possible subjects of experience: they must be capable of behaviour complex enough to reveal states of belief and desire, for experience always involves a causal process of acquiring belief and an appreciation of this in a 1st-person perspective. But there are no general constraints on what they can experience: depending on how they are made up they can experience things of any kind, and they need not know how they do it. We experience many things without knowing what we experience or how we experience them. Often we learn that we did experience things of which we had no idea because we lacked the means to detect them (x-rays) or the capacity and knowledge to describe and identify them in a proper way.

Thus it may well be that all the widespread evidence of God's non-apprehension shows is that *we* often lack the capacity and awareness to discern God's presence. But if God's presence cannot be discerned in principle, there is no substance to the distinction between God's existence, reality and presence on the one hand and our (lack of) awareness of God's presence on the other. If God really is present, God must

---

[36] Ibid., 59.

make a difference, and this difference must be such that it can in principle be discerned. A God who does not make any difference whatsoever to our life and who is in principle discernible only by others but not by us, is no God for us.

6. Experiential and Intellectual Modes of Apprehension

However, there are some important objections to all this. A long and important tradition in theology and philosophy has argued that God »cannot be known by hearing, nor made known by speech; nor can He be seen with bodily eyes, but with mind and heart alone«.[37] The reasons are, first, that God is immutable truth, and we grasp truth only through the operations of our mind; and second that God can only be discerned by thought because he is not present to our senses but has to be inferred from his effects in creation through an operation of the mind: Do »you say ›God is invisible‹? Speak not so. Who is more manifest than God? For this very purpose has He made all things, that through all things you may see Him. This is God's goodness, that He manifests Himself through all things. Nothing is invisible, not even an incorporeal thing; mind is seen in its thinking and God in His working«[38], and it is mind alone which discerns God in his working.

The idealist tradition has intensified this idea in the light of the epistemological dualism of experience and thought. Through experience we have access to the particular, individual or concrete, through thought to the general, abstract, universal or ideal. But God is neither a particular *datum* nor a *dabile* but a *cogitabile*. He cannot be experienced but only imagined and thought. However, God differs from all other thoughts in that he is neither a general concept nor an abstract idea nor a mere universal but a ›concrete universal‹ (Hegel) or ›the most individual of all universals‹ (Hartshorne). God makes a difference but this difference is not experiential but existential or *ontological*, it makes a difference by making those to whom differences are made. Without God, we wouldn't be different but wouldn't be at all. So the difference that God makes to our life is not just one among others but fundamental in the sense that without God's presence there wouldn't be a present life to which differences could be made. But if without God nothing exists, nothing is actual and nothing possible; if nothing

---

[37] From the Corpus hermeticum, quoted in J. Baillie, *The Interpretation of Religion*, New York 1928 (reprint 1977 Greenwood Press), 227f.

[38] Ibid., 228.

can be possible without something being actual[39]; if nothing can be actual without being actualised; and if nothing can be actualised without being actualised in the presence of God, then if anything is possible, God must be necessary, i.e. exist in every possible world. For either God exists necessarily or God is impossible, i.e. there is no possible world in which God exists. But this cannot consistently be thought because doing so entails that there is a world in which this is thought. Hence the attempt is self-contradictory, and God cannot fail to exist.

It has been concluded from this that the ontological difference can only be discerned by reason and rational thought. We cannot infer any knowledge about God from what we know in experience because – as Hume and Kant have shown in their different ways – we can argue from things experienced to things that might be experienced, but not to something beyond experience altogether. However, if God can only be a *cogitabile*[40], i.e. something discerned by thought, how can we decide whether what we discern as God is a mere fiction, a theoretical construct (useful fiction), or a rational reconstruction of a transcendental, practical or absolute necessity? What kind of reality has this *cogitabile*?

Some like J. Hick or R. Swinburne have argued that God is a contingent necessity or ultimate brute fact. Thus for Hick »the existence of purposive intelligence« is »an ultimate fact« which explains everything but is »not a candidate for explanation« itself.[41] Similarly, Swinburne has argued that God is the ultimate brute fact that explains the universe better and with a higher probability than any rival hypothesis. But he does not hold that God is a logically necessary being, not only because he believes this to be an incoherent idea but because »the non-existence of God is logically compatible with the existence of the universe«.[42]

Many philosophers have rejected this, but for different reasons. Some follow Kant in taking the idea of God to be a transcendental necessity demanded by the general conditions of possibility of human knowledge. »God is not«, as Kant put it, »a Being outside of me, but merely a thought within me«.[43] That is to say ›God‹ is not a concept

---

[39] Cf. Dalferth, *Die Wirklichkeit des Möglichen*, 116–168.

[40] F. Wagner, *Was ist Religion? Studien zu ihrem Begriff und Thema in Geschichte und Gegenwart*, Gütersloh 1986, 575f.

[41] J. Hick, *Arguments for the Existence of God*, London 1979, 50.

[42] Swinburne, *The Existence of God*, 120.

[43] I. Kant, *Opus postumum. Kant's handschriftlicher Nachlaß*, Vol. 8, AA XXI, Berlin/Leipzig 1936, 145 (my translation).

applicable to reality but an indispensable regulative idea of our knowledge of reality: We require it in order to give completeness and unity to our theoretical knowledge of what is true about the world of experience. But we must be careful not to reify this regulative principle and mistake it for an actual entity. The ideal of a unity in the explanation of the world may be necessary for our knowledge and a coherent conception of the world, but it »is not an assertion of an existence necessary in itself«.[44]

Others have followed Kant in taking God to be a practical necessity, i.e. a necessary postulate of practical reason. The highest good which is the object and final end of pure practical reason can only be attained if morality (the fulfilment of our moral obligations) and happiness coincide. But this is obviously not the case in this life. Therefore we have to postulate both our immortality and the existence of God or otherwise »would have to regard the moral laws as empty figments of the brain, since without this postulate the necessary consequence which is itself connected with these laws could not follow«.[45] God, then, is necessary not for morality as such but for the bringing about of the highest good. This, however, leaves us without any (theoretical) knowledge about God because we cannot make any truth claims about God.

This Kantian attempt to reconcile freedom and reason by distinguishing between knowing and acting, theoretical and practical reason and, accordingly, the impossibility of theoretical knowledge of God and the necessity of postulating God as a regulative idea of morality and the unity of knowledge has met with little approval. Philosophers in the onto-theological tradition like Hegel, Hartshorne or Ward have argued in different ways that God cannot be practically necessary but theoretically unintelligible. If God is possible at all, God is necessarily actual because God cannot fail to exist. The concept of God differs from all other concepts in that we cannot accept it as coherent and remain agnostic about whether it is actually instantiated or not: God is either impossible or a logically necessary being. For, as Keith Ward has argued, it »is a conceptual truth that any possibly necessary being is actual«.[46] However, the cogency of this argument depends on the interpretation of the notion of the possibility of God as ›It is possible that there is a necessary being‹ rather than ›It is possible that there isn't a

---

[44] I. Kant, KrV, AA III, B 647 (Translation: *Critique of Pure Reason* (1787). Trans. N.K. Smith, London 1933).

[45] Ibid., B 839.

[46] K. Ward, *Rational Theology and the Creativity of God*, Oxford 1982, 26.

necessary being‹. In the latter case the same type of ontological argument would establish not the necessary existence but the necessary non-existence of God. And we have already seen that there are no theoretical a priori reasons for choosing one of the two interpretations rather than the other.

But there is an even more deeply seated problem with this approach: the epistemological dualism from which it starts. Experience is not free of conceptual structure, and thought is not an independent source of knowledge and information. Thinking is our means of processing information, of drawing out its implications, and of testing the validity and truth of our beliefs, which we acquire through perception and communication. But then if God is to be discerned by rational reason as something real, he must exist independently of our thinking and believing; and if we find that we are rationally obliged to posit God as a necessary being, we must also insist that God must exist independently of our positing. Hence we are faced with the dilemma of choosing between foundationalism or fideism: either we argue for God's independent existence along the lines of cosmological, ideological or rational metaphysics (which is not convincing) or we presuppose it without argument in our analyses (which is not compelling). To take either kind of approach presupposes some prior theistic convictions grounded in some specific experience. Thus »an essential prerequisite for the construction of a theistic metaphysic« along these lines is some specific experience which not only requires us to posit such a being but in which »the nature of this Being is disclosed to a limited extent«[47].

However, there is no need to construct such metaphysics, and there is always more than one that could be constructed. But the argument is right in stressing that both our experiential and intellectual modes of apprehension are embedded in our complex interactions through feeling, perception, experience, memory and communication with our physical, biological, mental and personal environments. We live in concrete situations and are part of the ongoing processes in which given situations are transformed into new situations. We participate in this at all levels, with all structures and through all the functional operations of our being by selecting and actualising (some of the) possibilities that are available and accessible to us in a given situation. In combining the possibilities selected with what is actual at any given moment in the light of the capacities, needs, interests, desires etc. of the

---

[47] Ibid., 178.

operative structures of our life we are both made and make ourselves in the changes that occur from situation to situation. This is not primarily a conscious process but occurs differently at the various levels and in the different dimensions of the integrated physical, biological, emotional, mental and social structures and operations of our human life. In doing so we built up and sustain our *idem-* and *ipse-*identities by safeguarding the external and internal continuities of our life in the changing situations in which we live. This is how we become re-identifiable for others (*idem-*identity) and individual selves for ourselves (*ipse-*identity). Who we are and what we are for others and ourselves we become in and through these processes. They involve, with differing emphases, all our capacities of feeling, experiencing and thinking. There is a difference in function between them but not a principle divide. They are all embedded in the more complex and interdependent structures of our life as it is lived in changing situations, and just as there is no thinking for us that is not tied up with our feeling and experience, so our experiencing is not independent of our thinking and feeling.

But then if it is possible to apprehend God by thought, and if the difference between our intellectual and experiential capacities is not a principle divide but a difference of function and degree, then it is not a *prima facie* meaningless question to ask whether God, or something of or about God, can be apprehended by experience and feeling.

7. Perceiving God?

We are not now asking whether the »concept of God«, as John Macquarrie argues[48], »is an interpretative concept, meant to give us a way of understanding and relating to reality as a whole«.[49] Conditions of experience are not objects of experience, and if we are told that the concept of God is needed to synthesise the different spheres of our experience this may tell us something about the structure of our experience but not much about God. However, what we want to know is whether God is something that is or can be experienced, i. e. whether and, if so, in which sense it is possible that God's presence can be known from experience.

---

[48] J. Macquarrie, *In Search of Deity: An Essay in Dialectical Theism*, London 1984, 29.

[49] Cf. Hick's experiencing-as of a transcendental *noumenon*.

In a sense this question seems to be odd. Claims to have experienced God are intrinsic to many religious traditions. Consider only the various mystical traditions, the experience of the ›holy‹ or of the numinous described by R. Otto, W. James, N. Smart and many others, or the revelatory experiences characteristic of the theistic religions. They all involve claims to have experienced God. But can these claims be rationally sustained? Is not all experience ultimately based on perception, and is sense perception not an avenue to particular actuality in space and time but never to God? It is true, the critic may admit, that for the religious mind God cannot simply be a category of interpreting experiences that could be interpreted otherwise; but she also insists that God cannot be an object of experience among others. Religious claims to that effect cannot be taken at face value but must be re-interpreted or critically reconstructed.

To this we may reply that the critic wrongly assumes that all perception is sense perception, so that ›God‹ can figure only in the interpreting of perception-based experiences but not be a percept in its own right. But this assumption is misguided. Many from Calvin to Schleiermacher and R. Otto to W. P. Alston have argued that we posses a *sensus divinitatis*, a special *religious sense*, a religious *a priori* or a special *sense of God* that gives us direct access to God unmediated through our common sense perceptions. Hence we can apprehend God not only indirectly along with apprehension of creature but become directly aware of God.

In recent years, W. P. Alston has put forward one of the most widely discussed arguments to this effect.[50] There is no *a priori* reason, Alston

---

[50] W. P. Alston, ›Religious Experience and Religious Belief‹, *Nous* 16, 1982, 3-12; ›Christian Experience and Christian Belief‹, in: A. Plantinga/N. Wolterstorff (eds.), *Faith and Rationality*, Notre Dame, Indiana 1983, 103-134; *Perceiving God*. For critical discussions of Alston's argument cf. R.M. Adams, ›Religious Disagreement and Doxastic Practices‹, *Philosophy and Phenomenological Research* 54, 1994, 885-888; J.L. Schellenberg, ›Religious Experience and Religious Diversity: A Reply to Alston‹, *Religious Studies* 30, 1994, 151-159; P.L. Quinn, ›Towards Thinner Theologies: Hick and Alston on Religious Diversity‹, *International Journal for Philosophy of Religion* 38, 1995, 145-164; F. Ricken, ›Religiöse Erfahrung und Glaubensbegründung‹, *Theologie und Philosophie* 70, 1995, 399-404; E. Fales, ›Mystical Experience as Evidence‹, *International Journal for Philosophy of Religion* 40, 1996, 19-46; M. Steup, ›William Alston, Perceiving God – The Epistemology of Religious Experience‹, *Nous* 31, 1997, 408-420; Chr. Jäger, ›Religious Experience and Epistemic Justification: Alston on the Reliability of »Mystical Perception«‹, in: C.U. Moulines/K.-G. Niebergall (eds.), *Argument und Analyse*, Paderborn 2002, 403-423.

holds, why claims of direct awareness of God should be misguided in principle. To show this he outlines a general theory of perception, which he then applies not only to sense perception but also to what he calls »mystical perception«, i.e. cases of claimed awareness of God. The salient point of his »Theory of Appearing« is that »something (or so it seems to the subject) *presents* itself to the subject's awareness as so-and-so«[51], and this prior to all conceptualisation or linguistic expression. Alston does not deny the background beliefs that we bring to the construal of our experience as experience of something; but in contrast to Hick's analysis of all experience as ›experiencing-as‹ Alston insists on the prior presentation or givenness of the object of our awareness: Direct awareness »is a mode of cognition that is essentially independent of any conceptualisation, belief, judgement or any other application of general concepts to the object«[52]. And there is no principal reason, he holds, to deny this sort of experience in the case of God.

Now alleged experiential awareness of this sort does provide *prima facie* justification for the beliefs it causes: Normally, if I see a tree I am justified in believing that there is a tree – normally, because the validity of the belief is subject to certain conditions such as support from my background knowledge, absence of factors suggestive of alternative explanations and practical efficacy. The credentials of a given belief thus depend on the belief forming practice (the ›doxastic practice‹) in question, which is itself the result of the accumulated experience that beliefs formed in this way are usually true rather than false. Doxastic practices are socially established and at the same time subject to tests of coherence and pragmatic effectiveness; we all participate in more than just one such doxastic practice; and all religions include such doxastic practices as well.

All this is then applied to beliefs about God. They are justified by being based on putative experiential awareness of God. This is a direct, non-sensory experience of God, which involves an appearance of something to the subject, identified by the subject as God.[53] This identification is not independent of the religious and doxastic practices of a given community. However, it is only true if God not merely exists but is indeed among the causes of that experience.[54]

This, Alston argues, is no impossible thought: »there is not reason to think it impossible that God, if He exists, does causally contribute to

---

[51] Alston, *Perceiving God*, 36.
[52] Ibid., 37.
[53] Ibid., 5.
[54] Cf. ibid.

the occurrence of mystical experiences. Quite the contrary. If God exists and things are as supposed by classical theism, God causally contributes to every occurrence. That follows just from the fact that nothing would exist without the creative and sustaining activity of God«[55]. Hence it is not impossible »that at least some of these experiences occur only because God intentionally presents Himself to the subjects awareness as so-and-so«.[56]

The problem is, of course, to specify the precise nature of the alleged causal contribution God makes to such a direct awareness of him. This is not something Alston tries to do. He only points out that we »will have a chance of determining how God has to be causally related to an experience in order to be perceived therein only if we can first determine in a number of cases that God is being perceived«.[57] But this leaves open such important questions as: What would count as an effect of the alleged divine cause of God-belief? Where can such an effect be discerned? And are we justified in attributing it to God? Alston does not specify the kind of divine causality that he postulates, and he doesn't show how it differs from, and is related to, other kinds of causality in other contexts of our life. But without these specifications it isn't clear what he is postulating, or whether there is anything in what he postulates.

Besides, if God contributes to *every* occurrence, he must somehow be causally involved in sense perception as well. But this undermines Alston's sharp division between sense perception and mystical perception. He rightly protests against the »epistemic imperialism« that claims sense perception to be the normative standard of all perception. But if his argument holds then the reliability of sense perception is itself not independent of the reliability of mystical experience. That is to say, we must judge (the validity of) sense perception in terms of religious perception (not vice versa); and in this religious perspective sense perception grasps only a partial aspect of reality because it abstracts from the presence of God without which nothing would be.

Moreover, if God is present in particular perceptions, as Alston argues, then God is present in all our perceptions, actions and experiences. For if God is present with any of these activities, then God is present with all our interactions with our environment at all levels of our interacting, and then ›perception‹ becomes virtually indistinguish-

---

[55] Ibid., 64.
[56] Ibid.
[57] Ibid., 65.

able from ›feeling‹ in Whitehead's or Hartshorne's sense and God is causally involved with everything that is. But even in this broad sense God's divine causality must precede its effects; and this in turn implies, as R. Swinburne has argued, that just as God's »perception of events in the world must be later than those events«, so »his acting must be prior to the effects which his action causes«.[58] However, if God is present with everything as it occurs, then God is not present as a cause of what occurs. Causes are not only distinct but also temporally distanced from their effects, and if God were present as a cause God would in fact be absent from what is caused. So rather than making sense of perceiving God's presence Alston's (and Swinburne's) causal account of perception turns God into something absent from what is perceived as God's presence. This is so whether God's activity is seen as being mediated through physical causal chains as in sense perception (Swinburne) or through non-sensual causal chains as in mystical perception (Alston). In either case God's presence is causally mediated, and hence not the mediated (i.e. distinguished but not causally distanced) immediacy of God's presence with every presence. Or as Aquinas put it: »God is present in all things; not indeed as part of their essence, nor as an accident; but as an agent is present to that upon which it works ... Therefore as long as a thing has being, God must be present to it ... No action of an agent, however powerful it may be, acts at a distance, except through a medium. But it belongs through the great power of God that He acts immediately in all things«.[59] We only have to rephrase this as God being present not ›*in* things as long as they have being‹ but rather *with* the *occurring* of something and *to the presence* of someone in order to see why God's presence cannot be understood in terms of a causal account of perception and a temporal account of divine causation. ›Divine causation‹ must be something completely different from causation as ordinarily conceived. It cannot involve a temporal distance between God's activity and created agency. God must indeed be present for any present to occur. But God's presence to every presence cannot be a temporal relation. So it cannot be a ›causation‹, not even a ›divine‹ one, and distinguishing between ›physical‹ and ›metaphysical causation‹ is not clarifying but obfuscating the issue as we have seen.[60] The term ›causation‹ should be dropped when talking about God's relation to creation.

---

[58] R. Swinburne, *The Christian God*, Oxford 1994, 82.
[59] Aquinas, *Summa Theologica* Ia q. 8, a. 1. Cf. G.J. DeWeese, *God and the Nature of Time*, Burlington, Vermont 2004, 220-224.
[60] Cf. above chap. II, Anm. 76.

However, even when we restrict terms like ›causation‹ and ›perception‹ to created agencies, God is never present *per se* or in isolation in our particular perceptions but only in the particularising way in which God relates to a given situation of apprehension. God is present to *this* present, and while it is always *God* who is present, the determinations of God's presence differ with the situations to which God is present. God's presence provides the possibilities which allow us to live our lives by choosing from what is chosen for us. But not every situation has the same needs and desires, not every life the same requirements, and not all situations the same horizons of possibility. God defines and determines the horizons of a situation by the way he becomes present with it. God's presence provides different possibilities for different situations and although we always choose from what is chosen for us, what is chosen for us changes in time.

So in relating to God through the possibilities given to our present by God being present, we never become aware just of God but of the way God relates to us. We cannot discern God's presence without discerning how we, and everything present, depend on it, and we cannot discern this without taking into account the specific character and determination of the situation in which we become aware of God's presence. This does not stop us to be justified in claiming that we have apprehended or experienced God. But what we apprehend is God's way of relating to us in becoming present to our present in a particular situation, and this we symbolise in our conceptions of God. Since this always involves a co-presence of God and us, or of God and some present reality, we apprehend and experience God's presence always in some particular (epistemic) context. It is this context that allows us to form imaginative constructions of God, and at the same time accounts for the widely differing constructions of God which we find in religion, theology and philosophy.

Alston defends a more liberal understanding of ›experience‹ in order to allow for other kinds of experience alongside sense experience on which he can built his case for showing believers to be justified in relying on mystical experiences in their beliefs. But this move does not really help the religious epistemologist. Multiplying kinds of experience beyond necessity creates more problems than it solves, and postulating a special principle of explanation for every kind of experience, even when tied to an accepted ›doxastic practice‹, does not explain anything at all. It is not enough to argue: Since the claim that God has been experienced cannot simply be rejected as confused and since God is not the sort of being that could be apprehended by ordinary sense experience there must be another ›sense‹ for apprehending God. This claim is neither plausible nor warranted unless there are reasons to believe that we can indeed discern God's presence, at least in principle if not in fact.

8. Can We Discern God's Presence?

Charles Hartshorne has emphatically affirmed this. He holds that »[e]ither no one is aware of God and the idea is baseless, absurd, or meaningless, or everyone is aware of God«.[61] This absolute alternative follows from the universal range of God's reality which in turn distinguishes God from anything that is not God (i.e. the world): God – as we have seen – is either impossible (i.e. cannot exist in any possible world) or necessary (i.e. must exists in every possible world); but since God is possible (i.e. can exist in a possible world), he is not impossible and hence must be necessary.

This has epistemic implications for the possibility of our awareness of God. It is incoherent to think that God may be accessible to someone else but in principle not to us. We wouldn't know what we are talking about when using ›God‹ and ›us‹. It may well be, of course, that not all who could be aware of God, are in fact aware of God, or are aware of God in the same way or to the same extent. But if there are reasons to believe that at least some truly claim to be aware of God then it is not the case that no one is aware of God; and then we need to explain why this is the case only for some and not for all. If either no one is aware of God or everyone, how can anyone seriously deny to be aware of God even though everyone must be if anyone is?

Hartshorne's answer is that »[b]eing directly aware of God or not aware of God is a matter of degree and clarity, rather than an absolute yes or no«.[62] Some are more aware of God than others, but none can claim to be absolutely unaware of God even though he, she or it may not be able to become clear about it. To put it this way is to underline that Hartshorne's argument is not restricted to human beings but includes all sentient creatures. Being sentient is being capable of apprehending God's presence; and having this capacity is actually practising it. All sentient creatures apprehend God all the time; indeed, they only live because they do. But we alone of all creatures can become aware

---

[61] Ch. Hartshorne, *The Darkness and the Light: A Philosopher Reflects Upon his Fortunate Career and Those Who Made It Possible,* Albany, New York 1990, 121.

[62] Ibid.

of what we apprehend, and we do so if and when God chooses to open our eyes to it. What are we to make of this argument?

As noted earlier we are only able to discern what makes a difference to us. But to make a difference to us is not enough for being discerned by us. Many things make a difference to us that we do not notice. Sometimes it is enough to turn our attention to them in order to notice them; sometimes we need complicated technical means to discern what makes a difference to us; sometimes we know the phenomena but cannot explain their causes because we do not know the laws which they obey; and sometimes we do not even notice the phenomena because we are not aware of them.

Some of this may also be true in the case of God. There are differences which are or can be noticed by (some) others but not by (most of) us if we believe what mystics tell us; there are differences which we can notice in principle but not in fact if we believe Christian teaching; and there are differences that can be noticed in one way but not in another, e.g. in thought, but not in experience. So discerning God's presence is not a matter of all or nothing but something to be described in highly differentiated ways. If God is present at all, God is present to our presence at all levels and in all dimensions of our lives; and we cannot discern it without becoming aware of discerning merely an aspect of it.

It has always been a central tenet of Christian faith and theology that we are in principle capable of discerning God's presence. According to traditional Christian teaching about *sin* our difficulty or inability to discern God's presence is not due to an intrinsic deficiency of our human cognitive capacities but a failure that could have been avoided. Sin is the state in which we are unable or unwilling to apprehend God's presence, but since it is a state into which we have manoeuvred ourselves by the actual way in which we live, we are blamed for not achieving what we are made for, *viz.* to live consciously in the presence of God, that is, acknowledge and worship God by the way we live. Thus the notion of sin does not refer to any particular actions in our life, but to the fundamental disorientation of our whole life vis-à-vis God, which distorts our social, spiritual, rational, moral and emotional capacities by applying them for wrong ends. But – and this is what is important here – the very reality of sin is evidence for our human capacity of apprehending God's presence, and everything that is said about our factual human situation in terms of sin and its effects shown in human disunity, pride, jealousy, hatred or violence against others is a negative account of what human life could be like if consciously lived in the presence of God.

All this is supported by the doctrine of the *imago Dei*-character of human existence. The point of the metaphor of the image of God in the Jewish and Christian traditions is to underline the fact that human beings are in principle capable of living their lives consciously in the presence of God. We exist as persons-in-relation who are free to relate in free personal action to God and to the relational order in which we exist as part of God's creation.[63] Of all the beings we know we alone are able to relate actively to God, to ourselves in our social context, and to our natural and cultural environment. In neither respect we cannot choose not to choose. We all actively relate to God's presence with our life or, as Christoph Schwöbel puts it, »to the passive related-ness which is given for human life«[64], either by acknowledging our-selves as being grounded in God's creative presence or by acting as if our freedom were a sovereign and creative, radically self-produced freedom.[65] The *imago Dei*-doctrine reminds us that contrary to those who pride themselves on transcending religion and faith, being able to consciously relate to God is the opposite of primitive behaviour. Of course, as many are fond of reminding us, one can live without exer-cising this capacity. »Why not, since the lower animals do so? And we are all animals; the animal way is partly open to us still«[66]. But Chris-tian teaching is that we are in principle capable of discerning God's presence, can enter into a personal relationship with God, and if we don't it is our own fault.

However, it is precisely because we are made to live in a personal re-lationship with God that God cannot force us into discerning his pres-ence. In personal relationships no partner can simply be causally ma-nipulated as Vincent Brümmer has argued in detail. Personal relation-ships can only be realised on the initiative of both partners. But just as it is not unavoidable for God to enter into a personal relationship with us, so it is not unavoidable for us to enter into a personal relationship with God. The difference is, according to Christian teaching, that God has shown in Christ that he has determined himself eternally to have a personal relationship with each of us whereas we normally do not but live in sin and fail to discern God's presence and to live up to our pos-sibilities. Moreover, »if our salvation is to be found in a personal rela-tionship with God, we cannot achieve salvation by ourselves. We lack

---

[63] Chr. Schwöbel, *God: Action and Revelation*, Kampen 1992, 149.
[64] Ibid., 32.
[65] Ibid.
[66] Hartshorne, *A Natural Theology*, 5.

the freedom of ability, given that in a personal relationship we are by definition dependent for this freedom on Another with whom we enter into the relationship«[67]. For the same reason God cannot manipulate us into a personal relationship with him. All God can do is to »make it possible for us to enter into the relationship« and to »provide reasons which will motivate us to choose to enter into the relationship«[68]. But God cannot bring about our choice by himself. God can be present; God can make himself accessible to us; God can induce us to apprehend his presence; but God cannot do the apprehending for us, and he cannot make us draw the right conclusions from it. It is our choice, not God's, to live our lives consciously in the presence of God. If we don't, we are to be blamed for it, not God. And if we do, God is to be thanked for it because without him we could not have done it.

However, if we are in principle capable of discerning God's presence and if there is a way of how we can do it in fact then what exactly do we apprehend when we discern God's presence, and how do we discern it?

9. Discerning God

To the first question an answer has already been given. We never apprehend God *per se* or in isolation but only in the way in which God relates to us, i.e. changes us by becoming present to us. That is to say, *we apprehend not God* but *in God's presence*, and *we apprehend God's presence when we learn to apprehend ourselves to live and apprehend in the presence of God*. Our lives are the loci, the contexts and the media in and through which God makes his presence felt and in which and through which we can become aware of it. This is the opposite of religious subjectivism. For if God is present to our present then, according to the logic of presence, God is present with everything that is present to us. Therefore if we *apprehend ourselves to live in the presence of God*, then we *apprehend in and through apprehending this that our whole world in which we live with others exists in the presence of God*. God's presence is God's universal co-presence with everything present. God is not one of the things present at a particular time but the one who is present to every presence and with everything present at any present.

[67] V. Brümmer, *Speaking of a Personal God: An Essay in Philosophical Theology*, Cambridge 1992, 75.
[68] Ibid.

It is because God is present in this universal way that the sense of the presence of God takes many different forms. It occurs and originates not always as the spectacular or shattering experience that is sometimes associated with the idea of apprehending God's presence. It may slowly grow on us as the keynote and continual *basso ostinato* of our life. But it is always an experience in which we find ourselves to be existentially involved, and not only partially but totally; and it is an experience which allows for multiple interpretative processes that can lead to a deeper, clearer, better understanding of it in the course of time but also to distortions, misrepresentations and misinterpretations that need mutual clarification and correction in the religious practices and theological reflections of a religious community. Thus we apprehend *ourselves* to live in the presence of God, and like all apprehension this is a matter of degree and clarity; and we apprehend things that are present to us to be in the presence of God, and this again comes in varying degrees of intensity and clarity. We apprehend God in terms of the differences his presence makes to us, and in terms of the differences his presence makes to things present to us. We discern how God relates to us, or how God relates to others, and accordingly base our views of God on how we apprehend ourselves in our world, or how we apprehend the world in which we live in the presence of God.

The different ways of discerning and symbolising God's presence in the various religious traditions and beyond can all be understood to derive from here, and the same is true of the manifold attempts in the history of theology and philosophy to apprehend our apprehensions of God in more systematic ways. They are only in danger to lead astray if either (as has regularly happened) they are not seen as ways of *apprehending the presence of God* but are turned into questionable inferential strategies, or privilege *only one way* of apprehending God's presence at the expense of all the others and then become dogmatic. Yet even in these corrupt ways they show that the real problem is not the alleged lack of apprehensions of God's presence but their confusing richness and the difficulty of arriving at a clear, unambiguous, rationally defensible and religiously satisfying understanding of God on the basis of them.

The sense of the presence of God not only takes many different forms but also comes in many different degrees. Accordingly what we apprehend of God's presence differs as widely as the ways in which we apprehend it. At a basic level we live in God's presence without being aware of it: We ›feel‹ it, but not as a cause of what we are, as Whitehead thought, for causes are actual and earlier in time than their effects but as that without which there would be neither cause nor effect here and now. We do so by ›feeling‹ how (some of) the possibilities and chances provided by God for us and present in the situation to which God is present are actualised, and this contributes to the shaping of the basic processes of our life.

At a more complex level we experience God's presence in a way that leads to feelings, emotions, desires and unconscious beliefs on which we act and which influence the way we live. When we become aware of what we feel, experience, and believe, we begin to form conscious (›religious‹) beliefs about that without which we wouldn't and couldn't live although we may not be able to symbolise it adequately. By participating in the ›doxastic practices‹ of a religious community we may come to learn how to perceive the presence of God more adequately by acquiring more accomplished ways of discerning, symbolising and communicating God's presence with and to our lives. And finally we may use our powers of reflection and thinking to come to a clearer grasp of our manifold apprehensions of God's presence. These processes of apprehension through feeling, experience, perception or thought become increasingly more conscious, and just as all conscious operations they can be stopped at any point. But this does not stop God's presence to provide the possibilities and chances which define the potential of our lives in a given situation and whose partial and selective actualisation shapes the individual character of our life in the successive situations in which we live. And since apprehending it comes by degrees and not in a yes or no manner, what we apprehend as God and of God differs considerably.

Maybe we apprehend in a vague way that there is something present to our present, although all we may be able to say about it is that there is something that is ›not-nothing‹. Or we may apprehend in an already clearer way something on whose presence we feel to depend, or that it is (what in religious practice is called) *God* who is present, i.e. that *God really is*, without being able to give much content to our notion of God. But when it comes to apprehending what God really is, i.e. what *God's real nature* is, we must move beyond the niceties of negative theology if we want to be true to our experience. Thus we may become aware that something is present that is not simply part of our environment; or that it is God who is present; or what God's presence means for us; or how God is related to us and to others. Yet none of this we discern directly but only mediated through (in each case) a *particular way of understanding ourselves and our world*: There is no apprehension of God pure, neither of God's existence nor of God's nature or will.

Rather we apprehend *ourselves* and those co-present to exist in the presence of God; or we apprehend God in whose presence we find ourselves to exist, to be creative, self-giving love, the love shown in Christ. In every case the apprehension of God is insolubly linked to an apprehension of ourselves, and the apprehension of ourselves to an apprehension of our environment: We apprehend that *God really is* by apprehending *ourselves and everything else as being created by God*; and we apprehend *God's real nature* by apprehending *ourselves among all creatures as being singled out by God for a personal relationship of mutual love*.

In short, since God is *ubiquitous*, God's presence is somehow apprehended in all experience[69] as that without which no presence of anything to anyone would be possible; but it does not follow that we are aware of apprehending God in all our experience. If »being directly aware of God or not aware of God is a matter of degree and clarity, rather than an absolute yes or no« as Hartshorne has claimed[70], then we must distinguish between, on the one hand, *apprehensions* of God's presence in perpetually actualising chances in living our lives that are not of our making but given to us and, on the other, *conscious* apprehensions of God in which we discern God's presence with our lives as the source, provider and donor of the chances without which we couldn't live. Since these apprehensions never occur without some particular apprehension of ourselves and of our world, we have reason to believe that this is true of all apprehensions of God, whether conscious or not.

10. Discerning the Difference

It is part of a Christian meaning of ›God‹ that if God exists at all, then nothing that is will be or could be without God. But then the difference that God's existence makes cannot be a difference which some actual realities manifest while others don't, for if God wouldn't exist there wouldn't be anything to be discerned nor anyone to discern anything. So either there is nothing that could make a difference to anybody and nobody to whom any difference could be made, or everything that is, whether actual or possible, manifests God's existence. Thus the difference that God's existence makes is different in kind from any other difference that we can or could discern. It cannot in any way be discerned in the world but only, if at all, by becoming

---

[69] Cf. Hartshorne, *The Darkness and the Light*, 121.
[70] Ibid.

aware of the fundamental ontological difference between being and not being at all.

But this is a difference that we can only, if at all, experience because we are; and it is not a difference that is or could be exemplified only by some experiences but not by others within the horizon of our experience however much we enlarge the scope of the concept of experience beyond ordinary sense experience. It rather is that against which all actual and possible experience is marked off. If the difference to be discerned for apprehending God's existence is the ontological difference between to be or not to be, then apprehending God is not a particular experience or a special kind of experience alongside others. Anything that we apprehended could become an occasion for discerning this difference but there is also no need to discern the ontological difference in order to experience anything at all. We do not need to be aware of it in order to be able to experience. But if anything becomes an occasion for discerning it, then we become it ourselves: To be or not to be is a question that we cannot ask of anything different from us without thereby asking it of ourselves. But discovering the possibility and point of this question – so the argument runs – is becoming aware of the difference that is to be discerned for discerning God, whether we call it so or not.

Thus apprehending God's presence and existence is impossible without apprehending the contingency of our own existence: We and our world *might not have been*, but also – and this is important to add – our world and we *are* even though we could not have been. It is neither necessary nor impossible *that* we are, and it is neither necessary nor impossible *how* we are. But *we are* even though we need not and might not have been, and we are *in this way* rather than another that may also have been possible. We find ourselves thrust into a finite life with limited chances, and we experience this as a challenge, a burden, or a gift. This is how it appears to us in our perspective, and the way it appears to us is decisive for our way of orienting ourselves in our world and in dealing with the chances given to us. For although these chances are limited, and sometimes painfully so, and even though the distribution of chances among us is neither just nor equal, they offer each of us, within the limits accorded to us, opportunities to live a life that can be meaningful and enable us to discover and create continuities across the breaks, turns and twitches of our biographies. We know, or can know, that we haven't always been and shall not live forever. But we also know, or can know, that while we live there are chances, which we

can miss or realise, and that whatever we can and do become is related
to them and depends on them. We are, for a finite time, given the
chance to have chances, and this chance we cannot have without using
it: Even ignoring or dismissing it, is a way of appropriating and making
use of it. It was not our decision that we live, and we cannot live without permanently taking decisions at all levels of our embodied life. But
neither the chance that we have by living nor the chances that we are
given in the course of our life are of our making. We feed on something beyond our making in making ourselves. We might not have
been, but we are. We can live in this way or another, and we have to
choose one way rather than another.

We have a life of limited chances, but we must choose and we cannot avoid it. As long as we live even not to choose is a choice we take.
In many respects we are born into a world not of our making. But we
cannot live in it without making ourselves, within the limits of the
chances given to us. Our life might have been otherwise but it isn't,
and we could have been different but we aren't. We are what we have
been made, what we have made ourselves and what we have allowed
ourselves to be made within the limits of our possibilities and the
chances allotted to us. We might not have been here to have any
chances, and we might have been given different chances form those
we actually have. But these are the ones we have, because this is the life
we live.

So in either respect, with respect both to what might have been the
case (we could *not* have been) and what is the case (we *are*), discerning
God's presence is discerning something about *our mode of being*: *We are*
even though there is no reason why we should be rather than not be;
and we are given, for no reason whatsoever, *these chances* in our life and
no others. We may turn to God to bewail our limits or thank for our
possibilities and opportunities. We may lament that we live or be grateful for it. In either respect we turn to God not as the ultimate answer
to why we are or why we have these and no other chances but because
God is the permanent reminder that there is no ultimate why and no
final necessity of any sort but only sheer contingency and pure gift.

To discern God's presence, therefore, is not to discern the presence
of something called ›God‹ but to become aware of the precariousness
of our *condition humaine* and the unmerited, life-giving, life-enabling
and life-limiting mode of our presence and existence: We not simply
›are‹ but are granted a presence in which to live and exist; we are
granted it without an ultimate *why* or a final *what for* that we could dis-

cover in our life; there is no ultimate reason or final end inscribed into our existence; we live, here and now, in our finite present, in the presence of God; and we call ›God‹ the one to whom we address (if we do) our grateful surprise of having been granted a presence in which to live and chances which we can live in this presence even though we cannot see and find any reason for it.

In this sense, the sense of the presence of God is the ontological surprise to be rather than not to be and to be given, for a finite time, the chance to choose from chances that are not of our own making but from which we can and must choose in living our lives: We depend on them in living, and they enable us to live. Contrary to anything that could have been expected before we entered existence and beyond everything that can be explained about us and our life we have been awarded a presence of limited chances and finite opportunities in which to live and to be present to others and with others. And just as the limits imposed may (and will) occasion us to lament, so the presence awarded may (and should) occasion us to thank for a life that we have the chance to live.

Many theistic thinkers want to go beyond this. They want to discern *God* and not ›merely‹ (as they say) something about our life before God. But if we can only discern what makes a difference to us, and if God is such that he doesn't make a difference to anything without making it to everything, then we cannot discern *God* without discerning *the difference God makes to us and everything else in our life*, i.e. the way in which our life becomes different by God becoming present – different, on the one hand, by being changed from being merely possible to becoming actual (coming into existence) and different, on the other, from being changed from a life that ignores God (life of non-faith) to a life lived in acknowledging or rejecting God (life of faith or of rejecting faith).

This is not to say that God exists only if we discern God. God's presence is in principle quite independent of whether we can discern it or not. It is a mere contingent fact that we (can) discern God's presence: God could have existed without us, and God could have been present without any of us noticing. But if God's presence would not make any difference to anyone, then claiming God to be present, or absent, would be an empty manner of speech. And since the difference God makes cannot be noticed anywhere without in principle being noticed everywhere, we cannot come to discern God's presence without discerning ourselves differently in the presence of God. In short, as

Luther, Zwingli and Calvin unanimously held[71], there is no *cognitio Dei* without a corresponding *cognitio hominis*. And I have argued that this principle of Reformation theology is the key to show what it is for us to discern God's presence.

---

[71] Cf. G. Ebeling, ›Cognitio Dei et hominis‹, in: *Lutherstudien I*, Tübingen 1971, 221-272.

IV Modes of Divine Presence

1. Christian Realism

In an important sense Christians are realists. They believe that their dealings with God are not a purely one-sided affair and hence cannot be explained in purely psychological or sociological terms. They believe that one »cannot believe in God unless there is a God to believe in«.[1] They believe »that God is active in their experience at every point, ... they conceive their religious life as a bi-polar intercourse between him and themselves«[2], and they assert God's presence independent of their beliefs about it.

However, it is a peculiar sort of realism that they assert. To believe that God's presence and activity are independent of our beliefs about them is itself a belief; and this has been the perennial starting point for idealist objections against religious realism. But to believe in God's independence of our beliefs about God is not just one of the many things believers believe. It is not the sort of belief that could be justified by being deduced from more basic principles, nor is it an empirical generalisation that we would be prepared to give up in the face of adverse evidence. Rather God's presence is something believers take for granted in all their dealings with reality, even where they bewail God's absence. It is an absolute presupposition of their way of living, including their way of thinking, feeling and behaving. To abandon this belief is to cease to be a believer, and this, no doubt, is possible. The absoluteness of this belief is not a property of its content but of the way it is held: Believers treat it as absolute, i.e. as the organising principle of their large-scale cognitive map by which they integrate and unify the many different types of experience into a more or less coherent and consistent system of beliefs. It is the basic belief, inscribed into their very being as believers, about the central point of reference of

---

[1] D.Z. Phillips, ›On Really Believing‹, in: *Proceedings. Seventh European Conference on Philosophy of Religion*, Utrecht 1988, 83. Cf. M. Moxter, ›Wie stark ist der »schwache Realismus«?‹ In: J. Schröter/A. Eddelbüttel (eds.), *Konstruktion von Wirklichkeit. Beiträge aus geschichtstheoretischer, philosophischer und theologischer Perspektive*, Berlin/New York 2004, 119-133.
[2] J. Baillie, *The Sense of the Presence of God*, New York 1962, 127.

the new existential orientation, which they acquire by changing and being changed from a life of non-faith to a life of faith. Nobody has to be a believer, and nobody is born a believer. It is quite possible not to believe in the presence of God, and in one way or other we all do or have done so; but it is not possible to be a Christian (or Jew or Moslem) and not believe in it. Therefore to become a believer is to acquire this belief and to re-orient one's life accordingly.

What does this belief involve and what does it commit the believer to? Not to the absurd belief that God is now co-present to everything as we have seen. If I believe that God is present here and now, I am not committed to believe that God is now present to last night's dinner and at the same time to tomorrow's breakfast but that God was present then and will be present tomorrow. I am committed to believe in God's presence to every present and with every present occasion, i.e. with everything as it occurs.

This belief is not a hypothetical generalisation from the particular to the general. It affirms as true of each and every occasion what has been discovered in a special occasion: that God was present to it when it occurred. For there it became discernible to those who were not just present but changed by what they discerned to a new life and orientation *that* God was present; that God was present *as God*; that if this is what God truly is then there is no presence to which God is not present; but also, given our experience of us, our life and our world, that God is not present to every presence in the same way so that different modes of divine presence need to be distinguished. All this, of course, did not become clear to believers in the flash of a moment but by retrospectively pondering it, reflecting on it, discoursing about it, interpreting and clarifying it to others and to themselves in different respects and in changing situations. And all this not merely in an intellectual process of reflective labour and interpretation but above all by actually and actively living their life together with others in the light of this new orientation, by not merely believing but practicing it, and by experiencing the world and their lives, themselves and others in this new perspective into which they find themselves transposed and which they appropriate as their own new way of life by living it.

For Christians this special occasion was the life of Jesus and, in particular, his suffering and cross. This complex event became such a fruitful and creative point of reference for Christians not only because it was the decisive *terminus a quo* for the fundamental change of their life and orientation (occasioned by and ascribed by them to what they symbolised as God's Spirit) but also and importantly because it provided the interpretative means and framework for understanding it and everything else in the light of it in a specific way: From the beginning the cross was placed and understood in the perspective of the gospel which Jesus had proclaimed and for which he had died (God is becoming present even to those marginalized and outcast as forgiving, liberating, life-giving love); it became the decisive occasion that elucidated the eschatological point of Jesus' gospel expressed in the creative metaphor of the resurrection (a new life with God owed entirely to God's free and unmerited presence with those who ignored and despised his presence); and this in turn made the cross the decisive point of reference for elucidating and interpreting everything else in the light of its eschatological perspective.

The theological significance of Jesus' cross, therefore, is not that it marks the cruel end of a particular human life. This is true of each and every cross in human history, and it would not explain why Christians single out this cross from others. Its significance is that it stands for the decisive occasion in history where Christians find the most fundamental truth about God's relation to creation to be disclosed – most fundamental for understanding the reality of our life before God in the light of how God relates to us: *that God is present to his creation by re-creating it*, by calling new and everlasting life out of suffering and death, by ending the world not with a bang nor a whisper but by forcefully differentiating the world into the old and the new by his creative word, into that which is doomed for destruction and annihilation because it opposes, ignores or despises God's loving presence, and that which is saved, made right and privileged to live with God for ever. The cross discloses God to be creative (redeeming, liberating, justifying, saving ...[3]) love, a love that recreates the world by making it not merely better but good. This is why the cross stands for the end of the (old) world and not merely for the end of Jesus' life; its point is cosmological and eschatological rather than merely historical. In short, the reason why Christians affirm God's presence on the basis of the cross is not the discovery of a particular feature of the cross but an insight into the nature of God disclosed uniquely by this and no other cross: for God *to be God is to become present*[4], and *to become present as God is to become present as creative, self-giving and life-creating love.*[5]

---

[3] The plethora of descriptions reflects the many ways in which God's love is symbolised on the basis of the specific contexts in life in which it is experienced.

[4] In this sense, therefore, theology is the »science of the unique and singular«, whereas metaphysics is the »science of the abolition of the unique«, i.e. the craving for utmost generality.

[5] God is only present *as God* where and when God's presence is experienced and understood in the way disclosed by God's Word. For through his Word God

However, this by itself does not entail that the presence of God's love can be discerned at every presence, or is always discerned in the same way. There may be reasons for not becoming aware of God's presence even though one lives in and through it, and different modes of God's presence and activity that need to be distinguished. For God's presence is the presence of *divine activity*, and this activity is *divine* in that it is the activity of *God's love*: God becomes present in being *active* at this and at any other present in a particular way, the way of love, for God is love. But there is no love that is not active and actual: One cannot love without doing it, and one cannot be love without actually loving. By its very nature love is self-diffusive, it implies real and actual loving, and as such aims at mutual sharing, exchange, self-giving, and response. Thus divine love is not like a disposition that needs to be actualised but actual; it couldn't be possible unless it was actual love actually loving. But being active at a given present is (in a way to be clarified) relating to what is present there; what is present in one situation is not necessarily so in another; and since situations differ, relating to them results in different ways, and requires us to distinguish different modes, of divine activity.

2. God's Twofold Presence and Activity

This has long been known in theology. In his debate with Erasmus in *De servo arbitrio*, for example, Luther insisted on three theological principles:

(1) God is intrinsically active (*semper ubique actuosus*), his activity permeates everything so that God is intimately involved in whatever happens.

(2) God always acts in two specific ways: the Law and the Gospel, the way in which God is active in the creation and conservation of everything (e.g. by establishing orders in a chaotic world), and the way in which God acts in and through Christ for our salvation and final perfection.

(3) God is involved in everything that happens because his agency is a necessary condition for it to occur. But he does not intend or bring about everything that occurs. »There is much that is contrary to God's positive will. He may permit, but he does not countenance or con-

---

discloses love to be the true nature of his will towards his creation – a creation that blindly ignores its creator whose love unfailingly works at freeing and saving his creation from its deadly ignorance.

done. Angels and men are in open rebellion against him«.[6] Much of what happens is not positively willed by God but is rather (one might say) one of the unintended side effects of his intentional acts; and these in turn may be seen – in a speculative mood – to be one of the major reasons for the ongoing history of our world because they require God, in order to be true to his divine intention, continually to react to the effects of his own acting and in this way to work for a better and fuller realisation of the ends he intends. Therefore Luther insists that in order really to understand God we must concentrate not on his *opus alienum* (the ambiguous phenomena of creation) but on his *opus proprium*, i.e. on that which God not only brings about intentionally, fully and completely but also makes us understand as disclosing his heart towards us through the Spirit (the self-interpreting word of the gospel). For the one place where we can come to learn about the full and complete realisation of God's intentions is in Christ who discloses God's salvific will towards us, and the only way to come to accept this not only as a fallible human claim but as God's infallible truth about me and everyone else is through God's Spirit.

It follows that just as we cannot simply speak of God's activity, so we cannot simply speak of God's presence but have to distinguish different modes of God's presence and activity.

On the one hand, Luther argues, God is present but hidden everywhere and in everything that is; if God were not, everything would simply stop being: this Luther calls God's *natural presence*. On the other hand God is also *spiritually* present in particular occasions where he makes himself known to be present as redeeming love in such a way that it can be acknowledged in faith. This self-interpreting character and strict correlation to faith distinguishes God's spiritual presence in Christ and in the gospel from his natural presence in all things. For whereas God's natural presence, even where it is recognised, remains ambiguous as to God's will towards us, his spiritual presence reveals God's will to be that of a loving father who cares for his creation.

It is important to note that for Luther God's spiritual presence does not replace his natural presence nor is it simply that we come to be aware of his natural presence. We can know God to be naturally present without knowing about his spiritual presence[7]. Wherever God is spiritually present, he is naturally present as well, but not *vice versa*.

---

[6] P.R. Baelz, *Prayer and Providence*, New York 1968, 81.
[7] Cf. *WAT* 5, 368,21ff where Luther contrasts the *cognitio Dei legalis* with the *cognitio Dei evangelica*.

Yet in either mode God's presence is hidden from our eyes and has to be disclosed to us. The gospel discloses God's spiritual presence to us as being hidden under the contrary (*sub contrario*) of the cross; and only if we are moved by faith to see beyond the surface of Christ's suffering and death to the resurrection, do we become aware of it. Even then, however, God is still naturally present and hidden as well; and it is not easy even for faith to recognise God's natural presence in the world. Therefore it is not enough to hold, as Wiles does, that »God as Spirit is God as present«[8]. God as God is God as present. But God as Spirit is God as present *in a specific way*, viz. in his love for his creatures (the Spirit operative in creation) and in disclosing this love to be discerned and acknowledged (the Spirit operative in the life of believers). But this, as believers are painfully aware in the face of evil, pain and suffering, is often far from obvious. Sometimes we can hardly recognise God's presence there but have to maintain it contrary to what experience and reason suggest. Our experience is dominated by God's absence, and we cannot speak or think of God's presence in any other way than in the language of lament and of hope.

The different modes of God's presence distinguished by Luther correspond to *different modes of divine activity*. On the one hand God acts in all things by acting through all things according to his inscrutable almighty will; and even though God does not act directly but co-operates with the secondary causes which he has created, he is not simply the uniform power of action in all acting but remains the free agent who »can and does everything that he wills«[9]. However, simply to claim »that God brings about *all* events excludes the possibility of identifying particular events as acts of God as distinct from the rest which we ascribe to other agents«; and this not only »entails that we should hold God responsible for all events, both good and evil« but »would seem in the end to make all talk of divine agency vacuous«.[10] In order to identify particular events (including human actions) as divine acts we must know the intentions by which they are governed; otherwise we cannot ascribe responsibility for them to God. But how can we know God's intentions? The answer most commonly given is: Either by being told about them by God, or by inferring them from the character of God as known in the cumulative experience of a giv-

---

[8] M. Wiles, *Faith and the Mystery of God*, London 1982, 123.

[9] *WA* 18, 636,29f.

[10] V. Brümmer, *Speaking of a Personal God. An Essay in Philosophical Theology*, Cambridge 1992, 119.

en community of believers. Either way presupposes that although God's activity is a necessary condition for all that happens, there are particular actions, which God brings about intentionally and through which he discloses his intentions to us.

Thus besides acting in and through all things, God acts in and with particular things that he has ordained as vessels of his grace. This is the mode of the Gospel through which God makes himself known as saving love by adapting himself to the mode of the receptivity of his creatures[11] in such a way that they come to acknowledge his divine love. However, God co-operates with created activity in the realm of creation by not acting without and contrary to what he has created. He is the sole author of the acts of grace and, at the same time, the co-author of the created means in, with and under which he performs his acts of grace. The two realms of creation and grace are therefore not related as two stages of a monolithic creative activity. They are constituted by the two fundamental ways in which God acts in our world *in Christo* and *extra Christum.* And this entails that there are occasions in which God is present and active *in more than one way.*

If Luther's account is true, recent debates about divine agency in philosophy of religion have not come to grips with the nub of the problem. They concentrate on the question of how God's activity is related to created activity; and many have accepted Austin Farrer's *paradox of double agency,* i.e. the impossibility of specifying the causal link between finite and infinite agency. But if Luther is right, this is at best a side issue of a more fundamental problem that we may call the *paradox of divine double agency,* i.e. of God acting at one and the same time both in the realm of creation and in the realm of grace. This implies that God is present to us in two not necessarily homogeneous ways; and this in turn requires us to restate the whole problem of God's relationship to us in terms of the dialectics between Law and Gospel. For whatever may have to be said about God's relationship to creation in general, *with respect to us* God is present and active in more than one way because we can live in a state of grace or of sin, i.e. are capable of freely assenting to, or dissenting from, God's will towards us. God's relation to human existence is not monolithic but characterised by the dialectics between Law and Gospel, sin and grace, hiddenness and revelation.

Luther differentiates both terms of the divine-human relationship accordingly. Thus the dialectics of divine agency and presence lead him

---

[11] *WA* 43, 179,11-19.

to affirm the difference-in-unity between the *deus absconditus* and the *deus revelatus* to be an irreducible mark of every adequate conception of God. This difference is not the contrast between God as God is in himself and God as related to us; it is a difference in God's relation to human creation. But then human existence, the other term of this relation, has to be differentiated in a similar way. Corresponding to the paradox of divine double agency and its distinction between the hidden and revealed God we have a *paradox of human double existence*, viz. of existing either (as persons who are at the same time creatures and sinners) *simul creatura et peccator* or (as saved sinners) *simul iustus et peccator*. And just as the fundamental problem of the doctrine of God is to work out the unity-in-difference between God hidden and revealed, so the fundamental problem of theological anthropology is to work out the relationship between sin and salvation in human existence.

But could we not avoid these complications by refraining from differentiating God's activity in the way Luther does? Not if we take the cross seriously, i.e. if we take the cross to tell us something decisive about God and about our reality. If it were not for the cross, we might ignore the dialectical structure of God's hidden activity in and through the created things and his revealed activity in, with and under particular created things. But at the cross the two activities of God do not run parallel but contrary to each other, the one resulting in Christ's death, the other in his and our new life. The cross therefore marks a difference not only between divine and human agency but, more importantly, a difference also between God and God, between the inscrutable will of the almighty God who effects both life and death alike and the revealed will which shows God to be love and to be willing our life.

It is the dialectics of divine activity at the cross which requires us to differentiate God's activity and presence and to affirm the difference-in-unity between the *deus absconditus* and the *deus revelatus*. Without this distinction we either fail to acknowledge God at work in everything that happens, be it good or bad, or we are unable to safeguard the identity of the God who acts both *extra Christum* and *in Christo*. In any case, a theology which construes God's action on the basis of the dialectics of his saving act at the cross cannot bypass his twofold action in Law and Gospel (in the realm of creation and the realm of grace), and the dynamic tension between the world as old creation and as new that goes with it. If we ignore the two modes of divine activity or confuse the two realms, we shall fail to note the eschatological difference between »that which is the case« (*id quod res est*) and »that which is not yet but will be the case« (*id quod futura nondum est*) and thus fall prey to a rash identification of the world as it is with the world as it should be as God's creation.

Now I think there is a lot to be said for Luther's account as far as it goes, but we cannot leave it as it stands. Theologically it fails to relate the dialectical account of God's presence and activity to the doctrine of the trinity, that is, it needs a Trinitarian reworking. And philosophically it requires a much closer analysis of notions such as activity, action or mode of action before we can see exactly what it involves. Let us explore how this could be done.

3. Modes of Divine Activity

To hold that God is present with every present means that God is active at every present by becoming present with it. Now ›activity‹ is a term of art, and different artists use it differently. I take activity to be neither a particular (like action, event or thing) nor a fact (i.e. something that makes sentences, statements or propositions true) but a universal, i.e. a property that can be ascribed to someone or somebody: activity is always the activity *of x*. This property is actualised by performing an action, or by causing an event; it takes different forms depending on the kind of action performed; and it can be actualised in different modes, depending on the way in which it is performed.

Actions, on the other hand, like events, things or persons are particulars, i.e. entities picked out by names, definite descriptions or other singular terms. They are particular because they are tokens of a given sort or *type* of action. Types of action such as singing or eating or performing Mahler's 5th symphony are defined by a given *content* (what is done) regardless of who does it or when. Types of action are not so much another kind of action over and above particular performances of these activities, as properties that all their particular performances share. Thus we must be careful not to confuse *tokens* of action with *types of action*, nor *types of action* with *modes of activity*: Actions are particulars in that they are tokens of a given type (›*What* is she doing?‹), and the types are particularised by the concrete circumstances in which the action is performed. *Modes* of activity, on the other hand, are neither particular actions nor types of action but ways in which actions of a given type can be performed; and they are manifest in the way the particular actions are performed (›*How* is she doing it?‹). Whereas the first question (›*What* is she doing?‹) is answered by stating the beliefs (intentions, conventions) that govern what she does (or the belief s of those who interpret what they think she does), the second question (›*How* is she doing it?‹) is best answered in terms of adverbial qualifiers such as slowly, cunningly, contingently, necessarily etc.

Now *divine activity* is a unique and intrinsic property of God: It is God alone who exemplifies it, and God does so necessarily. That is, whoever exemplifies it is identical with God, and God cannot be without exemplifying it. How can this divine activity be characterised? Four points are important here:

(1) God's activity differs in character, scope and power from all other activities because it cannot be surpassed in any positive respect by anything different from God. It is, as Hartshorne put it, *unsurpassable by anything but itself*. Nobody can love more than God does, but God does not love always and everything in the same way.

(2) God's activity is not exemplified in only one way but comes in *different modes*. It never occurs *in vacuo* but in relating to situations and by continuing other actions: God's actions continue and connect with other divine actions. Insofar as these are relative to present situations of created agency by being present with their present (i.e. are immediate but distinct from them), they also react indirectly to the changing situations of created agency by continuing the corresponding divine actions differently relative to the new situation of created agency in the present.

(3) Since God is unique, none of God's actions instantiates an abstractable type of which there could be many different tokens but each divine action is unique, singular, irreplaceable and unrepeatable.

(4) God cannot be present and fail to be active, for God's being is his doing: God is not ›a being‹, nor even ›a person‹, God is pure activity – but activity of a very specific sort: Its unchanging, absolute or ›true‹ character which Christians find disclosed in Christ is *love*. It is not termed ›love‹ by way of analogy from our human loves but rather our human kinds and ways of loving have their norm and criterion in the love which God is. For God not only loves, God *is* love. But being love is practising and exercising love (*esse est operari*): God does not merely possess a potential for loving but loves actually; for a love that isn't exercised wouldn't be love. It may be, and indeed is, exercised in different ways for not everyone or everything is loved in the same way in all respects and in all situations. But if God, and God alone, *is* love, then this love is continuously being actualised in unique (not particular!) actions through which God creates and sustains, saves and perfects.

Therefore the most fundamental truth about God is that *God is love*. This is not to say that God is a property or that God's actions are an

[handwritten margin note: But God is a person!]

endless multiplication of boring and identical acts of love but it is rather that for God *to be* is *to be active*; that God's activity is *to actualise and
exercise his divine love* and that this is done in an infinite series of unique
acts of love, each new and different from all the others, yet for all its
difference it is an act of God's divine love nonetheless.

To understand God's presence and activity in this way has three important implications:

(1) Since God is *God*, he constantly actualises his love in the most
adequate way conceivable; and since *love* is relational, i.e. *love of* or *for
an Other*, the adequacy of its actualisation depends both on the love
which God seeks to realise and on the particular state of the Other for
whom he seeks to realise it. That is to say, whatever God does is determined, on the one hand, by his love and, on the other, by the particularities of the situation with respect to which God exercises and seeks
to express it. These are the two limiting or determining poles of everything which God does: God cannot contradict his divine nature of
love without ceasing to be God, and for precisely this reason God cannot realise his love without supremely adapting what he does to the
concrete situation to which, and to the particular needs of the Other
to whom, he relates. This is why *God is what God does* for someone,
and what God does, shows what God is.

This is in principal true of everything God does, although it is often
difficult if not impossible to discern it in creation because God does
not interact directly with created agency but with his own corresponding actions, and hence in, for us, hidden ways. For us »it is often
impossible to see the realisation of good purposes in the course of
events. We live in an emergent universe, drawn from nothing, through
the abyss of freedom, to a sharing in the divine life of eternity. In places, the picture we see will be very dark; it can even come to seem pur-
poseless«[12], not only in times of war and disaster, but also in the dark
turnings of an individual life. But there are also places where God's
love can be discerned, in particular in Christ in whom, as Christians
believe, God has unambiguously disclosed the nature of his self-giving
love in the face even of evil, suffering and death.

(2) All this is not to deny but underline the »Prior Actuality of God«,
as Austin Farrer has called it.[13] Talk of God cannot simply be replaced
by talk of divine activity because God is not just another feature of the

---

[12] K. Ward, *Holding Fast to God. A Reply to Don Cupitt*, London 1982, 96.
[13] A. Farrer, ›The Prior Actuality of God‹, in: *Reflective Faith. Essays in Philosophical Theology*, ed. C.C. Conti, London 1972, 178-191.

universe. But how are we to understand the »Prior Actuality of God« if all activity is mutual, and supreme activity supremely so?

The answer is that we have to distinguish two distinct but related contexts of divine activity: the *life of God*, and the *processes of the world*. In his acting God primarily connects to the unique actions of his own life, as the doctrine of the trinity reminds us. We may explain this in terms of the love that God is. Since one cannot love anything without loving oneself, God not only actually loves what is different from God but also himself. God's love of others is not independent of his self-love but, and this is important, neither is God's self-love independent of God's love of others. Indeed, God loves himself *by* loving others, and by loving others God loves himself. This could have been different, but it isn't. It is not impossible to imagine a pure self-love, i. e. a love that loves only itself and seeks exclusively its own good rather than the best for the other. But this wouldn't be the self-love of God and it wouldn't be the God in whom Christians believe and to whom they pray. God's self-love is not independent of his love of what is utterly different from him; indeed it is precisely in loving the most different that God loves himself. This is the message of the cross: God's love is supreme in that God loves what is utterly different and openly opposed to him, and he does so even in the face of the abyss of death where there wouldn't be anyone to be loved any more without God's love re-creating him or her. There not only is no limit to God's loving but his love intrinsically involves otherness in relating to the utterly different in such a way that God becomes present even to that presence, in life and in death; and this is also true of God's self-love, for God is God in loving in this and no other way.

But then relating to the utterly different is not merely a feature of God's love of others, but also of God's self-love. In loving himself God relates to what is utterly different from God without ceasing to be God; indeed God is God precisely by doing this and being so. This is why Christians have conceived God as trinity – as one who not only relates to himself *by* relating to others (as Hegel, Schelling or Whitehead have worked out in their different ways) but who is one God precisely by relating to utter otherness *in the very relating to himself*. God's self-love is the love of utter otherness which God is. Both with respect to others and with respect to God it is *God* who loves; and just as God loves others by relating to himself in relating to others (in his love for others), so God loves himself by relating to others in relating to himself (self-love). So God's love relates to God in no other way than by relating to others, and to others in no other way than by relating to God. God is creative love in that God is the one who loves everything and everyone, including himself, by loving others (as Father); is loved by God as God (as Son) or as different from God (as creation made to love God); and is the love through which others and God are loved by God (as Spirit) and love God (in and through the Spirit). This is what the (Augustinian) tradition has symbolized in the Trinitarian love of God as Father, Son, and Spirit.

Thus God, as the doctrine of the trinity points out, permanently actualises his divine love through the different yet interrelated activities of Father, Son and Spirit. What the Father does, or the Son or the Spirit, is not an action in itself but a necessary contribution to every divine action. Their unique co-operation constitutes each and every divine act as a concrete realisation of God's love; and since they can co-operate in an infinite variety of ways, God actualises his divine love not all at once or always in one and the same way but in the unsurpassable plurality of acts and ways of acting in which God continuously realises the unimaginable richness of love that he is.

This implies that *God has an eternal life of his own* which in principle transcends his relationship to any given (state of the) world: It is the infinite totality of ways in which God enacts his divine love, and no particular creation, no particular course of interactions with created agents, exhausts the richness of love and the possibilities of enacting it which are open to God.

But then God's eternal life is neither time-free nor temporal but *pluritemporal*: The infinite totality of ways in which God enacts his divine love includes an infinite totality of temporal orders between God's acts of love. In one of these orders God creates our temporal universe, but God does *not create time* (i.e. neither B-series nor A-relations). Rather each sequence of divine actions has its own temporal structure of ›earlier‹ and ›later‹; and since God's life consists of an unsurpassable plurality of such sequences, it comprises as many temporal orders as there are sequences of divine actions.

However, not only God's own life but also his actions with respect to the changing present of our created reality involve the distinct activities of Father, Son and Spirit as the three basic modes that determine God's acting. Every concrete realisation of God's love vis-à-vis a given state or situation of creation is thus determined as a creative, salvific and perfecting divine action; and since these modes can dominate a divine action in differing ways, we can speak of divine acts of creation, salvation and perfection provided we keep in mind that creation, salvation and perfection are distinct, but not separate modes of divine activity which are never realised in isolation from each other.

(3) *Divine actions*, therefore, are neither particular nor general but absolutely *unique* in that each is constituted by a unique combination of the activities of Father, Son and Spirit. Since this is also true where God relates to the present states and situations of created order, God continuously acts in two distinct respects: with respect to his own divine actions, and with respect to the situations of created agency. Thus at any present time God determines what he does in realising his love not only by adapting to the present state of activity of created beings but also by continuing his own prior actions with respect to creation: Whenever God is present with something present, he is completely aware of his former presences; he is aware of the possibilities, chances, and opportunities provided for created agents as well as of the successes, failures, and shortcomings in realising them in and through the activities of created agents; and he is aware of the best ways of continuing his work of transforming the world into a creation that freely responds to his love.

This is how God secures both that his acts constantly actualise his divine love and that they continuously actualise it in new ways by adapting to the changing situations and circumstances at each present to which he is present. In becoming present with each present in ever new ways, God has unlimited ability to adapt to varying states of the world without ceasing to be God or to exercise his love, and without directly interfering with created activity in any other way than by adapting the possibilities and chances provided in a situation for change, development, life and ways of living according to individual needs and circumstances. For God's eternal life, i.e. the everlasting interactions of Father, Son and Spirit, transcends all his relations to creation; and the internal differentiation of his divine life makes God supremely adaptable to the changing realities of situations. It enables him to continue and enforce the traces that his divine agency has left in created reality without ignoring or impairing the relative autonomy of creation.

This is why existing or living in the presence of God is not a monolithic relation. We are related not simply to God but to the presence of the triune activity of Father, Son and Spirit in the infinite interactions that constitute God's eternal life. We are involved in the presence of the activities of Father, Son and Spirit, and we are at each present involved in their present activities in different ways. There is nothing actual or possible at a given present that is not involved with God's presence and activity in this threefold way because God is unique and God's activity unsurpassable. Only the unique can be strictly universal, and since God's triune activity is unique in being unsurpassable, its scope cannot be less than cosmic. There can be nothing beyond the reach of the presence of Father, Son and Spirit, i.e. nothing that is not involved at each present in God's creative, salvific and perfecting activity. For God's love is actualised not in a uniform type of action but in different modes of divine activity and their corresponding actions. The doctrinal tradition has termed these modes *creation, salvation* (redemption, revelation, inspiration) and *eschatological perfection* (new creation, eternal life). All three are modes of actualising God's love but only together they specify the scope, content and end of God's love. We cannot take them in isolation without distorting our account of God's activity. And everything different from God is at each present involved in all three of them.

It follows that God cannot relate to us without relating to his own activity and ways of becoming present; indeed it is only in relating to himself that God relates to us. In relating to creation God connects to his own earlier actions, which he thereby continues. Since these divine actions differ in mode, God has to adjust his modes of creative, salvific and perfecting activity continuously in relating to creation: He never merely creates, or saves, or perfects but whatever he does is (in differing ways) a case of creating, saving and perfecting.[14] In short, God is pure, creative activity, but his activity is neither blind nor arbitrary but actualises God's eternal love so that God would not be the God he is without the actions he in fact performs.

What I am suggesting therefore is to understand God's presence in terms of God's activity, and to understand God's activity as the permanent and pluriform actualisation of his self-giving love: *God's presence is the presence of his divine love.* Since this love is actualised in all God does, we all exist in the presence of the triune workings of God's love in creating (Father), saving (Son) and perfecting (Spirit): this is the unchanging or absolute truth about God's presence. Since, however, it is actualised in different ways and relative to changing circumstances, God's presence takes on a different quality each moment because he recombines the different modes of his activity with respect to the particular state of the creation to which he relates and thus accommodates his love in continuously new ways: this is the changing or relative truth

---

[14] Perhaps we can say that the *eschaton* in which the ultimate purpose of God's agency is perfected, is the state in which the scope and content of these three modes of divine activity coincide so that God's acting in all its dimensions is coextensive and as such a perfect realisation of his love in the creation to which we belong.

about God's presence. God is changelessly present in actualising his love, and he permanently actualises it in the three distinct modes of creation, salvation and perfection (Father, Son and Spirit). However, God's presence constantly changes in the way in which God adapts his love to the changing situations of the creatures to whose presences he relates – not in completely arbitrary ways, of course, but in ways compatible with his divine love and in ways that contribute towards achieving its end of perfecting those to whom it is directed in making them become, in what they make or fail to make of themselves, individual images of divine love. God's love is unlimited, and God is completely free in the exercise of his love; but whatever God does is determined, on the one hand, by the love that he exercises (this is why God cannot sin, or do harm, or do evil) and, on the other, by the specific reality to which his love is addressed and accommodated.

4. Modes of Divine Presence

The different modes of God's activity that I have outlined thus correspond to different modes of divine presence. Wherever God is present, God is present in the different modes of Father, Son and Spirit. And since these go with different kinds of activity in shaping God's relationship to created reality, they imply different modes of Gods presence with what is present in time and space. That is to say:

(1) God is *time-free present* in his creative activity as Father: Creation is not a change; it does not involve any ›before‹ or ›after‹ and hence does not imply time. If the property ›*to be created*‹ is true of anything in time it is true of everything in time; and since it does not mark any difference within the totality of things, the localising predicate ›*being created*‹ signifies the same everywhere: that whatever is exists in the presence of God through God becoming present to it.

(2) God is *multi-present* in the perfecting activity of the Spirit. God not merely creates but responds to what is present as created reality and to the divine agency that is co-present to it; and the Spirit is God's dynamic presence with every present state of creation which at any given moment is actively engaged in transforming the world into God's creation. The Spirit does so not by force, or by directly participating in the ›drama of creation‹ herself, but by setting and adjusting the rules of the game at any given moment in providing the potential needed at each moment for changing from world to creation. For just as God exercises his divine agency in becoming present by creating the chanc-

es and possibilities of the situations to whose present he becomes present, so the Spirit continually adjusts this divine agency both to the actual state of created reality and to God's own acting as it has contributed to the shaping of it.

This raises some interesting questions about the nature of God's responsive presence as Spirit. If the Spirit is co-present with everything as it occurs, God responds not only to the changes in created reality but also to the divine activity that accompanies it; and since God is active both as creator and as Spirit, he at any present moment both continues his creative activity (which is always the same) *and* the specific accommodating actions by which the Spirit adjusts God's love to the presence of the particular reality in question. That is to say *God makes himself by making creatures make themselves.* This does not mean that God is »creating his own nature« as Thomas Morris has suggested,[15] but God does create his own biographies, and this plural is to be taken literally: As Spirit, God relates to present situations of entities in temporal relations and in doing so arranges his own acts in a temporal order relative to the created reality in question: *For the Spirit,* there is an ›earlier‹ and a ›later‹, *and* a ›past‹, ›present‹ and ›future‹. But since there are as many temporal orders as there are entities temporally related, God as Spirit is multi-present with creation. Therefore God orders his accommodating acts not only in one sequence but relative to the many different temporal orders of created realities: God is directly present to all that is present in whatever temporal order, and therefore God has not just one ›biography‹ in becoming present to the presence of created agents but as many as there are temporal orders of created entities. There is, however, no eternal ›Now‹ in which all the presences in different temporal orders are temporally co-present with each other; and there is no ›divine time‹ in which all presences are simultaneous. Rather God diversifies his divine activity by making himself present to each presence not only as time-free creator but also as multi-present Spirit who accommodates God's love to the particular needs and requirements of the temporal reality to which God responds by becoming differently present to and providing different possibilities for its changing presence.

(3) Finally, besides being time-free present as the creator of everything and multi-present as Spirit with the presence of everything created, God has also made himself *temporally present* to us *in a specific way* in human history. We among all creatures not only live in the presence

---

of God but can also become aware of it as selves who can live their
lives in loving God and their neighbours. Yet discerning the divine ac-
commodations to our present through which God becomes accessible
to us is a permanent source of ambiguity. No amount of empirical in-
vestigation or metaphysical analysis can disclose or show in an unmis-
takable way that experienced reality does indeed mediate the presence
of divine agency or give us an unambiguous sense of the presence of
God, to say nothing of God's true nature. The question cannot even be
raised if one doesn't move beyond a scientific description of experience to take into account the perspective of those experiencing: God
is present with every present situation and to every present, but only in
our own perspective can we discern God's presence, and if we do we
discern God's presence to our presence. But this is impossible without
either acknowledging it in faith or rejecting it in unfaith. And therefore there is no way of exploring the sense of the presence of God that
can avoid, escape or ignore the dialectic of faith and unfaith. Where
God's presence becomes a topic, there faith (trust in it), non-faith (ignorance of it) and unfaith (denial of it) also do.

   Now Christians believe that God has used a particular stretch of history to make his attitude towards creation unambiguously known to
humanity. Jesus Christ in particular is believed to have disclosed God's
self-giving love to be the ultimate ground and end of all there is. In
him God's love has become *self-interpretative.*[16] Thus – to summarise a
complicated hermeneutical process – *Jesus* has interpreted God to be
love, the *Spirit* assures us that Jesus' interpretation is true to God's nature, and this warrants us to believe that *God* has made Jesus interpret
God's love to us and continues to do so through the interpretative interplay between the proclamation of the gospel and the clarifying and
verifying work of the Spirit. That is to say just as Jesus and the gospels
give clarity and content to the activity and presence of God, so the
Spirit is the source of certainty about the truth of the gospel.

   The self-interpretative character of this hermeneutical process distinguishes it from the natural and historical processes of our world in
which God's presence is ambiguous. But it is important to see that the
point of the gospel is not to convey a historical truth about a past event
but to create a sense of God's presence in *our* lives. The truth of the
gospel is to be verified in the time and life of those to whom it is addressed but its content, i.e. the presence of the divine love whose work

---

[16] Cf. I.U. Dalferth, *Evangelische Theologie als Interpretationspraxis. Eine systematische Orientierung*, Leipzig 2004.

we are encouraged to discover in our life, is something Christians know from Christ.

In brief, I distinguish three modes of divine presence which differ in temporal modality as well as in scope:

(1) In his creative activity God is timeless and unchangingly present with everything that is present at all levels of reality. (As Creator, God is present in the same way with every presence.)

(2) In his perfecting activity, on the other hand, God is multi-present. He presents his love for the other in permanently novel ways relative to the changing conditions of created reality. (As Spirit, God is present in a uniquely singular way with each presence.)

(3) In his salvific activity God is present to human persons who can become aware of it and respond to God's love by loving God and their neighbours. Human life is the highest and most complex mode of being of which we are aware. We alone are capable of becoming aware of God's presence, of being affected by the difference between sin and salvation, and of consciously living our lives in God's presence or failing to do so. (As Saviour, God is present in a uniquely personal way to the present of each human person.)

The three modes of divine presence are not mutually exclusive but rather progressively more determinate ways of God's presence. Since God's salvific activity does not negate but perfect the other modes of his activity, every human presence is involved in all three of them: Whereas the processes of inanimate nature governed by the laws of quantum field-theory and relativity-physics do not express much of the salvific presence of God, it always makes sense to ask how our life relates to God's creative, salvific and perfecting activity. The answers differ and therefore help believers to orient themselves in reality. Whereas all events express God's creative activity (which is identical everywhere), it is often difficult if not impossible to see the realisation of the purpose of God's love in the actual course of events. This is why most religions distinguish some events as revelations where God's salvific presence can be more adequately discerned and experienced than in other occasions, even though these events become revelations only in being perceived as such by those who are changed from non-faith to faith by the salvific presence of God's love which they disclose.

Perhaps we can say therefore that parallel to the emergence of human life in creation God's presence and activity becomes more diversified. It takes on new forms and differentiates itself into new modes relative to new emergent realities. Before there were selves God was *present with* the occurring of events. With the emergence of selves God is not only present with them but also becomes *present to* them, that is, present to them in their 1st-person perspectives so that he can be experienced and known to be present.

The difference between the three modes of divine activity can thus be conceived as an ›effect‹ of the process of creation on God, an ›effect‹, however, which only occurs because God freely decides to differentiate his ways of becoming present with the present of created realities relative to the changing situation of creation. In God's eternal life they are in perfect correspondence and equipoise. We can even define God's eternity as the dynamic unity of the three modes of divine activity and presence both in content and scope. Relative to creation, however, they are differentiated.[17] They operate differently and have differing effects. Thus it is not nature that is perfected by grace but *God's creative activity is perfected by his salvific, perfecting and consummating activity.* God progressively perfects himself by adapting his activity to a changing creation, and his perfection consists precisely in adjusting the realisation of his divine love to the needs of the increasingly more diversified Other. Just because God is perfect and unchanging love, he upholds the unsurpassable standard of his perfection by permanently adjusting the realisation of his love to the differing realities of those whom he loves. What is adequate to microphysical processes is not sufficient for sentient creatures or human persons. God's love must be actualised in very different ways in order to be in each case the most appropriate help to perfect those to whom it is addressed. The final perfection of creation, therefore, will not be a state of a monotonous identity and sameness of love, but an ongoing process of pluralist individuality beyond imagination. God's love is inexhaustible in its powers to adapt, and the objects that God creates for his love are limitless.

The theological implications of this account of God's presence are wide-ranging. Let me draw out just a few for the understanding of *creation* and of God's *omnipresence, omniscience, omnipotence* and *love.*

---

[17] So it is just the other way round from the Augustinian principle *opera ad extra sunt indivisa*: There is indeed no divine activity in which not all three modes of divine activity are involved but, relative to creation, they take on different emphases and need to be distinguished.

5. God's Creative Presence

Since God is actively present with everything present, deism, as commonly conceived, is ruled out. God did not once create the world but is no longer active in it. On the contrary, God's presence and activity is necessary for every other presence and activity, and it is sufficient for itself. This is the point of the doctrine of *creatio ex nihilo*. It is primarily a doctrine about God's creative activity, not (or only indirectly) about God's creation: The property of *being created* does not help to discriminate anything within the universe (if anything is created, everything is created) but defines the universe as ontologically depending on God. The world – any world – could not exist without God: it wholly depends on God who creates and sustains it by becoming present with its presence. God, one the other hand, is not just adjectival to the world; he is not just an aspect of the world which could not have existed without the world. God does not exist because there is a world but the world *is* only because there is God who makes it make itself.

Thus the doctrine of *creatio ex nihilo* states that God is fundamentally active, that God's activity is fundamentally creative, and that without it nothing that is would be. Whatever is, from the processes of inanimate nature governed by the laws of quantum field-theory and relativity-physics to the emergence of life in all its complexity and variety, the development of human culture and history and the highest forms of personal life and to the emergent future which the human race is now beginning to hold in its own hands – everything that is, was, and will be present – rests on God's activity, whereas God's activity rests on no other condition than on his nature of unconditional love. Since God's love is a reality that is necessarily actualised (otherwise God would not be), and since it is actualised in different modes (otherwise God would not achieve the end of his love, i.e. the free loving response of the created Other), all modes of God's activity actualise God's unconditioned love, and nothing that is exists outside the scope of God's love. Just because God's love is essentially creative, salvific and perfecting, God's activity is universal in scope: Everything that exists presupposes God's creative, salvific and perfecting activity as the condition for its being, well being and perfection. Therefore *unconditioned creativity* – together with *unsurpassable perfectibility* and *unlimited salvific intention* – are *the fundamental modes of divine activity.*

To hold this is to posit a radical distinction between God's creative agency and all created agencies whose being and activity depend on God's creative agency. But can we say more than this? In particular, is there a way to specify in more detail how the relationship between divine creativity and created activities is to be conceived? There is, as Austin Farrer has pointed out, no »action *in vacuo*, that is, action without interplay«[18]. But it seems impossible to conceive the relation between creator and creation in terms of interacting activities. Seductive as the model of causal interaction may be, it is hardly appropriate. Createdness has to do with ontological dependence or, rather, existential empowering because it provides the potential for finite freedom. However, it has nothing to do with temporal beginning. Whereas causes precede their effects, God is co-present with every presence of his creation. Moreover, to conceive God as cause is either to obfuscate the notion of a cause by creating an abyss between ›metaphysical‹ and ›physical causation‹ or to make God an aspect of creation. The first results in an ontological dualism between the physical and metaphysical that is neither needed nor helpful to make sense of the sense of the presence of God. If on the other hand we conceive God's creative activity in causal terms as interaction between creative and created activity, it is hard to avoid the process–fallacy of identifying the activity of God with the temporal process of the world. We then seem to be faced with either of two options:

Either we turn God into the creative aspect of a self-sufficient ›nature-in-process‹ — an idea traceable in different forms from Spinoza's *Deus-Natura* to Whitehead's World-God or Derrida's *différance*, the ›absent presence of the trace‹ that some identify with the infinite and the divine.[19] Or we distinguish between divine and created activity not merely in degree but in kind; and then paradox seems inevitable as is shown by Austin Farrer's theory of double agency. If ›God makes creatures make themselves‹, the activities of the creator and of the creature cannot be actions in the same sense or on the same level; and it would be wrong to construe the cosmological interaction of finite and infinite activity as the co-operation of two polar agents on a scale ranging continuously from unconditioned will through to conditioned will and inanimate agencies. Yet if the two activities are utterly incommensurable, is it really appropriate to speak of a *causal relationship* or even of

[18] A. Farrer, Faith and Speculation. An Essay in Philosophical Theology. London 1964, 167.

[19] Of course, the differences between these positions are enormous: In Spinoza or Whitehead God is conceived in a positive sense as the creative aspect or dimension of reality; in post-modernism it is the *via negativa* that triumphs: just as shadow is the mark of absent light so, we are told, God's absence is the trace of his creative presence. Cf. *Shadow of Spirit: Postmodernism and Religion*, ed. Ph. Berry

interaction between omnipotent creativity and creaturehood? It is hardly surprising that Farrer admits to be unable to specify the causal joint between divine and created activity and contends himself with the *paradox of double agency*, i.e. with the rule that wherever there is created activity, there also is creative activity.

Can we move beyond this? Farrer rightly insists on the fundamental asymmetry between God's creative agency and the agency of created beings. But if we want to escape the barren alternatives of *finitum capax infiniti* or *finitum non capax infiniti*, God's creative activity must itself be differentiated in such a way that it comprises both infinite and finite activity. Creation is a timeless divine activity, which differs from causation in that it does not imply any temporal relation between creator and creation, creative ›act‹ and created ›result‹. There is no ›before‹ and ›after‹ here, no change from one state of the world to another; there is »nothing that is at any time some distance in time from the creator or in space at any distance in space«[20]. What is created depends upon the act of the creator, but this act is (onto)logically, not temporally prior to it: God is co-present to what he creates, and as creator God is not the sort of ›being‹ that can have temporal relations with anything distinct from him. Thus Hartshorne is right that there is no logic in making God cause only, and not also effect. But contrary to what he thinks it does not follow that »God is both before and after, both cause and effect, of all events«[21], but that *as creator* God is neither cause nor effect: God is not the cause of all things, but their creator. Creating, however, is not a change[22], and hence no matter of causation if this is taken to imply temporal relations of before and after, earlier and later: It is the time-free positing of ontological dependence or existential empowering.

How is this ontological dependence to be conceived? If God's activity were the sufficient antecedent condition for the actions of created agents, then everything that happens in the world would be completely determined in the divine decree and »Neither the relative autonomy of natural processes in the world which we express in the probabilistic statements of natural laws nor human freedom would be possible«[23]. We can avoid this if we »understand God's creative action as sufficient condition for the existence of the world and as necessary condition for

and A. Wernick, London/New York 1992. But since there are good reasons not to believe in negative facts I see no reason to follow this line of reasoning.

[20] P. Helm, *Eternal God. A Study of God without Time*, Oxford 1988, 20.
[21] Ch. Hartshorne, *A Natural Theology for our Time*, La Salle, Illinois 1967, 60.
[22] Cf. Thomas Aquinas, *Summa Theologica* Ia q 45 a2 ad 2.
[23] Chr. Schwöbel, *God: Action and Revelation*, Kampen 1992, 31.

every occurrence in the world«[24]. Schwöbel, therefore, follows the Aristotelian pattern of thinking in traditional Lutheran theology by distinguishing an initial divine act of *creatio ex nihilo* from a subsequent divine act of *creatio continuata*. However, if God's creative activity is time-free present activity, the distinction between creation and conservation in a temporal order is devoid of content. There is no time before which God was not creative; there was no time at which God decided to create; and there is no time at which God wouldn't be creative, although creativity is not the only mode of divine activity.

But doesn't this imply that God wholly determines everything that is? If God essentially acts, and if it is impossible for God's actions not to achieve their end, then God does what he wills and achieves what he does. But this is not so. All that is entailed is that God wholly determines *whatever he does*, not that God wholly determines everything that is. »As creator, it is within God's power of free decision to create a universe containing partly self-determining beings«[25]; and since all self-determination must of logical necessity be made by the agents themselves, the prize for God's creating beings that are self-determining to some degree is that he cannot wholly determine them. No agent can be a sufficient cause of the free act of another, not even God. Every agent, on the other hand, is a necessary cause of his own action, whereas God, and he alone, is a sufficient cause of what he does. Agents originate their own actions in the sense that their free choice to perform them is a *necessary* condition for their occurrence. I would not be here if I had not chosen to come. However, »I cannot perform an action merely by choosing to do so. Unless my factual circumstances are such as to enable me to do what I choose to do, I cannot perform the action ... The *sufficient* condition for an action being performed therefore consists of the conjunction of the agent's choice and the complete set of factual circumstances which make possible for the agent to perform the action in question«[26]. But not so for God. God can perform an action merely by choosing to do so. There are no factual circumstances that would either enable or hinder God to create what he chooses to create. If God chooses to create beings that are partly self-determining, he wholly determines himself to create such beings, but he cannot (logically cannot) wholly determine those whom he wills to be self-determining. That God wills to create such

---

[24] Ibid.
[25] Ward, *Holding Fast to* God, 62.
[26] Brümmer, *Speaking of a Personal God*, 114.

beings is a sufficient condition for his creating them but it is only a necessary condition for the self-determining acts of those he creates. In short: If there are agents that are not completely determined by God's creative activity, then this is because God has completely determined his activity not to be completely determining.

The picture of creation that emerges could then be sketched as follows. At any given time created reality is in transition from one a state of the world to another. Each state is a complex situation that comprises a plurality of complex situations, and each situation is a particular state of the world at a given time that differs from other contemporary situations in certain respects that determine its character. Thus a situation can be described as, on the one hand, the totality of what is actual at a given time in a given respect and, on the other, the totality of what is possible at this time, given this totality of actualities. Some of these actualities are only loosely and externally related, others more strictly embedded in complex agencies of different orders so that internal structures and operations become differentiated from external relations and operations. So at any given time a situation is a complex field of interacting actualities at different levels of complexity and order pulling and pushing, as it were, in different directions and about to change the situation in different and incompatible ways. Since all these activities cannot permanently be harmonized into a coherent whole, some break down and cannot be continued when others become more effective and dominating. So the totality of what is actual is permanently in flux and in transition to another state; and this is impossible without feeding on possibilities.

Now what is possible in a given situation with respect to the totality of actualities at a given time is not the totality of the logically possible but only, on the one hand, the really possible (real possibilities), i.e. that which could become actual in continuing the situation without resulting in incoherence and inconsistence because it is compossible with the given actualities and, on the other, that which might have been possible if the actual state of the world would have been different (counterfactual possibilities). However, even though every given situation allows for an infinite variety of possible continuations, not even all the real possibilities in a given situation will be actually possible (actual possibilities) in the light of what is actual. Some will be very unlikely, some more unlikely than others, some more likely and some neither likely nor unlikely but completely unavailable, unachievable and inaccessible and simply beyond all imagination. At any given time there is more possible than what is likely or unlikely, for this depends on what is actual and therefore comprises only a selection of the possible at any given time. And while the actual doesn't determine what will become actual but allows for a large though not unlimited range of possible continuations, the state of the actual at any given time determines what is *not* possible now because it would be incompatible with what is actual. However, while some possibilities will thus not be realised and may remain unrealised forever, this is not so with all of them. What is not a real or actual possibility now may become one with a change of situation. The sun cannot rise now because it is noon and the sun has been shining for hours. But when, after the appropriate series of changes, the next night has passed the sun can rise again, and what is not possible now will be possible then.

Against this background God's creative activity can be seen as providing, for each situation at a given time and with respect to the various levels and kinds of activity that define its actual state, the possibilities that are real, or actually real, or counterfactually possible. God does not change the situation by directly interacting with what is actual in it. But by becoming present to its present in a specific way God determines the range of possible continuations of the situation by selecting those possibilities that make it possible, if actualised, to change it in such a way that something that wasn't possible before may become a real or actual possibility. God does not determine what will in fact become actual of the possibilities provided. This depends on the contingent causal processes of created reality in which some of the possibilities selected but not others are selected and actualised. By becoming present to the present of a situation God determines the horizon of its possibility, not what is actualised in this horizon, and God does so by investing a situation with the possibilities that make some but not all possible continuations possible. On the one hand, there is always more possible in principle than what is provided as a real or actual possibility for a situation, and in this sense God determines the range of possibilities that become available in a situation but not what is selected from them to be actualised. On the other hand, there is also always more possible than what is likely or unlikely to become actual, given the actual state of a situation, and in this sense God creates, and keeps open, room for novelty and surprise.

So God determines the range of possibilities allotted to a given situation but not what created agencies actualise of these possibilities. He is the poet of the possible, not the cause of the actual. But God is the sole author both of what he does and what he refrains from doing. So if God determines possibilities relative to situations, it is because God determines himself to do so. If God refrains from determining which of the possibilities provided will in fact be actualised by created agency in a given situation, then because God determines himself not to determine this.

Does this imply divine self-limitation as some have claimed? Only if our ideal is that God determines everything completely. But why should it be? If the divine nature is essentially love, God's creating free creatures is not a matter of divine self-limitation or self-renunciation but of *enhancing the range of divine activity and the opportunities for divine love.* By determining himself not to determine everything completely, God opens up ways of acting such as his salvific, inspiring or perfecting activities, which would have been closed to him otherwise. Just because he creates what he does, he determines himself to act not merely in the way of timeless creation but also in response to the state of created reality. More precisely, *by timelessly creating a universe containing partly self-determining beings,* God determines himself to be active not merely as Creator but *differentiates his activity into the time-free activity of creation, the multi-present activity of the Spirit in creation and the particular temporal activity of the Son in salvation.* Thus God is not limiting, but enriching his divine life by not completely determining everything. Or if he ›limits‹ the exercise of divine power in respecting the existence, structure and processes of creation, then this is because it permits him to exercise his divine power in ways that are more appropriate to his divine love than mere dominance and determination. This enrichment of the divine life is the reason both for God's creation and for his salvific and perfecting activities in creation: God acts for the sake of some good, i.e. for the sake of bringing about a state which realises some desire; and the only good which it makes sense for God to desire is to enhance the variety, opportunity, and degree of clarity of the exercise of his divine love. Just as it is better to be than not to be, so it is better to be pluriform than uniform, and to be clear than vague; and this is as true of God as it is of us.

I conclude, therefore,

(1) God's creative activity is the sole and sufficient condition for the bringing about of the existence of everything different from God; and since this includes God's free decision to create a universe containing partly self-determining creatures, it is at the same time the necessary condition for all created activity;

(2) just because God creates this sort of universe, he does not content himself with being timelessly creative but determines his activity by responding to the changing realities of his creation through the time-relative workings of the Spirit and of the Son; and

(3) for precisely this reason God is co-present with all the presences of created beings not only in his time-free creative activity, but also in the multi-present activity of the Spirit and, to human persons, in the way of the specific temporality of the Son.

Nothing therefore exists outside the range and presence of God's love. God is actively present to each and every presence, and as creator God is always present in the same way. Therefore we cannot have a temporal or historical relationship to the Creator but only to the co-presence of particular workings of God the Spirit and the Son with particular presences that for us are past, present or future. God is never in any temporal or spatial distance from any of us, he is always close to each and every present of us, in fact, God is closer to us than anything else: Without his presence nothing could be present to anyone because there just would not be anything or anyone. Just as nobody can escape his or her own presence so nobody can escape the presence of God. Every attempt to overcome the immediacy of presence and to distance oneself from what is present at a given moment necessarily takes place in the presence and hence in the presence of God.

6. Divine Omnipresence and Omniscience

This is the point of the doctrine of God's universal presence or *divine omnipresence*: It does not mean that God is present at the same time to everything, for this would result in absurdities. Rather it means that there never was or will be a presence to which God is not present: *God is present to every presence*. This neither implies that God has temporal location and/or temporal extension as some (e.g. Stephen Davis) have argued, nor that »the distinctions among past, present and future, and between before and after, can meaningfully be applied to it«[27], nor that God is ›eternally present‹ in the sense of having an »infinitely extended, pastless, futureless duration«, as E. Stump and N. Kretzmann interpret Boethius' account of God's eternity. God's presence to every presence is not a matter of temporal simultaneity: it is the time-free co-presence of his creative activity with the occurring of the event in question without which this event could not occur. It is not one of the causes of this event (events in time are caused by other events in time) but it is the necessary condition without which neither this event nor its causes nor its effects could be possible and actual.

---

[27] S. T. Davis, *Logic and the Nature of God*, London 1983, 22.

Since God is actively present with every presence, God is directly aware of what goes on everywhere without any intermediaries. That is to say, the »divine awareness of events does not depend upon the transmission of information over physical distances by physical processes«[28]. God knows everything immediately, not by inference nor by acquaintance but *by being present with its becoming*. The very occurring of all that occurs is internal to God's presence because God enables it to be made or to make itself. God's *omniscience* is thus best understood as a kind of *practical knowledge*: *God knows what God does in becoming present to what thereby becomes present*, and since nothing occurs to which God is not actively present, God knows everything that can be known. Thus God's omniscience follows from his omnipresent activity: it is his all-inclusive awareness of his divine activity with respect to everything that is present. More precisely: God is omniscient *not* because for any state of affairs that occurs God knows that it occurs, why it occurs, what it is that occurs and what it in turn can cause to occur; but because God knows with certainty what he does, or does not, in the occurring of everything that occurs. In this sense nothing whatsoever can occur without God knowing it to occur for the simple reason that *God knows what God does*. God knows what is knowable at any particular time because God is present to every presence and hence present both to what he does and what others do: God knows what God does and what others do, and just as God knows the first by doing it he knows the second by being present to it.

On this account, the problem of divine foreknowledge, much discussed in recent philosophy of religion, seems to be misconceived: God does not know now what will happen tomorrow but only *what he does* with respect to the actual situation and the possible types and probable range of situations which it includes: Since divine omniscience does not include foreknowledge there is no genuine problem of reconciling divine foreknowledge with human freedom. Of course, if we define omniscience, as Stephen Davis does, ›for every proposition p that is true at T, God knows p at T; and for every proposition q that is false at T, God does not believe q at T‹; and if you hold, as Davis does, »that there are true and false propositions about future states of affairs«[29], then we are stuck with a problem about divine foreknowledge. But the problem disappears if, as I have suggested, God's omnis-

---

[28] D.A. Pailin, ›Panentheism‹, in: S. Andersen, D.Z. Phillips, *Modern Theism and its Alternatives*, Aarhus 1994, 95–116, 112.
[29] Davis, *Logic and the Nature of God*, 52.

cience is understood in terms of *practical knowledge*, i.e. as God's knowing what *God is doing*: For then God's knowing reaches as far as his doing, and his doing occurs whenever something occurs, i.e. is present.
Thus God knows unfailingly what is the case (because he is present to
it) and what has been the case (because he has been present to it), but
not what will be the case (because it has not yet occurred): God knows
future possibilities *as possibilities*, i.e. as something that may be true, in
fact, he knows the whole range of the possible at any given moment
without distortion. But God is not present now to what will be true
tomorrow but will be present to it when it occurs.

It follows that God does not have what has been called ›middle
knowledge‹ in the sense of knowing with certainty what every possible
free creature would freely do in every situation in which that creature
could possibly find itself (›If I emigrated to Iceland, my wife would not
join me‹). What God does know with certainty is what he would do
with respect to every possible free action of his creatures in every situation in which they could possibly find themselves: He does not determine our actions but his own activity. That is to say, God has complete
control not over the free actions of his creatures but over his own actions, and in this sense God always knows what he does. Thus God's
omniscience does not involve a single, absolute, privileged perspective
on the whole process of reality; but it does involve a complete grasp of
his own activity in every actual and possible occurrence because of his
co-presence to all that is present and his immediate awareness of every
aspect of its internal and external relations without distortion.

7. Divine Love and Omnipotence

This does not imply that for God all presences are equal. God relates
to all that is present as love, i.e. creates and sustains it as an object of divine love. But not everything to which God is present discloses the
presence of God's love, or discloses it in the same way. There are situations, which do not display or contradict God's love, even though
there wouldn't be any situations without God, and no God worth the
name if God were not love.

This, at least, is Christian conviction. Christians believe that God has
disclosed the real character of his divine activity in Christ, and what he
has disclosed there is his ceaseless, unwavering and limitless *love*. But if
it is true there that this is what God is, it is true everywhere. God is actively present to every presence as love: He not only loves (among other things) but he *is* love, and being love not only means having a dispo-

sition to love but actually doing it. Love is the unchanging character of God's presence and activity in all its modes: Whatever occurs, God's love is operative in it, and wherever God is operative, it is an operation of love.

This has two important implications. First, if divine activity in all its modes is an operation of divine love, and if love operates not by coercion but by persuasion, patience, suffering and hope, then Whitehead is right in pointing out »that the divine element in the world is to be conceived as a persuasive agency and not as a coercive agency«[30]. More precisely (and different from how Whitehead develops the idea), it is persuasive not by interacting with created agencies ›in the world‹ but by playing again and again the chances and possibilities in their way that are needed here and now for (partly) self-determining beings to make a free and unforced response to the divine love in and through whose presence they are. Where love hopes for a response it cannot enforce it, for nothing that is not done freely and out of love could count as a response to love. The upshot of this is, that divine omnipotence is not a divine property alongside or alternative to divine love but a particular feature or aspect of this love: In theology ›God is omnipotent‹ is always to be understood as an abbreviation of ›God's love is omnipotent‹, and the point of almighty love is not that it can do everything that is not logically impossible but that it will not give up under any circumstances to hope and work for a response of love from those whom it creates and sustains out of love.

Second, God's love does not operate uniformly as it does in timeless creation. It adapts to circumstances. It is sensitive to the specific needs of those it loves. It reacts in the workings of the Spirit to the actual state of that which God creates as object of his love. It thus takes different forms with respect to the particular persons, situations, events to which it is directed; and it changes with those circumstances. Just as God's presence comes in different modes of divine activity, so God's love is multifaceted and various – not uniform, but pluriform. As David Pailin has put it: »When, for example, I say that ›Mary loves Sarah‹, I imply that in whatever situation Sarah may find herself, Mary will respond in a loving way. The appropriate expression of that love in practice will, however, vary according to Sarah's situation. When Sarah is suffering from influenza, Mary's love for her will involve sympathetic nursing; when Sarah is exuberant after winning a race, loving her means sharing her joy; when she is wanting to be alone, loving her

---

[30] A.N. Whitehead, *Adventure of Ideas* (1933), New York 1967, 166.

means respecting her privacy; and so on«.[31] God's love differs from Mary's in that it is supremely adaptable to the particularities of the case in question: It is not distracted by other concerns but brings that into being which it loves. Or, as Luther put it following Augustine: God does not love the loveable but what God loves is and becomes loveable. God, as it were, ›loves into being‹.

It is precisely in this radical sense that the doctrine of God's intrinsic love conflicts with the horrors and tragedies of our actual experience and lives. Where is the presence of God's love in the agony of a child that dies of aids? Answers such as Swinburne's that there is something positive in all suffering and that even death can be seen as an institution of God's love because it stops endless suffering may comfort the theoretical mind. They are of little help to those who suffer. The problem of evil, i.e. of all the unnecessary evil and suffering in our world, is a challenge to the Christian faith (or any faith in a loving God) that cannot be answered by a cunning conceptual operation.

This is also true of attempts such as Hartshorne's to limit or remove the omnipotence of God.[32] That the power of God's creative activity is limited because it necessarily interacts with created activity (as he believes) does as such not show how horrendous evil and unjust suffering is overcome. It is not enough to argue that »[e]ven divine power cannot create the good without the risk of the evil«[33], or that it can and will be overcome in the long run, for the suffering takes place now, and the evil is experienced in the presence by those who are present. It is here, if at all, that evil is to be overcome, not at some other time and for someone else. What has to be envisaged is »the active transformation of creatures«[34] not by limiting the workings of divine love but by stretching and surpassing it in the transformation of the other to which it is directed. The Christian reaction to this need is the hope, based on Christ's resurrection, that this is not the only life there is; and unless this hope is taken seriously, Christian theology has little helpful to say about the problem of evil.

---

[31] Pailin, ›Panentheism‹, 100.

[32] Ch. Hartshorne, ›The Logic of Panentheism‹, in: Ch. Hartshorne/W.L. Reese, *Philosophers Speak of God*, Chicago 1953, 499–514; *Omnipotence and Other Logical Mistakes*, Albany, New York 1984.

[33] D.R. Griffin, ›Panentheism: A Postmodern Revelation‹, in: Ph. Clayton/A. Peacocke (eds.), *In Whom We Live and Move and Have Our Being. Panentheistic Reflections on God's Presence in a Scientific World*, Grand Rapids, Michigan 2004, 36–47, 45.

[34] N.H. Gregersen, ›Three Varieties of Panentheism‹, in: Clayton/Peacocke (eds.), *In Whom We Live and Move and Have Our Being*. 19–35, 33.

V The Gift of God's Presence

1. The Distinction of Human Beings

God's love is creative. What God loves he creates by loving it. He does so in the myriad of ways shown in creation. By unceasingly exercising the creativity of his divine love God is the maker of an emergent world whose growing complexity opens up new ways of God's relating to it and calls for new modes of God's presence with everything as it occurs and to every presence of those present at what occurs. For while God's creative activity is the sole and sufficient reason for the existence of created reality (*that* there is a world), every given state of creation (*how* the world is at a given time) is governed by the double contingency of the (selected) possibilities provided by God for a given situation and the possibilities selected from this selection by created activity in that situation. God continuously makes new realities with new and unforeseen possibilities make themselves. He does so by relating to the presence of created realities in such a way that he plays possibilities and chances in their way that could help, if chosen and appropriated rather than ignored and negated by created reality, to preserve and strengthen what agrees with God's love and end for his creatures, and to overcome and transform what opposes or contradicts to them.

This is not a lamentable deficiency of an incompetent creator who continuously has to repair what he has managed to create only imperfectly. It is rather precisely the way in which love almighty overcomes ills unlimited. By providing possibilities that do not impose themselves but can be negated God opens up a space of alternatives at each moment of time from which created reality has to choose in continuing and progressing through time. At every present created realities change by continuing in some respects (becoming) and not continuing in others (passing away). In both respects not everything is possible at any given moment. But what is possible depends on the possibilities provided to created reality at a given present, and what becomes or ceases to be actual depends on how a given state of created reality is actually continued by choosing certain options available rather than others or their negations. There is always more than one possibility in which a given state of the world can change by becoming something new or ceasing to be something that is not or cannot be continued. These alternatives and the corresponding decisions become more complex with the range of freedom and decision open to created realities of increasing complexity. But since at every given moment myriads of decisions are taken not all of which result in coherent and consistent actualities, any given state of the world is unstable and in transition to another one. This is true both with respect to fact and value. The world is not only continuously changing but also becoming better or worse as the case may be. At any given time the world is far from being perfect. There are an infinite number of ways in which it could and should be better. It clearly is not the best world, and it is a very long way from being even the best possible. However, no actual state of the world is solely due to God who provides the range of possibilities available but is always a result of contingent moves in a game that would have been impossible without God but are not performed by God. God is not a player in the game of creation but its inventor, the creator of its rules and the poet of its possibilities.[1]

The point of all this is, briefly put, to enable creatures to live their lives both as creatures and (in our human case) images of the divine love to which they owe their existence by living a life of love according to their capacities and in the ways open to them. But the only way in which creative love can hope to achieve its end of a free response from those created for love is by making creatures make themselves; and there is no built-in guarantee that they will actually choose and become what they could become by choosing that which would realise the end of God's love in their lives. But just as love cannot be en-

---

[1] The triune God creates but as creator God does not interact with creation. This is not to deny that God reacts to what goes on in creation but God reacts to his own re-presentation of the changing reality of creation and is not causally involved with created reality. God's creative activity is continually attuning to the changing states of creation in terms of the activity of the Spirit who re-presents the changing situations of creation to God and presents God to the changing situations of creation. So God is intimately involved with creation, more intimately than anything created. But God is involved by playing possibilities in its way and not by causally interacting with created actualities. He does not directly determine what happens but takes the risk of opening up a field of options for created freedom by providing a range of possibilities – at least one possibility *and* its negation beyond the range of possibilities given with a given state of creation – which requires creatures to chose and take risky decisions for which they are responsible and can be taken to account. In this way God creates by making creatures make themselves, and this in turn creates creatures to whom God relates not only as creator but also in the personal terms of salvation and perfection.

forced but has to be given freely and returned gladly, so divine love is given freely and not on condition of being returned. Because it is given independently of the reception and response it receives, it will not give up or despair by being despised and ignored. It clings to its end with respect to each and every creature and hence individualises endlessly. For precisely by continuously adjusting his divine love to the changing states of the world and of each creature in its changing situations, God is true to the love he is. If God stopped to do so, the world would cease to be. And whenever God stops to do so with respect to specific created realities, they dissolve into nothingness and are reduced to a mere trace in the past history of creation.

This divine responsiveness is true at all levels of created reality, but it takes on a different quality and mode at more complex levels of the emergent universe. In many or even most cases in the history of creation God's loving has been a rather one-sided affair by creating realities that beyond their own intrinsic ends serve to provide possibilities necessary for other realities. They are, as everything created, willed by divine love, otherwise they would not have been. But they are willed not only for their own sake but also for achieving something else. For if God's love seeks to create x, and the reality of y is necessary for x to be, then loving x entails loving y for you cannot love x and not love what is necessary for x to be. This is not to say that y is loved only as a means for x. It may well be loved for its own sake as well. Indeed, as a specific reality it *is* loved for its own sake if what I said about the individuating power of God's love is true. But it has a point and function in creation beyond itself by providing the possibilities without which something else could not have been.

Perhaps everything created is to be seen in this double perspective, as something to be cherished for its own sake and as a necessary means for something else.[2] But the theological tradition has commonly distinguished within creation between creatures that are ends in themselves (i.e. rational beings such as angels or, less obviously, human beings), and others that are not. The distinction is misleading when it is abused to degrade everything that is not human to a mere means at the disposal of human beings, as if *we* were the centre or the end of creation rather than God. But this is not Christian teaching and a misunderstanding of the Christian doctrine of creation and its view of human beings as images of God. The end of creation is the glorification of God, not the apotheosis of human being, reason and power.

---

[2] Whitehead's actual entities exemplify both perspectives.

With respect to *being created*, therefore, there is no difference between human and other creatures; they all owe their existence exclusively to God and depend for what they can and do become on the possibilities which God provides by becoming present to their presence. The difference is rather that each of them has to choose from the possibilities provided in its specific situation, and hence respond in its special way to the divine love to whom it owes its existence, and that human beings are expected to respond *as human beings* to it, capable of apprehending, acknowledging and praising God, and not as something else. There is more to human life than to other kinds of life not because human beings are superior creatures to whom everything else is given at their free disposal but because they have a capacity of responding to God's love that is different from that of other creatures. What is distinctive about them is not that they have a higher status but that they exist under a higher expectation and obligation. God's love expects more of them than of others. Whereas in most cases God's love is a rather one-sided affair, this is not so with respect to human life. The emergence of human life in the history of creation has brought about beings, whom God loves in such a way that his love hopes for a return. God's love not only makes them exist but also expects and enables them to return his love.

This is not something that can be enforced, not even by God. Love can only be given freely or it wouldn't be love; and it cannot be freely given without knowing what one does and why one does it. If human beings are singled out from other creatures by being expected to return God's love freely, by loving God and their neighbours whom God loves as well (and of whom he expects the same return of love by loving God and their neighbours with all their heart, and soul, and mind), then the human capacity to know truly, decide responsibly and act freely is a necessary prerequisite to a loving return of God's love. Only creatures with this capacity can be expected to return God's love in loving God and one's neighbour as oneself. Yet God's love cannot enforce such a return but only hope for it and enable it, and his love can enable it only by being present, by providing possibilities for a loving response, and by creating occasions for becoming aware of living in the presence of God's love.

Human beings are singled out from other creatures by being able to become aware of God's presence and acknowledge it as the present or gift of God's life-giving love to them and to all creation. They can pray to God, and they can thank God for the gift of his presence. They are created by God's love in no other way than all other creatures, but they alone are created to love God in loving God and their neighbours as themselves, i.e. as those who owe their life with its changing possibilities to God's love, live their lives in the presence of this love, and are able and expected to do so with all their hearts, and souls, and minds, i.e. consciously, freely, gladly and comprehensively. In short, human beings are made to become aware, acknowledge and appropriate in their way of living that they live through, off and for a present gift: the present of the presence of God's love. God's love is the gift to which we owe our lives, and the presence of God's love is the gift that enables us to live the life of responsive love for which we are made.

2. The Impossibility of the Gift

It is a fundamental tenet of Christian theology to conceive God's presence as the gift of divine love that initiates and sustains all relationships to created life and human beings, not only in the order of grace but also in the order of creation. For Christians there is nothing more real than the reality of this gift. God is conceived as love, God's love as gift, and the gift of God's love as present reality. To quote just one of a plethora of examples: »God, who is rich in mercy, out of the great love with which he loved us even when we were dead through our trespasses, made us alive together with Christ ... and raised us up with him and seated us with him in the heavenly places in Christ Jesus, so that in the ages to come he might show the immeasurable riches of his grace in kindness toward us in Christ Jesus. For by grace you have been saved through faith, and this is not your own doing; it is the gift of God – not because of works, lest any man should boast« (Eph 2:4-9). For the writer of the letter to the Ephesians God's gracious, unconditioned and unbounded love is the fundamental reality; it is the most present of all realties, and it is a pure gift.

However, if God's presence is pure gift, what if a pure gift is strictly impossible? A pure gift is a gift given unconditionally. It is not given because of something done by the recipient (›not *because of* works‹) nor by expecting anything in return (›not *for* being honoured or loved or admired‹) nor by being given *as* a gift by the donor or by being recognized or accepted as such by the recipient. Indeed, in the strictest possible sense a gift is unconditional only if there is no donor, no recipient, and nothing given. As J. L. Marion argues, »un don peut s'accomplir comme don sans aucun donateur ... sans le moindre donataire ... enfin sans donner aucun objet susceptible de revenir à une valeur d'échange.«[3] But if a gift is *truly unconditional* only where no one gives, no one receives and nothing is given, then a *pure* gift seems to be possible only where there is *no gift*. Pure gift is »une contradiction dans les termes«, a »contradiction formelle«.[4]

Marion here summarises an argument that has most effectively been put forward by J. Derrida in recent years.[5] *Nothing that is given and received as a gift is a gift.* Not because there is no giving and receiving of gifts in human life, but because whatever is given, received and recognized *as* a gift is not given unconditionally and hence not a pure gift. The gift, Derrida argues, is structured as an *aporia*.[6] That is to say, the »conditions of the possibility of the gift (that some ›one‹ gives some ›thing‹ to some ›one other‹) designate simultaneously the conditions of the impossibility of the gift.«[7] You cannot give something as a gift to someone without producing, at the same time, »the annulment, the annihilation, the destruction of the gift.«[8] If a donor who gives something as a gift anticipates some kind of return, he does not give unconditionally. If a recipient receives something given to him as a gift, he has already responded with recognition and hence with acknowledging that he is indebted to the donor. And if something is given as a gift, what is given loses its character as gift because »its very appearance, the simple phenomenon of the gift annuls it as gift, transforming the apparition into a phantom and the operation into a simulacrum.«[9] In short, if »to give a gift means to give something freely, without return, then in its identification as a gift in the present, no gift is ever accomplished.«[10] A gift can only be a past or perhaps a future (promised) but never a present reality. It may be described as gift retrospectively or expected prospectively, but in the present it cannot be identified as such without being dissolved. A gift, so it seems, is a present that can never be present.

---

[3] J.-L. Marion, ›La raison du don‹, *Philosophie* 78, 2003, 3-32, 14f.

[4] Ibid., 3ff.

[5] J. Derrida, *Donner le temps: 1. La fausse monnaie*, Paris 1991 (engl.: *Given Time: 1. Counterfeit Money*, trans. P. Kamuf, Chicago 1992); *Sauf le nom (Post-Scriptum)*, Paris 1993. Cf. H.-D. Gondek/B. Waldenfels (eds.), *Einsätze des Denkens. Zur Philosophie von Jacques Derrida*, Frankfurt am Main 1997; R. Horner, *Rethinking God As Gift. Marion, Derrida, and the Limits of Phenomenology*, New York 2001, esp. chaps. 1, 7 and 8.

[6] Derrida, *Donner le temps*, 27f; *Given Time*, passim.

[7] Derrida, *Given Time*, 12.

[8] Ibid.

[9] Ibid., 12-14.

[10] Horner, *Rethinking God As Gift*, 9.

Derrida's argument is not derived from an analysis of giving and receiving gifts in everyday life. Rather it is modelled on his criticism of Husserl's analysis of »the original self-giving evidence, the *present* or *presence* of sense to a full and primordial intuition.«[11] If evidence is understood as the perfect presence of the intended object to consciousness, then nothing is ever perfectly, fully or actually present to consciousness. There is no presence without presentation, and no presentation without the retention of a present past and the protention of a present future. Presence involves presentation, and presentation the temporally devisive movements of re-presentation and appresentation.[12] So for x to be present to consciousness it must be present *as* x. But this is possible only if x is followed or anticipated by y, i.e. by being identified as x by being differentiated from y. Hence nothing that seems to be present is so actually. Its presence is always a play of presence and absence. It is present to consciousness as something absent because what is present to consciousness is its presentation, and what its presentation presents is what is absent. Since presentation always involves a selection of aspects and not the totality of all the possible aspects of what is presented, pure and perfect presence is strictly impossible. Whatever is supposedly present is tinged with a difference and present only as a trace of the absent. This is just as true of the perfect presence of something to consciousness as of the perfect self-presence of consciousness itself. Derrida does not deny that there is presence but that presence can present itself. So whatever is present cannot be intuited in the present or perceived as present. To be perceived it must be inscribed, and being inscribed bars it, in principle, from being perceived in the present as present.

Apply all this to the case of gift and you can see why Derrida conceives the gift as an *aporia*. A gift may be present, but it cannot be present as a gift without being dissolved and undone. If a gift is recognized in the present *as a gift*, whether by the donor or the recipient, it is no longer given or received unconditionally but always and inevitably (expected to be) returned. If I give something as a gift to you, I expect you to receive or accept it as a gift and not as something else. If you do so you comply with the obligation to receive or accept it as a gift and not as something else. In either way the unconditionality of the gift is undermined or undone. The gift is no longer gift but obliga-

---

[11] J. Derrida, *Speech and Phenomena and Other Essays on Husserl's Theory of Signs*, trans. D.B. Allison/N. Garver, Evanston 1973, 5.

[12] Ibid., 7.

tion, return, payback, or whatever. It becomes part of the economy of
exchange and hence is undone as gift. In short, a gift that is present,
i.e. can be identified as such, is no longer gift but commodity, value, or
obligation. Derrida shows this for each aspect of the gift: A donor who
intentionally gives, invariably receives. A recipient, who perceives
what he receives as gift, responds with recognition and recognizes an
indebtedness to the donor. An object (whether a thing, a symbol, a
value, or whatever) that is given or received as a gift loses its gift-aspect
and becomes an obligation or a debt.[13] One cannot give or receive a
gift intentionally without annulling it. And so Derrida concludes »The
truth of the gift is equivalent to the non-gift or to the non-truth of the
gift.«[14] For a gift to accomplish its work as a gift, it must remain unrecognisable as a gift, but if it remains unrecognisable it is not present as a
gift, neither to the donor nor to the recipient. The gift is possible only
by being impossible.[15] And »it is perhaps in this sense«, Derrida holds,
that the gift is not merely impossible but »that the gift is the impossible.«[16]

3. The Unavoidability of the Gift

But what exactly is declared to be impossible here? Not the possibility
of the gift but of a gift appearing or being present *as a gift*. What Derrida denies is that gifts can appear as phenomena. This allows for a
number of reactions. Some agree with his analysis and conclusion:
Gifts are not phenomena. Others criticise it and argue: *Gifts are phenomena.* And some, such as Marion, strictly object to it and offer a different
sort of analysis altogether. Whereas Derrida holds that *no gift is a phenomenon,* Marion argues that *every phenomenon is a gift.*[17] To see this we
have to concentrate our analysis not on whether gifts are phenomena
or not, but on the horizons in which gifts appear, or do not appear, as
phenomena. If we analyse gifts, as Derrida does, in the *horizon of economy and exchange,* or *of causality and intention,* they will not appear as

---

[13] Cf. Derrida, *Given Time*, 12-14.
[14] Ibid., 27.
[15] Cf. J.D. Caputo, ›Apostles of the Impossible‹, in: J.D. Caputo/M.J. Scanlon
(eds.), *God, the Gift, and Postmodernism*, Bloomington, Indiana 1999, 185-
222,210f.
[16] Derrida, *Given Time,* 7.
[17] Cf. in particular J.-L. Marion, *Etant donné. Essai d'une phénoménologie de la donation,* Vendôme ²1998.

phenomena. But if we analyse them in the *horizon of giving* or *giveness*, as Marion proposes, they will. Gifts have their own proper horizon in which they are to be understood, the horizon of *givenness*. In this horizon nothing appears that does not appear as something given. And since there is nothing that could not appear in this horizon, Marion concludes not merely that gifts are phenomena but that all phenomena are gifts.

But there is a price to be paid for this saving of the phenomenon of gift. If every phenomenon is a gift, then to describe gifts as phenomena is not very illuminating. For all practical purposes Derrida's proposal *No gift is a phenomenon* and Marion's counter-proposal *All phenomena are gifts* amount to the same. The difference between them cannot be sorted out phenomenally, i.e. in terms of particular phenomena, but only phenomenologically, i.e. in terms of the appropriate method of phenomenology. If everything given is a gift, then the term ›gift‹ does not help to identify a particular set of phenomena and there is no way of phenomenally distinguishing the giving of gifts from other acts or processes of social interaction and communication. If the true gift consists in the givenness, then the gift appears to be saved as a phenomenon by being dissolved into the being given of phenomena and thus made dependent on the method of phenomenology.

However, to reduce the gift to the givenness of phenomena appears to be as much due to a problematic and abstract approach in phenomenology as to reject the gift as a phenomenon. In either case what is described as gift is not what we know as the giving and receiving of gifts from everyday practices in our culture and in others but what a specific sort of phenomenological reduction makes of gifts.[18] Derrida's

---

[18] Cf. J.-L. Marion, *Being Given. Toward a Phenomenology of Givenness*, Stanford, California 2002, 113ff. J. Milbank, *Being Reconciled. Ontology and Pardon*, London 2003, 156 is right in pointing out that »gift-giving is a mode (*the* mode in fact) of social being, and in ignoring this, Derrida and Marion remain trapped within Cartesian myths of prior subjectivity after all.« But he wrongly concludes that if »there is a gift that can truly be, then this must be the event of reciprocal but asymmetrical and non-identically repeated exchange« (157). In siding with Derrida »that a unilateral, purely sacrificial gift can never occur« (156f) Milbank limits the application of the notion of ›gift‹ to the social and ethical situation of actual and potential reciprocity and plays down that in faith and religion its primary application is creation and the experience of being created: *To be* or *to be present* is pure gift, i. e. something utterly unlikely for any of us to occur and, for us, absolutely beyond any sort of ›exchange‹. We come into being and continue to be through the totally unmerited gift of God's presence for God becomes present to our present in a purely one-sided self-giving and self-presentation. There is nothing whatsoever that we could give in return or in exchange for God's presence

analysis leads to the *annihilation of the gift* and thus results in the *aporia* that a social reality that nobody denies is negated as a phenomenon on phenomenological grounds. A gift can only be present if it is not present as a gift, but if it is not present as a gift, it is not a present gift for us. The gift is structured as an *aporia*, and ›pure gift‹ is an aporetic idea. It is said to be possible only where there is no donor, no recipient, and no thing given. But what is left of the gift after this operation that amounts to a death by unrestricted negation? Derrida's answer is:

---

because everything we are and have we owe to God our creator. There is nothing, which we have not received, and hence there is nothing, which we can return as *our* gift to the one who has given us everything. Creation, as Milbank occasionally sees, is »an entirely one-way gift« (66). But he misses the point of this insight by turning it in the ethical obligation of »an absolute exchange, since the gift is only received in its return to God« (66). This emphasis on reciprocity is nothing less than the modernist claim that the sinner has not received the gift of creation – that he ›is‹ without having been created. But this is either to ignore that the sinner too is God's creature because he couldn't sin without being created (*simul creatura et peccator*) so that we must distinguish between the *person* and the *deed* of the sinner (the first is whom God loves and wants to save, the second is what God hates and seeks to overcome). Or it is to miss the point and gravity of sin (*nondum considerasti quantum ponderis sit peccatum*) that there is nothing we can give that we do not owe to God anyway: There is not the slightest possibility of exchange, neither for the sinner nor the justified sinner (*simul iustus et peccator*), for what he has received in being created and in being redeemed is God's unilateral gift and cannot be returned, not even in a »non-identical repetition« (xi), to God as the creature's gift. Or it is to fall prey to the very divorce between ›being‹ and ›being created‹ or ›being in the present of God‹ which Milbank is so much at pains to unmask as the disastrous consequence of the Scotist fallacy of a unitary notion of being untouched by the difference between the creator and the created. The »divine donum« is not to be reduced to »the notion of a participation of reciprocal exchanges in an infinite reciprocity« (x) for the divine gift is *not* »an exchange as well as an offering without return« (xi). Milbank's attempt to describe the divine gift as a »gift-exchange« in terms of »participation« misses the very point of the divine donum by describing participation as »participation of the created gifts in the divine giver« and as the creature's »participation in a Trinitarian God« (xi). But it is all-important here to see that it is not the creature that participates in the Trinitarian God but God who becomes present to the creature. God ›participates‹ in created reality and not the other way round; and God does so by opening up his divine life and makes space for created reality to be present in a way that cannot be described in terms of ›gift-exchange‹ since the only one who gives here is God and not the creature: Both *that* and *what* the creature can return is God's gift, and only God's gift. Throughout his argument Milbank's obfuscates the important difference between a divine love that hopes for reciprocity and a God who loves only where there is reciprocity. God gives freely and for the best of his creature, not for an exchange that is primarily or exclusively or finally good only for God.

nothing, and hence he negates the gift as a phenomenon. Marion, on the other hand, holds against it that such operations of negation and modification wouldn't be possible without something given to which and through which they are applied. Hence he arrives at exactly the opposite conclusion: *everything* given as a phenomenon is, as a self-giving, a being given, i.e. a gift.

4. Save the Phenomena – or Phenomenology?

Both positions, Derrida's as much as Marion's, use figures of thought and argument that are well known in theology: How we approach something, i.e. the mode and the horizon through which we explore, understand and symbolise something as something, decides to a large extent on what we perceive, what we can say, and how we think about it. What seems to be at stake in the debate between Derrida and Marion, therefore, is not so much a particular phenomenon, or a particular set of phenomena (gifts), but the relationship between phenomena and method of approach. For does Derrida really reject gifts as phenomena or is he not rather using an intentionalist analysis of the gift for criticising and deconstructing the intentionalist approach in phenomenology by pushing its analysis to (or even beyond) the limit? And does Marion really save the gift as a phenomenon or is he merely demonstrating a methodological presupposition of his phenomenology of givenness? In either case what they differ about is not the gift or the limits of the gift as a phenomenon but the limits of phenomenology or a particular phenomenological method and approach. Their phenomenological debate about the gift as a phenomenon is not a debate about the gift but about phenomenological method.

Central to this debate is the method and mode of phenomenological reduction. Since its invention by Husserl, phenomenology has had a problem with the fact that there is a world. The phenomenologist, Hans Blumenberg has argued, is defined »by a fearlessness of infinite regress«[19] but he is »permanently threatened with the fact that there is a world as the totality of all that is the case, and that this bars him from having direct access to his essences.«[20] The method of phenomenological reduction demands of the philosopher the ability »to inspect an ob-

---

[19] H. Blumenberg, *Lebenszeit und Weltzeit*, Frankfurt am Main ²1986, 374 (my translation).

[20] H. Blumenberg, *Zu den Sachen und zurück*, Frankfurt am Main 2002, 241 (my translation).

ject independently of its existence in nature, in the world, in time. Essence is always what is left over when existence has been subtracted from an object.«[21] In this respect phenomenological reduction is based on an »elementary indifference to the existence of objects« which in Husserl's case may be due to his background in mathematics[22] since the mathematician »is indifferent to the existence of his objects even when he speaks about it as significant in one way or another.«[23] It is precisely the point of phenomenological reduction to isolate the essence of a phenomenon for essential or eidetic intuition (*Wesensschau*) by disregarding or bracketing its existence.[24]

But this was »fostering a methodological illusion« as has been borne out not only by the whole »history of Husserl's difficulties with his method of reduction and its multiple alterations«[25] but also by the continuation of this problem in the later phenomenological movements. Even modes of reduction that do not follow Husserl's pattern of pure intuition of essences in their ideational universality in mathematics are infected by this illusion. This is true of Blumenberg himself and his method of a free historical variation of the ideas embedded in the metaphors and concepts of our cultural heritage. In order to delineate the essence of what is under examination by exploring the possibilities of a phenomenon in the history of language and culture he does not de-

---

[21] Ibid., 240 (my translation).

[22] Cf. E. Husserl, *Logical Investigations, Introduction to Volume 2*, trans. J.N. Findlay, ed. D. Moran, London/New York 2001.

[23] Blumenberg, *Zu den Sachen und zurück*, 243 (my translation).

[24] Blumenberg is oversimplifying here. The danger of this account of phenomenological reduction in terms of the medieval distinction between essence and existence is to take the beginnings of phenomenology in Husserl's *Logical Investigations* and (in part) *Ideen I* to be normative. But Husserl corrected this misleading impression in his later writings. The point of phenomenological reduction is not to grasp essences independent of the existence of things but rather to insist that what we grasp are *phenomena*, i.e. something whose essence or existence is inaccessible to us independent of the way in which it appears to consciousness. There is an open debate about the status and character of the *noema* resulting from the reduction. Some take it to be a mental representation of the thing or object intended (Føllesdal, Dreyfus, Miller, Smith, McIntyre), others understand it to be the worldly object itself as given in our experience (Sokolowski, Drummond, Hart, Cobb-Stevens). But it is clear that for the later Husserl the world of phenomena was not different from the world of existing things. Cf. his self-criticism in Hua 15/287; cf. Hua 16/162, Hua 29/160-165 etc. The problem is discussed in detail in D. Zahavi, *Husserl's Phenomenology*, Stanford, California 2003, 43-77. I am grateful to D. Zahavi and C. Welz for drawing my attention to this important point.

[25] Blumenberg, *Zu den Sachen und zurück*, 240f (my translation).

scribe and analyse what is the case but explores and imagines what might have been the case. He concentrates not on the reality of the phenomena under examination but on their possibilities.

It is precisely this that results in the *aporia* in the case of the gift. Derrida seeks to explore the essence of the gift by bracketing the existential realities of a donor, a recipient and a gift-object and by concentrating strictly on the possibilities of its essential structure. But he comes to discover that what is left after the bracketing is not a purified essence of the gift for phenomenological intuition but simply nothing at all that could be inspected. The reduction ends where it begins: with noting the mere fact of something that cannot be described as a phenomenon but only as the absence of a phenomenon, a trace of something that never was or will be present.[26]

Marion, on the other hand, seeks to avoid this result by declaring exactly that which disappears with the bracketing of the realities of the gift for the essence of the phenomenon under examination: The gift is what makes phenomenological reduction possible in the first place, and whatever is assumed as given in phenomenological reduction is a gift.

They both share in common the fact that they stick in principle to the method of phenomenological reduction, but whereas for Derrida its use results in the annulment of the gift as phenomenon, for Marion the gift becomes an essential part of the method itself. *Nothing is a gift that phenomenological reduction presents for intuition*: The gift is not a phenomenon (Derrida). *Everything is a gift that phenomenological reduction presents for intuition*: Phenomena are given, they give themselves, and their givenness is the gift (Marion).[27]

---

[26] C. Welz has pointed out to me that a different way of putting this is to say that Derrida draws attention to the difficulty of phenomenological attempts from Husserl's ›gebende Anschauung‹ through Heidegger's ›es gibt‹ to Marion's ›auto-donation‹ to describe that which appears to consciousness as gift. The *gift* is neither a phenomenon in either of these senses nor is it simply not a phenomenon. The ›essence‹ of the gift is not that it is impossible for the gift to be present as gift, and its ›existence‹ is not the absence of the gift as phenomenon. Rather the distinction between essence and existence becomes highly problematic in the case of gifts: It is drawn from things (substances) that exist but gifts are not things (substances) but (as I shall argue) *specific practices*.

[27] Marion, *Being Given*, 68ff.

5. Essence and Existence: The Interference of the World

Phenomenology is the study of phenomena, and phenomena are everything whatsoever insofar as it appears or is given to consciousness.
But phenomenologists have always known that there is more to the
world than phenomena. Phenomena are not all there is, and not everything is a phenomenon. *Horizons*, for example, are not phenomena
even though every phenomenon is a phenomenon-in-a-horizon. One
cannot isolate and inspect horizons by bracketing everything of which
they are a horizon. The horizon behind the lake of Zurich is not a
property of the mountains that I see over there, but if I disregard these
mountains there is no horizon left either. Horizons limit a perspective
in which phenomena appear to a consciousness, but *perspectives* also are
no phenomena. It is even a question for debate whether everything
that appears in a perspective and its horizon is a phenomenon. Are
rainbows phenomena? Or are they water drops reflecting sunlight that
have the phenomenal structure on which a phenomenological analysis
of rainbows has to concentrate?

Similarly with the gift: When analysed as a phenomenon it disinte-
grates and disappears under the impact of phenomenological reduction
(Derrida). But is it really a way of saving the gift as phenomenon
when, just as in the case of *horizon* or *perspective*, its *being given* or *givenness* is turned into a methodological presupposition of phenomenological reduction (Marion), that is to say, if the gift is described as the very
givenness of phenomena that is presupposed in every phenomenological reduction because otherwise there wouldn't be anything that could
be reduced? Derrida pushes the phenomenological reduction to or beyond its limits by showing (1) that there is no *essence of the gift* left for
eidetic intuition if you bracket the *existence of gifts* in real life, and (2)
that the giving of gifts in real life cannot clearly be distinguished from
economic exchange so that there is no essential difference between the
order of giving and the order of exchange. Marion, on the other hand,
seems to opt for precisely the opposite conclusion by identifying the
essence of the gift with the very *existence of gifts*, i.e. with their *being given*:
The mere fact of *givenness* or *being given* of anything whatsoever is the
gift whose phenomenal essence we seek to describe. Whereas the
method of phenomenological reduction strictly annuls the gift as a
phenomenon for the one, it turns all phenomena into gifts for the other.

They both react to the interference of the world with phenomenological intuition by opting for one of the two extreme positions possi-

ble under their common methodological assumption: that we can, in a phenomenologically viable way, distinguish between the essence and the existence of the gift. If it is the point of reduction »to abandon *existence* in order to keep the *essence*«[28], then this results either in the loss of the gift as a phenomenon (the *aporia* of Derrida's negative phenomenology of the gift) or in the phenomenological act of despair of identifying the essence of the gift with its existence, i.e. of saving the phenomenon of the gift by reducing it to the givenness of phenomena and by thus turning all phenomena given to consciousness into gifts (the universalising approach of Marion's phenomenology of givenness).[29] The first position reacts to the interference of the world by limiting the world of phenomena and by opening it towards something beyond itself: *There is more to the world than that which appears or can appear to consciousness.* The second position reacts to the interference of the world by describing phenomena as such as the interruption of consciousness by something different from it: *There is more to the world than that which appears or can appear to consciousness, because whatever appears must be given, but its being given or givenness is nothing that either could or could not appear.*

6. Saying and Showing: Beyond the World of Phenomena

If we look at it in this way we can see that both Derrida's annihilation of the gift and Marion's universalising of the gift are ontologically motivated. The first seeks to show that there is more that we can truly say than what appears to us because not everything that is also appears. The second insists that we can only say what appears because that which appears to us shows us more than actually appears. For Derrida there is more to the world than that which appears or can appear to us. Marion agrees but adds that there is more to the world because nothing could appear to us if that which in principle cannot appear as such were not the case: that which is given *to us*, *gives itself*, i.e. is self-giving givenness. Just as it is in vain even to attempt to show what cannot be shown because it does not appear but always disappears, so it is in vain to attempt to show what even in what we show cannot in principle be shown: the fact that that which appears to us, is *self-appearing*. Thus

---

[28] Blumenberg, *Zu den Sachen und zurück*, 254 (my translation).
[29] This is not to say that gift is a mere intra-mental reality. What is given is given to consciousness but this does not imply that it is merely intra-mental but rather that it is a reality for consciousness precisely if and insofar as it is a *self-giving*.

both Derrida and Marion try to depict the way in which the world is
more than merely a world of phenomena. But their common interest
results in two fundamentally diverging ontological orientations:
Whereas the one underlines the principal *openness of the world* towards
something beyond the phenomena, the other emphasises in a no less
principal way the *givenness of the world* in the self-giving of phenomena.

The gift is annulled as a phenomenon, Derrida argues, because the
very conditions of the possibility of the gift designate simultaneously
the conditions of its impossibility. The gift is not a phenomenon that
can appear to or be present to consciousness as a gift but only as something that is indicated as absent by something present. It may be remembered (as having been given) or expected (as promised) but cannot be identified in the present. For our consciousness it is accessible
only as a trace of something that does not appear to but disappears
from consciousness; a trace of something absent that, if it ever was
present, never was present to consciousness *as* a gift. This is why it is
not a phenomenon. In Derrida's analysis, the gift cancels itself because
as soon as it appears as a phenomenon it disappears as gift. It cannot
become present without ceasing to be a gift. The reason is that it cannot break free of the cycle of return. Whatever appears in the present
to consciousness, appears in the horizon of exchange and economy
and hence not as a gift. Yet only against the background of economy
and the cycle of exchange can we describe the gift as that which does
not appear but disappears, is *not* present but absent. For the gift never
appears to consciousness in the present but neither it is simply not or
nothing at all. It rather appears in and through that which is different
from it as something *disappearing, withdrawing, absent*.

This is why gifts cannot be *shown* to be present but only *spoken of* in
the present[30]: They are present not in the showing but only in the saying. This makes the gift ontologically precarious. It is not a phenomenon in the world of phenomena, but marks the limit of the world of
phenomena for although it is not a phenomenon it is not nothing either. But then the world must be more than a world of phenomena:
There is more to the world than what appears or can appear to consciousness. There is a ›beyond‹ or ›behind‹ or ›before‹ of the world of
phenomena that cannot be shown or described and is referentially inaccessible. We can speak of gifts in terms of memory or promise but
we cannot show or present them. This gives a ring of fictitiousness or

---

[30] Not, of course, by describing it but by (for example) remembering it or
promising it.

illusion to our talk of gift because we can never identify a gift in the present but can only speak of it or promise it, announce it or remember it, thank for it or recall it. The limits of our language, not the limits of the phenomena, are the limits of our world.

Derrida's annihilation of the gift as a phenomenon thus turns out to be a pleading for a ›beyond‹ of our world over and above that which appears or can appear to consciousness. The gift is the prime example of the fact that phenomena point beyond themselves to a dimension of the reality of the world that is not one of its possibilities but presupposed by all possibilities of the world of phenomena. Phenomena do so not by what they show but by what is appresently present and presupposed in their showing without ever being able to become a phenomenon or be shown itself. There is more to the world than that which appears or can appear in the world. For if it were not, there wouldn't be a world and nothing would appear. The world of phenomena depends on conditions of possibility that can only appear as impossibilities in the phenomenal world. This is why the world of phenomena is not closed but exists with an open horizon – not only in the sense that more and other phenomena are possible besides and beyond those that are actual but in the more radical sense that the world is in principle more than the totality of what is or could be a phenomenon in the world.

Marion agrees. He too argues that there is more to the world than the totality of actual and possible phenomena. But he does not stop, as Derrida does, by pointing out that there is something of which we can speak in the present but which we cannot show to be present because it is present only as something absent, and appears to consciousness only by disappearing. For Marion, describing the problem of the gift in this way indicates only that it is described in the inappropriate horizon of the economy of exchange and the cycle of return. Understood in this perspective and horizon there is nothing wrong with Derrida's account of the gift. But why confine its analysis to this approach? So Marion proposes a change of perspective and an analysis of the gift in a different horizon: There is indeed more to the world than that which appears or can appear in the world as a phenomenon. But not merely because there could always be other phenomena, or because the phenomena could appear to us differently, or because there is something appresent to their appearing that becomes present only as absent and appears only as disappearing. The reason is rather that something can appear *to us* only by *being given* to us, and that it is given to us rather than constituted by us only *by giving itself.* Without the givenness of phenomena to consciousness there is no world of phenomena, and without this givenness being a *self-giving* of the phenomena there is nothing *given to us*.

However, and this is the nub of his argument, this *self-giving* is in principle not something that could appear to us as a phenomenon. There is no phenomenon, i.e. nothing given to us, that is not a self-giving, but *self-giving is not a special phenomenon in its own right*. It is here where Marion's analysis arrives at a very different conclusion from Derrida. Whereas for Derrida the gift is the exception to the rule of phenomena, for Marion it is the rule: That there is more to the world than the world of phenomena is shown most clearly not in the rare occasions when something does *not appear* to us but can only be noticed as *disappearing* in the appearing of something else, but rather in the common situation in which what *appears* discloses itself to be *self-appearing*: The fact that everything *given to us* is a *being given* only in so far as it is *giving itself to us* is the decisive pointer beyond the world of phenomena, rather than the fact that there is something that is *not given to us* but only appears as disappearing (or is present as absent) in what is given to us. The trans-phenomenal openness of the world is not denied but is said to depend on something more fundamental: that the world proves to be more than what appears to us even in what appears to us. There is not a world beyond the world of phenomena that appear to us but rather the world of phenomena itself is more than what appears to us because all that appears (is given) to us is something that discloses itself (gives itself) to us.

Yet precisely the fact that the *being given* of phenomena is a *self-giving* is not a phenomenon itself. It rather is the intrinsic truth about all phenomena that does not allow us to distinguish between phenomena, i.e. between those that are given and those that give themselves. A phenomenon is something *given to* consciousness-, not merely a self-affection of consciousness. So in order to avoid the pitfalls of Husserl's Cartesian transcendentalism that conceives everything given to consciousness as being constituted by transcendental subjectivity, Marion argues that whatever is given to consciousness is *given to* (rather than constituted or created by) consciousness only if and in so far it is strictly *self-given*: If there are *phenomena* (i.e. something *given* to consciousness rather than merely constructed by it) at all, they must be *self-giv-*

---

[31] The whole argument has to be taken with a pinch of salt. Husserl was quite aware of the importance of passive synthesis in the constitution of phenomena not only *by* but also *for* consciousness. And Marion doesn't really escape the pitfalls of transcendentalism by insisting not only on a self-giving of phenomena that is a *gi-*

en.[31] However, the fact of phenomena then proves that there is more to the world than phenomena. The world is what there is, and it is our world only in being given to us. But since what there is *is given* to us only if it *gives itself*, the world is what there is only if it gives itself. This is not a truth of something in the world but about the world. It does not *show* in the world because this would require us to draw a distinction which we cannot draw, viz. distinguish between phenomena that are given to us and phenomena that give themselves to us. It can only be *said* about everything that shows in the world, i.e. be maintained as a fundamental truth without which there wouldn't be a world for us. For us there is a world only if what there is for us gives itself to us. This self-giving is not a phenomenon itself but without it there wouldn't be any phenomena.

For both Derrida and Marion, therefore, the paradigm of the gift shows a way of coming to grips with the disruption of phenomenological contemplation by the interference of the world. For Derrida the analysis of the gift brings out the *ontological openness* of the world in that it points to something that appears only as disappearing in the appearing of something else, i.e. is present only as absence, withdrawal, or trace. For Marion, on the other hand, the analysis of the gift brings out the *ontological givenness* of the world, and since nothing is really *given* to us unless it is *giving itself*, the givenness of the world is analysed to be a *self-giving* of the phenomena given to us. Thus not only what does *not* appear to us (but is present only in its disappearing) but also everything that *appears* to us proves the world to be more than the world of phenomena. The trace of the absent as much as the structure of the present point beyond the world pf phenomena. Both are paradoxical features of the world, and in both cases a hermeneutics of suspicion will find it easy to detect misguided tendencies to questionable metaphysics. But both positions are clear-headed and straightforward attempts at a critical phenomenology, i.e. a phenomenology that seeks to come to grips with the interference and interruption of the world without abandoning the phenomenological approach or ignoring its limits.

---

venness to consciousness but also on consciousness itself as *given*: The distinction between *being given* and *being self-given* is to be drawn in terms of the consciousness to which it is given – and here all the problems re-occur.

7. From Exchange to Giving: Gifts as Social Phenomena

But what is to be learned from these controversies about phenomenological method about the problem of the gift? It is a common conviction of both positions discussed that *gift* has to be marked off from *exchange* and that there are only gifts in so far as they can be distinguished
form the economic cycle of return. Wherever the distinction is
blurred, as is often the case in anthropological, sociological and ethno-
logical studies, the gift is seen as »The Form and Reason for Exchange«.[32] Marcel Mauss famously analysed gift-giving in this sense as
a system of exchange that creates bonds with others and operates in
certain societies to create and preserve relations between people. Gift-
giving is a common operation in particular economies. It is part of the
circle of reciprocation that maintains social cohesion through the re-
distribution of wealth.[33] But it goes beyond a mere economic exchange in that it creates and expresses relationship between people. For
Mauss the explanation of why gifts must be returned is a spiritual one:
the gift is part of the giver and creates a bond with the recipient that
requires him to return the gift as part of the bond. Later anthropologists, such as R. Firth, C. Lévi-Strauss, and M. Sahlins have concen-
trated more on reciprocity as a basic feature of social cohesion. But
they all are criticised by Derrida for at least two reasons. The first is
that he questions »the very existence of something like *the* gift, that is,
the common referent of this sign that is itself uncertain.«[34] The second
is that for »there to be gift, it is necessary that the gift not even appear,
that it not be perceived or received as gift.«[35] The donor must radically
forget what he or she gives, and the recipient must not receive or perceive it as a gift. For only if the cycle of return is broken, can the gift
be identified *as gift* and distinguished from exchange.

On the other hand, Derrida seems to agree with the anthropologists
he criticises that the gift can only be identified and described against
the background of a highly developed economy of exchange. Whereas
exchange is an operation or relation that is reciprocal, symmetrical and
equivalent, *gifts* differ from exchange in that they are *not* equivalent, *not*
symmetrical and *not* reciprocal. However, understanding the gift in
this way exclusively against the background of an economy of ex-

---

[32] Cf. M. Mauss, *The Gift. The Form and Reason for Exchange in Archaic Societies*,
trans. W.D. Hall, London 1990.

[33] Ibid., 31.

[34] Derrida, *Given Time,* 26.

[35] Ibid., 16.

change is to understand only what the gift is *not*, and not what it is. Precisely this is born out by Derrida's analysis. In the horizon of an economy of exchange, there is no gift. It does not nor cannot occur because all there is are kinds and forms of exchange.

There are a number of ways in which one can react to this. One is to turn the argument around and universalise the giving of gifts rather than the cycle of exchange to be the basic reality against which all other forms of giving and taking are to be understood: *Only because there is gift, can there be exchange.* Another is to distinguish sharply between gift and exchange by offering different and unrelated accounts of the giving of gifts and the economy of exchange: *If the gift is understood as gift (and not merely as exchange), it is seen to be a social reality in its own right independent of the economy of exchange.* Or one can go even further and differentiate different kinds of giving by identifying the specific practices and life-world occasions where the giving of gifts is not a case of exchanging goods, and vice versa: *Not every giving is a case of exchanging something.*

Marion combines the first and the second line of approach. He seeks to understand the gift by changing from the horizon of exchange to that of *givenness*. Whereas in the horizon of exchange gifts can only be characterised negatively as that which they are not (they are *not exchange*), we must go beyond this and characterise gifts positively as a reality in their own right. This, he argues, is possible if we start from the *givenness* of gifts. There are no gifts if they are not given, but being given is something that does not just characterise gifts as a particular social reality but everything that is: Only what is given is, for without being given to someone it would not be anything for anyone.[36]

The result is a *radical phenomenology* that no longer seeks to intuit the essence of the gift by bracketing its existence but rather identifies the very existence of gifts to be their essence. But if we follow this line of approach we have to go beyond Marion. For in doing so phenomenology is forced to re-conceive itself as a *hermeneutical phenomenology of human life-world*. For if the gift can be identified and be described as gift only in the horizon of *givenness*; if *givenness* is the *existence of something for someone*, that is, not the existence of something *as something* for someone but simply its existence for someone, the mere being given of something to someone; and if a *horizon* is nothing but the scope of a domain of possibilities which delimits or defines how something is and

---

[36] Cf. J.-L. Marion, *Réduction et donation. Recherches sur Husserl, Heidegger et la phénomenologie*, Paris 1989; *Etant donné*, ²1998.

can be given to someone, i.e. does and can exist for someone; then the
horizon in which something is given to someone is at the same time
the hermeneutic condition of understanding something *as* something:
It is the condition for those to whom something is given to understand what is given to them in a particular way.

However, if nothing can be given to me that cannot be understood
as something by me, then there can be no gift unless something is giv-
en to someone *and* if those to whom it is given can understand it as a
gift, i.e. as something given not only *to* them but *for* them. There is no
gift if it cannot be perceived and received as a gift by those to whom it
is given. It is not enough for it to be given, nor to be given to someone. It must be possible that those to whom it is given understand it
not merely as something *given*, nor as something *given to them*, but as
something *given for them*, i.e. as something given to them *as a gift*. It is
true that without something being given there is no gift. A mere possible given, i.e. something that may or might be given, is not a gift. But
neither is everything actually given. It must be given to and for someone. And while it may be given *to* someone without being noticed
(something can be given to someone whether or not it is noticed by
her), it cannot be given *for* someone without being able to be noticed
(a gift would miss its point if it were in principle impossible to notice
it, and it has missed its point, if in fact it isn't). Giving a gift entails
that the recipient can perceive it as being given *to him or her* (rather
than to anyone else), and as being given to him or her *as a gift* (and not
as something else).

8. From Intention to Interpretation:
Gifts as Hermeneutical Phenomena

In this sense gifts are not merely social but hermeneutical phenomena.
Something is a gift for me only if it is given to me as something for me
(›This is for you‹), and this entails not only that I can understand it as
such (›This is a gift for me‹) but also that I cannot do so without at the
same time understanding myself as the recipient of the gift (›I am a
donee‹). For participating in an economic process of exchange it may
be enough to know the value of the objects exchanged and the rules
of the exchange of values. But to receive a gift I must be able to understand what is given to me as given for me, i.e. as a gift, and myself
as its recipient.

This is why gifts are hermeneutical phenomena – not because they
have to be understood *as gifts* in order to be gifts but because they

would stop being gifts and mutate into something else in the communicative practices of our life-world if they couldn't be understood as something given to us that is not given by us nor through us but for us. Something is not a gift because I understand it as a gift but the other way round: Something given to me proves to be a gift by making me the recipient of a gift, that is, by making me understand, on the one hand, myself as the recipient or donee of a gift and, on the other, what I receive as something given for and not only to me. It is not me who turns something given to me into a gift, but the gift that turns me into a donee.

This has some important methodological implications. If gifts are what they are by provoking a certain understanding of themselves and of those to whom they are addressed, they are hermeneutical phenomena and must be studied accordingly. Now hermeneutics differs from phenomenology in method and approach.[37] It is not based on phenomenological reduction but on interpretation. It does not reduce phenomena to an ideal essence that can be studied by eidetic intuition as saturating a specific intention, and it does not investigate the essential structure of what appears or is given to consciousness by bracketing the existential, historical or empirical aspect of our experiences and by concentrating on the ›ideal types‹ that the contingent phenomena before us allegedly exemplify. On the contrary, hermeneutics starts from contingent phenomena that belong to particular cultural contexts, linguistic practices and social or communicative situations. It seeks to illumine the complex network of meaning and practice to which the phenomena under consideration belong and trace the changing ways in which they participate in a changing reality with its varying dimensions of possibility. It starts from phenomena that are interpretative and as such already understood or misunderstood in one way or another; it seeks to clarify these interpretations by interpreting them further; and it does so by exploring the background of meaning

---

[37] In what follows I oversimplify in order to bring out a difference between the methods of phenomenological reduction and hermeneutical interpretation that is important even though both phenomenology and hermeneutics exist in many different and sometimes overlapping versions. Phenomenology – even in Husserl – is much more varied and aware of the contingency of phenomena and the perspectivity of our perception of them, and in Blumenberg it takes a ›hermeneutical turn‹ to a historical phenomenology of the life-world in which it becomes virtually indistinguishable from hermeneutics. Cf. Ph. Stoellger, *Metaphor and Lebenswelt. Hans Blumenbergs Metaphorologie als Lebenswelthermeneutik und ihr religionsphänomenologischer Horizont*, Tübingen 2000.

in which they participate, and the dimensions of possibility that are opened up by them. Whereas phenomenology tends to idealise and oversimplify phenomena by abstracting them in phenomenological reduction from their actual contexts in real life, it is the point of hermeneutics to concentrate on the particular, individual, even singular in the very contexts in which it functions, lives or exists. It does not bracket the contingent dimensions of phenomena but on the contrary describes them in their contingent and changing contexts. It sees phenomena as being embedded in and constituted by processes of interpretation that need permanently to be rehearsed and readjusted by understanding and interpreting the actual against the background of the possible and the possible as the changing domain of the actual. By interpreting what is the case in the light of what could or might be the case, we can arrive at a new and better understanding of our world and our place in it, and this in turn allows us to explore new ways of living and acting in it. This practical interest is central to hermeneutics, and it can achieve its end only by concentrating on the concrete particularities of life.

9. Communication: Gifts as Life-World Phenomena

This is also true in the case of gift. A hermeneutical approach will not try to isolate *the gift* as the common referent or essential meaning of the sign ›gift‹ but rather concentrate on the actual processes of giving and receiving gifts in the social practices of our life-world and culture. It is here that what we call ›gift‹ is marked off from other practices of giving and receiving, and it is only by reference to these practices that we can trace similarities and distinctions between the giving and receiving of gifts and other practices. Gifts do not occur as isolated phenomena open to abstract inspection. They are part and parcel of social interaction and communication in human practices.

To disregard the life-world practices in which gifts occur is to loose sight of what one seeks to understand. Any attempt to describe the gift as gift independent of the particularities of life in which gifts occur is doomed to failure. The term ›gift‹ does not denote an object or a thing or an entity, that is distinguished from other objects, things or entities by a particular set of properties. Gifts are cultural artefacts, not natural kinds, and they occur in the form of social practices and in no other way. The term ›gift‹ refers not to particular objects or things but to a *particular social practice* of using objects or things, that is, to a *particular practice of human interaction and communication.*

My point is not that there is a difference between *giving a gift* and *a gift given*, between the practice or activity of doing something and the result of what is done in doing it. This is true as far as it goes. But gifts are not the result of a particular activity (*giving*), they are a particular activity: the *giving and receiving of gifts.* This activity or practice is misunderstood if analysed into a generic activity (*giving and receiving*) and a special case of it (giving and receiving *gifts*). It rather is a social practice or activity in its own right; the *giving and receiving of gifts:* You cannot separate or distinguish the *gift* from the *giving and receiving* without loosing both the gift and the giving and receiving. Giving gifts is not giving a special sort of thing but a special sort of activity, and receiving a gift is not receiving a special sort of object but participating in a special kind of practice. There are no objects that are gifts while other objects aren't but anything can become a gift when it is appropriately included in the practice of giving and receiving gifts. Similarly, there is no general giving and receiving which becomes a giving and receiving of gifts when tied to the appropriate object, or when performed with the right sort of intention, or in the right sort of way. There are no gifts independent of the giving and receiving of gifts, and the giving and receiving of gifts is not a special sort of giving and receiving but a communicative practice in its own right. What it involves cannot be illumined by a general analysis of giving and receiving but only by looking at the particular cases of giving and receiving gifts in our life-world, culture and society. To learn about gifts we have to study these concrete communicative practices.

This is why traditional phenomenology is of little help in understanding gifts. Its method of reduction as a means to study the phenomenon of the gift by bracketing all its concrete social occurrences is bound to end in an *aporia* as Derrida has shown. If there are no gifts independent of the particular social practices of giving and receiving gifts, one cannot disregard these practices and keep the phenomenon of the gift. And if gifts are to be distinguished from exchange in a more than merely negative way, one has to identify and delineate the social practices and cultural places in which gifts are actually given and received. To disregard these practices and places does not leave us with a ›pure gift‹ but with no gift altogether. If the giving and receiving of gifts is to be distinguished from the economy of exchange one has to concentrate on the concrete giving and receiving of gifts in our life-world practices.

This practice can be differentiated from other communicative practices in our culture by a number of features.[38] The giving and receiving of gifts is a form of social interaction between persons that is not a means to an end but an end in itself. It is not normally tied to special expectations of the recipients but allows them a wide range of reactions, including the reaction of not reacting at all. In this respect it regularly transgresses given orders of exchange and establishes a relation between persons that may include but cannot be reduced to relations of exchange. How one communicates in giving and receiving gifts is more important than what is communicated, or who communicates, or about which one communicates. It is the mode of communication by which we establish and sustain bonds of friendship, family ties and other personal relationships in our culture and society.

Paradigmatic for this type of communication is the social practice of giving and receiving of *presents*.[39] Giving a present to someone cannot be reduced to the laws of exchange but is anomalous because it disrupts the established orders of exchange. »Giving a present is an emphatic form of giving which is characterised by a surplus of giving over and above what is given« as B. Waldenfels put it.[40] Examples of this form of giving gifts are Christian acts of love, forgiving other persons, giving one's life for someone else and similar acts and activities. They all express or manifest personal relationships that go beyond economic or political relations.[41] The giving and receiving of presents or gifts differ from all forms of economic exchange or political order in that they are personal forms of communication in life-world practices

---

[38] Not all of what follows will be true of the giving and receiving of gifts in other cultures as well. Cf. the different account of Mauss, *The Gift*.

[39] Vgl. R. Comay, ›Gifts Without Presents: Economies of »Experience« in Bataille and Heidegger‹, *Yale French Studies* 778, 1990, 66-89; G. Clausen, *Schenken und Unterstützen in Primärbeziehungen. Materialen zu einer Soziologie des Schenkens*, Frankfurt am Main 1991; Fr. Rost, *Theorien des Schenkens. Zur kultur- und humanwissenschaftlichen Bearbeitung eines anthropologischen Phänomens*, Essen 1994; H. Berking, *Schenken. Zur Anthropologie des Gebens*, Frankfurt am Main/New York 1996; G. Schmied, *Schenken. Über eine Form sozialen Handelns*, Opladen 1996; G. Dressel/G. Hopf (eds.), *Von Geschenken und anderen Gaben. Annäherungen an eine historische Anthropologie des Gebens*, Frankfurt am Main 2000; B. Wagner-Hasel, *Der Stoff der Gaben. Kultur und Politik des Schenkens und Tauschens im archaischen Griechenland*, Frankfurt am Main/New York 2000.

[40] B. Waldenfels, ›Das Un-ding der Gabe‹, in: Gondek/Waldenfels, *Einsätze des Denkens*, 385-409, 399.

[41] Cf. M. Godelier, *Das Rätsel der Gabe. Geld, Geschenke, heilige Objekte*, München 1999, 291.

which underlie all others social and cultural activities in our societies. They go beyond economic and political orders because they help to establish and sustain the social identity of human persons or, more generally, the symbolic identity of the agents (persons, groups, communities, societies) in life-world interaction and the spheres of social and cultural communication in our society without which the orders of the market and of politics would not and could not work. Giving and receiving gifts creates the symbolic identity of social and cultural agents that cannot be produced, but it has to be presupposed in the economic exchange of goods or the political exchange of power.

10. Being Given

There is no general answer to what gifts are or how they differ from exchange. It depends on the social practice of giving and receiving gifts in a given society, and the practice differs across cultures and societies. So we cannot begin with general features but have to start from particular examples.

In our culture the paradigmatic case of this practice is *making someone a present of something* or, in Old French, *mettre une chose en present à quelqu'un.* »A gift is made present, it is brought before its intended recipient, it enters into the presence of the one who is to receive.«[42] While an exchange takes time in a reciprocal process of giving and taking (i.e. in a B-series activity involving two agents acting at different times), gifts occur in the present and although they are directed from a donor to a recipient (i.e. are performed in a B-series of giving and receiving) they become what they are in making someone a recipient of a gift (and not of something else) by being received in the 1st-person perspective of the recipient as a gift in an A-determined present that is distinguished from a past without the gift and from the future opened up by the gift.

But this is at best a beginning. For what exactly is meant by the phrase ›in the presence of‹? »If I am present to a present do I have to be completely aware of it, or aware of its value as a gift?«[43] Does a giver need do know that he or she gives a present to someone in order for it to be a present? Does knowing it mean to know the present *as* present, and the person to whom it is presented *as* its ›intended recipient‹? In

---

[42] Horner, *Rethinking God As Gift*, 3.

[43] Ibid. In what follows I summarise some aspects of Horner's analysis in my own terms.

this case for something *to be* a present it must be *intended to be* a present. But is this true? Can't I make a present to someone without intending to? Or is intending something to be a present enough to make it a present whether or not it is identified as such by the recipient? Then there couldn't be presents that were never intended as such. But there are. The student happily accepted the book that I pointed out to her on my shelf as a present even though it was never meant to be one. It seems to be neither necessary nor sufficient for a present to be a present that it is intended as such by the giver. But if it is possible for a gift to be given without being intended as such, why should it be impossible for a gift to be received without being identified as such? Does the recipient have to receive it *as* a present for it to be a gift? Wouldn't this blur the important distinction between receiving and accepting, i.e. taking a present into one's possession and consenting to receive it? Or is it enough to say »to the extent that I perceive a gift to be a gift, on one side or the other, it functions as a gift, and this may well be sufficient to define it as a gift«?[44] This still leaves us at a loss as to what it is to perceive a gift to be a gift. For even if we agree that a gift is something put into the presence of someone, it is clearly not the case that everything put into the presence of someone is a gift. But what else has to be the case for a gift to be a gift or a present to be a present?

One important answer is that it must be a presence or presentation of something that is given *gratuitously* and changes our situation *for the better.* A gift or present is not merely something put into our presence. So is the book just bought, or the letter bomb received by the president. Neither would be called a gift. What is made present to us is a gift only if it is given gratuitously, i.e. freely and not in answer to anything we expect or deserve, and if in receiving it our situation is improved in that we passively become what we had not been before by being enriched or enabled to live in some respect or other better than would have been possible for us without the gift. Receiving gifts makes us recipients, that is, changes us for the better and improves our situation by what is gratuitously made present to us, and thereby allows us to live and act in ways that are preferable to those before but were not open to us without to the gift.

Now to be a recipient is to be a recipient *of something*, and what is received is the *gift* that makes the recipient a recipient. From the recipients' point of view the important thing about gifts is not that they are

---

[44] Ibid.

given nor merely *what* is given but, on the one hand, that they are given *to them* and, on the other, that they are given to them *in a special way* that improves their situation in some respect without committing them to anything or indebting them to anyone. Anything I accept as a gift because I understand and receive it as something gratuitously put into my presence, whether it is given by someone or not, in effect operates as a gift for me. Anything that can be accepted in this positive way can function as a gift for me, but unless it is a gift *for me*, i.e. something with which *I* am presented, it cannot be a gift. It is no gift unless I become a passive recipient by what is presented to me, receive it gratuitously without becoming indebted to anyone, and find my situation changed for the better by what I receive.

So not *what* is given (the gift-object) nor *by whom* it is given (the donor) nor *to whom* it is given (the recipient), is the decisive aspect of the making of presents or gifts, but *how it is received* and *what is effected by it* (the mode of receiving): A gift is a gift only if received in the beneficial or wholesome mode of doing me good and serving me well. Whether this is the case or not does not depend on what is given, or by whom and to whom it is given, but on when and where it is received: A gift is a gift for someone in a particular situation, and just as not everything given to someone in a particular situation is a gift, so a gift in a particular situation is not necessarily also a gift for me in other situations or for other persons in this or another situation. It depends on the situation in which someone is presented with something that he or she accepts as a gift, and these situations of receiving gifts vary not only between persons but also for the same person. If the specific situation and its particular mode of receiving are not taken into account, there may be subjects who give and receive and objects (things, signs, feelings, values) given or passed on between them, but no gifts. The decisive aspect of a gift is not the object given, nor the intentions of the donor or of the recipient but the mode and situation in which it is received. Gifts are nothing apart from the practice in which they function, and they function as gifts only by being made present in such a way that they become received as wholesome and beneficial presents made for a particular person in a particular situation. It is not my decision nor intention as the recipient that makes something presented to me a present for me but, before I can relate to it in any way, it has to be presented to me in a particular way, namely as a present *for me* that makes me the recipient of a gift. In short, it is not the recipient who makes the gift but the gift that makes the recipient by making him or her receive it in a particular way – the way of the gift.

So mere givenness is not enough. A gift that is made present to someone must be received in a way that is determined by the gift received and not by the receiver of the gift. Just as being given is not enough for something to be a gift so what is there or presents itself to me is not for this reason alone a gift. Not everything present is something made present by someone, and not everything present to me is a present for me. Whether or not this is the case depends on the actual situation. For a gift is not a gift by being given but by making someone the recipient of a gift, and it is not the recipient who makes the gift but the gift that makes the recipient. This needs to be elaborated.

11. Basic Passivity

The social practice of giving and receiving gifts has a variety of functions, including economic ones. If we focus on the actual performance of the practice and describe it in the perspective of those who actually participate in it, one aspect appears to be particularly important: Those who receive gifts are changed into something that they were not before and to which they couldn't have made themselves. Of course, any activity changes those who perform it in some way or other. But in the case of the gift it is not the receiving that changes me, even though in a certain sense this is true as well, but the gift. Receiving is a particular activity and not different in kind from other more ›active‹ activities. Both giving and receiving are activities, performed by those who give or receive. It is my doing when I give or receive something. I hand the book to you when I give it to you, and I take the book that you give me. Without my taking it there is no receiving, and without my handing it to you there is no giving.

This is not only true of particular activities but also of the underlying capacities, even of the most basic ones. Spontaneity and receptivity are both faculties to do something, viz. to change my surroundings and to note being changed by it. They are polar activities, as Schleiermacher and Levinas have pointed out in their different ways; there is no spontaneity without a minimal receptivity and *vice versa,* but they are both activities.

However, while this is true of *receiving*, it is not true of receiving *gifts*. *Receiving* something is my activity, receiving *a gift* is not. Whatever I do I cannot make my receiving become a receiving of a gift. If I receive a gift, it is the gift that turns me into a recipient, not my receiving. I am made a receiver by the gift but I do not make the gift by receiving it.

Receiving gifts involves a *fundamental passivity* on the side of the recipient, a passivity that is not just the polar opposite of an activity and as such an activity itself but something more fundamental, namely that without which my receiving would not be a receiving of a gift. The gift makes me its recipient, not by denying or obliterating all activities on my part but by qualifying everything I do or receive by what it does to me. I am passively made into a recipient of the gift by the gift I receive, and I am thereby enabled to be and to do what I couldn't have been or done on my own.

This is not mysterious but something we all know from experience. Falling in love, receiving honorary doctorates, being knighted or becoming a Christian, for example, have all in common that they change me, that is, my personal or religious identity (who I am) or my social status (what I am for others). They do not end my activities or stop me from living the life I live, but neither are they or can they be achieved by anything I do or decide to do. They are not the result of my own doings but qualify and change me with all my doings. My life may continue as before but I live in a new way and with a new identity. Not necessarily my actions but the agent and my mode of acting has changed. On the other hand, I am also enabled and entitled to do things that I couldn't have done before like writing love poems, going to senate, sitting in the House of Lords, or receiving the sacraments. In some important respects I have become someone else and something new, not through my own doings but through a gift.

There are three things to be noted here. The first is that gifts *make us into* something or someone into which or whom we couldn't have made of ourselves. They break the circle of self-reference and the logic of the knowing and acting subject (*I* experience; *I* know; *I* act) and bring out what has been called the *me-* or *dative*-structure of human existence: It is *me* to whom the gift is given, and I am the one *to whom* it is given. Existentially more basic than the ›I do‹ is the ›It is done to me‹. In this respect human beings are not subjects or agents who are what they are by actively perceiving, feeling, experiencing or acting, but recipients who passively become who or what they are by what they receive: *donees* or *recipients* (in the case of gifts); *heirs* or *successors* (in the case of inheritance); *pardoned* or *justified persons* (in the case of forgiveness); *saved persons* (in the case of rescue, deliverance or salvage); *reconciled persons* (in the case of reconciliation); *acquitted, discharged* or *exonerated persons* (in the case of acquittal, exoneration, absolution) etc. In these and many other cases who or what I am does not depend on what I do but on what is done to me.

However, not everything done to me is a case of receiving a gift. The second point about gifts is that receiving a gift is receiving something *positive,* something that is desirable to have or to be and not something that harms or burdens me. A gift makes me ›gifted‹, i.e. talented, apt or capable for something that enhances my life. It plays possibilities into my way that enlarge what I can do and how I can live and does not reduce or curb it. It achieves this by making me into someone whom I couldn't have become by myself but who I am grateful to be, and by enabling me to do what I couldn't have done on my own but what I am happy to be able to do. Whether something given to or received by me is something positive and hence a gift is not an intrinsic quality of what is given or received. What may be a gift in one case may be a burden in another, and what has been received as a gift originally may become a nuisance later on. So not what is given (in the broadest possible sense) as such but the situation in which it is given decides on whether what I receive is a gift and not something else. The same possibilities played into my way in one situation as a gift that enhances my life may turn out to be a hindrance for a better life in another situation. Becoming pregnant may be a long waited for gift for one couple, and a disaster for another. Gifts are sensitive to situations, and not everything is a gift in every situation.

The third point is that receiving something positive is not enough either. If I graduate *summa cum laude* from college because I have written the best thesis in the past decade I receive what I deserve. What I receive makes me a graduate, something I couldn't have made myself; it is something positive, but it isn't a gift. The same is true in many other cases: My salary is not a gracious gift given to me by my university but the return for my work to which I am legally entitled. I am not grateful to my university for it, because what I receive is based on a contract that defines our mutual rights and commitments. It is a case of economic exchange, not a gift, and it should not be mixed up with it. So over and above being something positive, what I receive must not be something I deserve or merit, not an exchange or compensation for something I have done or have committed myself to do. A gift is something positive which I do not merit, to which I am not entitled, and which I do not deserve. It is not given as a return for something I have given or done, and it is not given with the purpose of making me do something I wouldn't have done otherwise. There are no ties attached to a gift because if there were what I receive would be positive, but it would not be a gift.

12. The Ambivalence of Passivity: Deficiency or Chance?

The passivity that goes with the gift precedes all our choosing and deciding. Before we can decide whether to accept or reject a gift, it must have become present to us, and this is not a matter of our decision. We cannot produce a gift by anything we do, and we cannot undo it after we have been presented with it. Of course, I might have bought the book myself which was given to me as a present, but it wouldn't then have been a present. Gifts are intrinsically tied to social practices, as we have seen, and in these practices the recipients of gifts are basically passive. Before we can relate to a gift, we find ourselves presented with it, and this prior passivity precedes all possible activity and passivity, spontaneity and receptivity with respect to the gift in question.

Since this basic passivity is not merely beyond the contrast of activity and passivity but grounds and enables it, it has again and again be described or symbolised in terms of the contrast that it grounds. Schleiermacher described it as *dependence*, and marked it off from relative dependence in contrast to freedom as *utter* dependence. Leibniz, on the other hand, identified it as *finitude* by which finite substances are marked off from infinite substance, and since he understood finitude to be a deficiency compared to infinity, he interpreted it as *metaphysical evil*. Others again describe it as the *utterly unavailable* that differs from the available by being chaotic, not ordered, uncontrollable, dangerous or perilous. In each case one side of the relative contrast (dependence vs. freedom; finite vs. infinite; availability vs. unavailability) is used to characterize the basic passivity prior to and beyond that contrast. And in each case the basic passivity is interpreted in a one-sided and negative way as a kind of deficiency.

However, what is described as *utter dependence* can be understood negatively as something utterly devoid of all freedom and activity, but also positively as an endowment or empowerment that grounds and enables all relative freedom and dependence. Similarly with *finitude*, it can be described as metaphysical evil because of what it lacks compared with infinity, but also as *creation* or *createdness* which is not an evil but a fundamental good since it does not divorce the created from the creator but relates it to him. In the same vain, what is described as *utterly unavailable* may be experienced in actual life as an inscrutable evil or an unexpected stroke of luck, as a surprising and delightful discovery or a paralysing loss of the world. In each case what is experienced is something utterly unavailable, but this on its own does not tell us whether it is to be described in negative or positive terms.

13. Religious Interpretations of Passivity

This is particularly obvious in the case of religious understandings and accounts of this basic passivity, not only as they are explicitly stated in theological doctrines but also as they are implicit in central religious practices and activities such as worship or prayer. When believers thank God for something, they react to events in their lives, or to their whole lives, as a gift given by God. Similarly when they pray to God for something they turn to God as the one from whom all help and everything good is to be expected. They thank God for what they believe to have received from him, and they pray for something that they cannot achieve on their own or by themselves.

However, they do not thank God for everything, and they do not pray indiscriminately for just anything whatsoever. They turn to God as the giver of the good and the saviour from all evil. But they do not assume that the mere happening of something shows it to be a gift of God, and they do not thank God for just anything that occurs. Not all believers are as sophisticated as Thomas Aquinas who can praise even evil to be a sign of God's goodness: »*si malum est, Deus est*«.[45] For if *omne ens est bonum* because it is created by the good God, and if evil (*malum*) is not something (an *ens*) but rather the lack of something (*absentia, remotio, privatio boni*), then there can only be evil if there is something good that manifests this lack or evil: Without something good, there is no evil, and this entails conversely that wherever there is evil there must be something good and hence God. But Thomas never even thought of concluding wrongly from this that evil should be praised and not God, or that believers should be thankful for the gift of evil rather than praise the good God who is even manifest where we encounter evil. Evil is not a gift to be thanked for but at best an occasion for thanking the good God for living in a world in which the good is always ›greater‹ than the evil because it is God's good creation.

So it is not the general givenness of things, the being given of just anything, that makes believers turn to God in prayers of thanksgiving. Rather they are careful to distinguish between God's gifts for which they are grateful and the harms and pitfalls of life from which they seek to be saved. The given may be a gift, or it might not be; and whether it is a gift for which one ought to thank God depends on whether what occurs does or does not concur with God's good will for us and all creation.

---

[45] Thomas Aquinas, *Summa contra gentiles* III, 71.

So believers typically distinguish between situations of thanksgiving and lament, situations in which they react to what they experience by thanking God for his gifts, and situations of crying to God for being delivered from evil. It is difficult to see why they should do the second without having some experience of the first: You cannot turn to God without some inkling of who it is to whom you turn, and this inkling arises in situations in which we are overwhelmed by the good that opens our mouth to thank God rather than in situations in which we are silenced by the evils that hit us or our neighbours. This is why memory of the great acts of God in the history of his people is so central in Jewish, Christian and Moslem worship. The reason for turning to God in the face of evil is the memory of God's commitment to fight evil and free his people from it. But this is not the only reason for which God is remembered.

In situations of thanksgiving believers look back not only on the evils and calamities which God has overcome but also on the excess of unexpected happiness by which the have been surprised and overwhelmed. They thank God for something positive in their own life or the life of their community (people, nation, church or humanity) but they do not necessarily or exclusively thank God for delivering them from a situation of evil. Christian believers at least understand and interpret the sense of passivity that makes them turn to God not always or exclusively as the passivity of an inescapable evil but often and even primarily as the passivity of an overwhelming good. It is not just the evil from which they have been freed but the good by which they have been overwhelmed that makes them turn to God in praise and thanksgiving.

14. Towards a Theology of the Gift

This is at odds with a theological and philosophical tradition that understands the basic dependence, finitude and passivity of human beings to manifest their fundamentally deficient nature and constitution and their anthropological need of social and cultural compensation. They interpret their utter dependence as an absolute need, their finitude as a metaphysical evil, and their experience of the unavailable and uncontrollable as a permanent threat or menace by fundamental meaninglessness. Understanding gift as gift is prevented and blocked here not by an economy of exchange but by an anthropology of human deficiency.

But this is misleading even where one agrees with the biological, social and cultural data and phenomena adduced. Human beings indeed
become human by what they receive from others, by the possibilities
that are played into their ways and which break or interrupt the established patterns of behaviour in such a way that their lives are opened
up towards the new, the unforeseen, the unexpected. We develop from
primates into human beings as the biological processes of our life are
interrupted by the presence of others and are thereby opened up towards the life of others in mutual feeling and interaction. And we develop from self-centred human beings into human fellow-beings in the
same measure as others interrupt and keep interrupting the social
processes of our life in such a way that we cannot ignore their presence
in our life but have to react to it as a menace or endowment, an en-
largement or restriction of our own chances and possibilities. We are
and live as human beings not merely together with others but through
the presence of others, that is, through that which they make present
in our life by entering into our presence, through the possibilities they
play into our ways of life, through everything we receive from them as
gifts that continuously enrich and change our lives. In short, it is impossible to live a human life in total isolation from others: we depend
and feed on others and their otherness even where we live the life of a
Robinson on an island or of a stylite on a column.

Now to describe this basic human passivity and need for others as
our fundamental *dependence on others* is to contrast it to the *independence
of human freedom and self-determination*, and this casts a negative light on
the phenomenon under discussion. This is how the idea of basic passivity or utter dependence has often been understood and elaborated
in philosophy and theology: It is seen as a defect, a deficiency, a lack, a
need for something that one doesn't possess, a shortcoming and a want
of the higher good of independence and autonomous activity. This is
supported by reference to the fact that, with respect to their biological
outfit, human beings are underspecified, lack instinct and are exposed
to the world without predetermining behavioural mechanisms. And
these biological facts are in turn seen to result from the metaphysical
deficiency of human finitude, passivity and utter dependence on
something without which they could not be and would not be able to
live.

But to understand the fact that human life depends on others and
lives on what it receives from others by contrasting it to the ideals of
independence, freedom and self-determination inevitably leads to a
negative view of our basic passivity as a deficiency rather than under-

standing it in a positive sense as the anthropological resource of human change and progress, as that basic structure inscribed into human existence which continuously enables new developments, opens up our life towards new possibilities, and empowers us to leading a human life by transcending the limits of what we know and can do and by stretching out for the new and as yet unrealised. To describe human passivity in negative terms of dependency is to understand humans as basically deficient beings, and this in turn serves as a basis for philosophical, sociological and theological approaches designed to overcome or make up for this basic human want. Religious faith is then presented as the awareness of and answer to our insurmountable deficiency, and it is argued to be intelligible, rational, probable, or at least not wholly improbable, precisely in so far as it can be shown to make up for what we lack in biological specification and organic adaptation to our dangerous and threatening surroundings. Since the human experience of pain and suffering is universal, and the need for comfort, hope, and salvation is no less, religions in general, or Christian faith in particular, are said to provide this comfort, hope and salvation.[46] Alternatively, it is sometimes argued that religious faith is not merely possible but necessary in human life because it answers to the basic need of our human existence. Although not everybody lives with the right faith nobody can or does live without faith.[47] Human existence is first described as basically problematic and deficient, and religious faith then presented as answer to these problems and as remedy for our deficiency.

But this type of argument, widespread as it may be, is seriously misleading. It seeks to show religious faith to be valid and legitimate by presenting it as an answer to the basic needs and deficiencies of human life and existence; and it describes human life and existence in such a way that faith can be presented as making up for its deficiencies. The validity and legitimacy of faith is not shown in its own terms or in terms of the truth of its content and beliefs, but in terms of its anthropological function and a negative anthropology of want, need, defect and deficiency. But this seriously misrepresents the reality and character of both human life and Christian faith. What the New Testament calls ›faith‹ is not merely or primarily a substitute for a human deficiency but something quite different.

---

[46] H. Maier, ›Die Überwindung der Welt. Auf dem Christentum liegt kein Fluch. Eine Antwort auf Herbert Schnädelbachs Polemik‹, *Die Zeit* 27, 2000. (http://zeus.zeit.de/text/archiv/2000/27/200027.replik_.xml).

[47] Cf. I.U. Dalferth, ›Theological Fallacies. A Contribution‹, *The Heythrop Journal* 16, 1975, 389-404.

In the New Testament, faith is not a remedy of deficiency or cure of evil but a phenomenon of abundance and excess – the abundance and excess of grace. It is not, at least not primarily, seen and described as an answer to questions posed by human life but left open by it. It refers to the overwhelming experiences of something utterly new and totally unexpected, the abundance of unexpected good, unhoped-for happiness, surprising discoveries, unforeseen riches, and undreamed of possibilities that have broken into a human life and have changed it radically into a new life of faith. Faith, in short, stands for everything new and unexpected that the gospel effects in human life. Its point is not so much the overcoming of human defects and deficiencies but the inclusion and incorporation of human life into the excess of God's grace.

This includes but goes beyond the healing of human suffering and pain, but it is not the human deficiency that defines the answer to it, and it is not the human situation that determines the character and content of God's grace. On the contrary, faith goes far beyond anything missed or hoped for. It originates not from the overcoming of our existential deficiencies but from the occurrence of goods that were not even thought of as unavailable before they occurred and from the unexpected discovery of possibilities and chances in and for life, which nobody had hoped for or imagined or even missed before they were discovered.

Faith, in short, goes far beyond anything needed in human life. It is not human life and its deficiencies that define faith but faith responds to a gift that was neither missed nor expected but exceeds anything hoped for, longed for, needed, wanted, wished for, imagined or dreamed of. Faith is always more than what is or was needed, wanted or missed in human life; it manifests the excess of God's grace and does not merely answer to a human deficiency.

It is a misleading attempt to show this excess to be necessary by presenting it as God's answer to our human quest, as that for which we have all along been longing, consciously or unconsciously. We have, as a rule, not longed for it and we have not missed it, and not merely because we haven't paid much attention to what we have longed for and missed all along. It simply wasn't part of our life, not even a missed or missing one.

But then it is a mistake to present it as such and to claim something to be an anthropological necessity, which we do not need in order to live a good, humane, and happy human life. A theology worth its name should not argue from allegedly biological and metaphysical deficiencies of human life to God's amending grace but rather from the contingent and overwhelming fact of God's grace arriving in and breaking into a human life, of God becoming present in it and playing more into its way than anything it would ever have expected, hoped for or needed. The gift of God's grace is gratuitous not only because we need not and cannot pay for it (true as this is as well) but above all because *it goes far beyond anything we needed or missed* in our life before it occurred. We had no inkling that something was missing or what we were missing before it occurred, and it is only in retrospect that we can describe our life as having been poor without it.

However, not everything one doesn't have is a lack or deficiency; not everything what we become actualises an ability or potentiality that we have always had; and not everything we receive satisfies a need or answers to a want. Who would even begin to argue for a human need or potentiality or faculty to experience music by Mozart, or music, or at least something, or ... as if one could ground the right and legitimacy of Mozart's music by showing it to satisfy a basic human need or want. But, on the other hand, who would want to deny that Mozart's music has enriched human life, that it has made it better, more beautiful, more worth living, more hopeful, more interesting and more adventurous than it would have been without it?

Similarly with God's grace and the gift of faith. It is not something that has always been felt missing and now at last has been found, nor something for which we have been looking out all the time because of the unrealised potentials of our finite human life and our longing for fulfilment, perfection and eternity. On the contrary, we had no idea what we should have been looking for before it occurred and became a reality in human life and history. This, at least, is what we can learn from Jesus' theology of the ›more than necessary‹ or from the corresponding Pauline theology of ›gratuitous grace‹ and ›faith alone‹. [48]

Consider, for example, the feeding miracles of the gospels: Jesus not only appeases the hunger of thousands but there is such an excess of bread and fish that baskets full of the leftovers are carried away.

Or the calling of the disciples: The disciples are not portrayed as frustrated unemployed who had been looking for just any job in vain or sought to escape their midlife crises for some time. Their calling is

---

[48] For the following cf. H. Weder, ›Komparative und ein parataktisches kai. Eine neutestamentlich orientierte Skizze zur transzendierten Notwendigkeit‹, in: I.U. Dalferth/J. Fischer/H.-P. Grosshans (eds.), *Denkwürdiges Geheimnis. Beiträge zur Gotteslehre. Festschrift für Eberhard Jüngel zum siebzigsten Geburtstag*, Tübingen 2004, 555–579.

rather presented as a new creation and not merely as a new job offer by
Jesus, as Caravaggio shows beautifully in his ›Calling of the Publican
Matthew‹ by quoting Michelangelo's creation of Adam in the Sistine
Chapel.

Or the miracle stories of the gospels: Jesus' miracles are not portrayed as answers to human queries, short cut solutions to problems
that could have been solved otherwise, or expressions of uncontrolled
wishful thinking on the part of those who reported or narrated them.
The evangelists rather tell stories about the unexpected and surprising
ways in which God's grace brakes into the life of ordinary people and
enters into their presence as proclaimed by Jesus; and they use the narrative pattern of miracle stories to bring out the gratuitous and overwhelming character of the gift of God's presence in human life.

Or consider the prologue of St John's gospel: The world was not
waiting for the Logos to become incarnate. It didn't even notice what
was going on when it happened because it was too busy with its own
affairs and didn't feel any lack or deficiency that had to be overcome
and made up for.

Or Paul's teaching about sin in Romans 5: The argument is not that
what Jesus did is important for all of us because we are all sinners, but
the other way round: What has happened in and through Jesus is of
such overwhelming importance and significance that nothing in creation remains unaffected by the abundance of grace and the free gift of
righteousness which Jesus manifests; or the reception of this teaching
in the 3rd article of the Apostles' Creed where it is not sin but the *forgiveness* of sin, and not death but *eternal life* that is the topic.

Wherever we look in the New Testament and beyond in the continuations and receptions of its message in the history of the church we
can discover traces of this logic of grace, of its abundance and excess,
its being more than necessary and beyond all need, its gratuity and dynamics of renewal, its provision of possibilities which were not sought
but found, and not waited for but played into our ways.[49] This is what
one has to unfold if one seeks — *per impossibile* — to ›ground faith‹, explicate its point and argue for its rationality. And to do so one has to
start from the fact of faith and the occurrence of grace rather than
from the experiences structures, dispositions, needs, wants or deficiencies of those who have been overwhelmed by the unexpected abun-

---

[49] ›I don't seek anything, I find it‹ said Picasso. ›I was found even though I wasn't
aware that anyone was seeking me‹ replies faith and goes beyond Picasso in that it
knows not even of a continuous I that is changed from old to new.

dance of grace and the host of possibilities which it has opened up in their lives. Only after the event they began to notice what had happened, and even then only by noticing that it was something *maius quam cogitari posit*. Before it they did not expect nor miss it. There is no way of ›quantifying oneself into‹ faith before it occurs, as Kierkegaard's Climacus knew. It is only after, not prior to, the arrival of faith in a life that one can begin to discover signs of what was to come in the life before; signs and facts that can be taken up, strengthened and elaborated in the life of faith, but also facts and signs that need to be corrected, modified, overcome and forgotten because they do not contribute but hinder or harm the new life. They are incompatible with it, not because they have been so all along but because life has changed, and changed radically. Only *a posteriori* can we identify the ground of faith, and only *post festum* we can show it to be reasonable and to make sense – if indeed it does.

VI Re-Presenting God's Presence

1. A living God

For Christianity, Judaism and Islam alike God is a *living God*. Only a living God can be God for us. If there is no God for us, there is no one worthy of worship, i.e. no God. But if there is a living God, God *is present* (for whoever lives, lives in the present). If God is present, God is present *to the present of someone* (for whoever is present, is it to someone present). And if God is present to the present of anyone different from God, God must be present *to the present of everyone* different from God (for if God were present only to some and not to all present, God would not be worthy of worship, i.e. not be God). God may be present in more than one way, and Christians, Jews and Moslems may understand God's presence in different ways, but for all of them there is nothing actual nor possible without God being present. If there is anything at all, God is present.[1]

The importance of God being present has not always been rightly understood to be central to the Christian understanding of God. Richard Swinburne, in his *The Christian God*, includes omnipresence among the divine properties, but mentions it only in passing[2] because

---

[1] This is not to say, as we have seen, that God is omnipresent, if by »»omnipresent‹ is meant ›everywhere present‹« (R. Swinburne, *The Coherence of Theism*, Oxford ²1993, 99). God is not present everywhere in an unqualified sense but *present to every presence*, i.e. with every event as it occurs and to everyone present at its occuring. Just as unfailingly as everything that occurs occurs in the present, so for those who find themselves placed in the presence of God everything that occurs occurs in the presence of God: Not because God is a cause of what happens (a cause is what makes its effects more probable than in the circumstances they would have otherwise been) but because God is that without which there would be neither cause nor effect. »Apart from God«, as Hartshorne put it, »not only would this world not be conceivable, but no world, and no state of reality, or even of unreality, could be understood« (*A Natural Theology for Our Time*, La Salle, Illinois 1967, 53). But if God is compatible with every world or state of the world, God's presence does not raise the probability of any of them and hence does not causally explain anything.

[2] R. Swinburne, *The Christian God*, Oxford 1994, 125.127.150. Neither his discussion of time (72-95) nor his brief account of omnipresence in his earlier *The Coherence of Theism* (104-107) can make up for this remarkable lack.

he is more interested in God's »limitless intentional power«.[3] Richard E. Wentz, on the other hand, takes divine presence to be the fundamental reality, more basic than any imaginative human construction of God. For him the divine is »a sense of *inexhaustible presence* … that gives rise to the use of the word God or gods, but also to concepts like love, hope, trust, and honor.«[4] It is the presence not *of something,* nor of something *unique* such as »an *ens singularissimam*« (sic!)[5], but of an indeterminate and inexhaustible reality that underwrites all our existential acts, emotive determinations and cognitive objectifications. If we try to think it, we cannot but think it *as* something, *as* (a) person, power, reality, god. But we must not mistake our signifying acts for the reality signified. One »does not *think about* God, but *thinks with* God«[6], i.e. »*in the presence* of an other whose reality forces us to deconstruct our self-understanding«[7] as cognitive subjects and rational agents vis-à-vis an objective reality. With respect to God »we do not stand *in front of,* or *below,* or alongside a singular other, but *in the presence*«.[8] To ask ›In whose presence?‹ is for Wentz the first step on that slippery slope that leads to the misleading »domestication of the divine«[9] and »objectification of God«[10] which he finds to be characteristic of »the pragmatic mind« of Western modernity. Swinburne's »divine individual«[11] is a perfect case in point. But God is *being,* not *a* being, *presence,* not the presence *of something, reality,* not something real.

If Wentz is right, and I think he is[12], then God was never more present than he is today. There never was a time when God's presence

---

[3]　Swinburne, *The Christian God,* chap. 7.

[4]　R.E. Wentz, ›The Domestication of the Divine‹, *Theology Today* 57, 2000, 24-34, 24.

[5]　Ibid., 33. (Wentz's Latin throughout his paper is very idiosyncratic to say the least.)

[6]　Ibid., 33.

[7]　Ibid., 32.

[8]　Ibid.

[9]　Ibid., 24.

[10]　Ibid, 26.

[11]　Swinburne, *The Christian God,* 125. For Swinburne, God is »a person essentially bodiless, omnipresent, creator and sustainer of any universe there may be, perfectly free, omnipotent, omniscient, perfectly good, and a source of moral obligation.« Cf. *The Coherence of Theism,* 1.

[12]　This is not to say that I agree with his rather sweeping account of the Medieval, Renaissance, and Reformation periods. There is more to Protestantism, for example, than »manipulating the divine to conform to its individualistic desires and its concern for utilitarian Salvationism« (30), indeed, this is precisely what Protestantism protested against.

was more obvious, or less hidden, than today. It is a modern myth that God has vanished or disappeared from human life in our post-Enlightenment world. And it is a religious myth that Apostles, Patriarchs, mystics, or martyrs were in a better or a more privileged position vis-à-vis God than we are. Perhaps we are less interested in God than former generations were, though I doubt it. Perhaps our culture is more obstructive to becoming aware of God's presence than others, though the evidence is far from clear. And perhaps some persons are more sensitive to discern God's presence, more eager to apprehend it, or more patient to wait for it being disclosed to them than we are. But as far as God is concerned there is no difference: »God is no more silent today than he was in the past. God spoke no more transparently to our ancestors than he does to us today.«[13] God was no less hidden then than he is today.

For us God's presence is accessible only as an absence within God's presence, a reality that allows us to see God's very absence within the world as a trait of God's presence to the world. To do so we must be able to distinguish between God *being absent* and *not being at all*, and this requires some prior grasp of God's hidden presence. But we cannot move beyond the presence/absence of God within the world to a *direct awareness* of God without failing to becoming aware of *God*. The reason is not that God is wholly other, the infinite that cannot be grasped by the finite. What stands between God and us is not epistemology but sin. God is not »the *ens alterissimum*« that infinitely transcends all our finite cognitive capacities so that we can approach it only in terms of negative theology.[14] On the contrary, as Merold Westphal has pointed out, »God becomes wholly other only when the self-estrangement of fault renders God a stranger«.[15] We are divided from God by sin, not by being created. There has always been a human desire and yearning for direct encounter with God, for the Garden from which we find ourselves expelled, and for the final overcoming of all that stands between God and us. Yet a direct vision of God in his glory is something we can never attain, neither in this life nor in another. For God is creator, and we are his creatures.

---

[13] B. Zelechow, ›God's Presence and the Paradox of Freedom‹, in: A. Loades, M. McLain (eds.), *Hermeneutics, the Bible and Literary Criticism*, London 1992, 162-176, 173.

[14] M. Westphal, ›Faith as the Overcoming of Ontological Xenophobia‹, in: O.F. Summerell (ed.), *The Otherness of God*, Charlottesville/London 1998, 149-172, 149ff.

[15] Ibid., 161.

There is nothing wrong with wishing to become aware of God's presence. What is illusory is the hope for a directness that is unmediated, or for a divine presence that is open for direct inspection. We cannot discern God directly, and we shall never be able to do so. Not because God is too distant or far off but because God is nearer to us than anything we can see or hear or touch or feel or can ever hope to discover by more refined technical means. God is present and active, in the most intimate way, at every present moment of our life; and in each moment God acts in a singularly unique way that for us is utterly unpredictable and uncontrollable.

This is not to say that we cannot become aware of God's presence or that there is nothing on which we can rely with respect to God. Believers who experience life in terms of divine presence are rationally entitled to trust that each moment of our life is immediately sustained by the presence and power of God; and Christians who find God's self-giving love disclosed in Christ have every reason to expect this love to be at work in whatever happens. But none of this enables us to predict any of God's actions. We know the rule, but not its application. We know that God is love, but we do not know and never will be able to know the unique way in which this love will be actualised at any given instant. God's acting is too unique to be accessible to our human techniques of explanation and control. God is too close to us for inspection. We cannot distance ourselves far enough from God to objectify him and discern his presence directly. But we can become aware of it because God ›makes his presence felt‹ in *mediate immediacy.*

2. God's Mediate Immediacy

Awareness of God's presence »is immediate in so far as it is direct; it is not the product of discursive reasoning. At the same time it is mediated by signs.«[16] We can only become aware of it by apprehending the media through which God presents his presence to us.

It is a fundamental insight of Christian theology, encapsulated in the central tenets of Christology, that there is no unmediated access to or awareness of God. We can discern neither God's presence nor its true character without mediation: It is a hidden presence, for both soteriological and epistemological reasons. God is present whether we are aware of it or not. We become aware of it only if God mediates his presence to us. And what we become aware of in this way is that God's

---

[16] H.P. Owen, *The Christian Knowledge of God*, London 1969, 135.

presence is hidden. It is not one of the things present to us but that which is present with their presence to us and to our presence with them in such a way that without it there wouldn't be anything present or anyone to whom anything could or would be present. So God's presence is not directly accessible to us but only as mediated through our presence and the presence of what is present to us, and there are at least two reasons for this.

On the one hand mediation safeguards our freedom of assent: God presents himself in ways that allow us freely to respond to him, even though whatever we do or don't do will be a response to his presence. On the other hand God's acts are so singularly unique that they are in principle beyond our powers of discernment. We cannot discern the divine life *per se* but only the ways in which it effects and affect us. God mediates his presence to our particular situations, i.e. relates to our present in his creative, perfecting and salvific activity in ways appropriate to our particular circumstances; and we become aware of God by apprehending how we depend and feed on the possibilities and chances played into our way by God, i.e. by consciously apprehending both our prior apprehensions of God's present with our present and God's present to our present in apprehending it. The first is our becoming aware of the gift of God's creative presence with our life without which we couldn't live our life at all: Without God's presence we wouldn't be and be able to live. The second is our becoming aware of the gift of God's illuminating presence to our mind without which we couldn't become aware either of God's presence with our presence (that God is present) or with the nature of God's presence (how God is present): Without God's presence we wouldn't be aware of the gift of God's presence and of why God's presence is a gift for us. The first discloses that we are creatures who owe their life to the prior gift of God's presence with them. The second makes us aware that we do not live the life that we could and should as God's creatures without the gift of God disclosing his presence and clarifying its nature to us. Therefore the sense of the presence of God is typically expressed not only by thanking God for the gift of his presence (*we are* because God is present with us) but also for the gift of making us aware of his presence (*God* is present to us), and of the nature of his presence (God is present to us *as creative and self-giving love*).

Thus we become aware of God's presence by apprehending ourselves to live in God's presence. We cannot do this, on the one hand, without becoming aware that it is only in and through God's presence that we can and do become aware of God's presence. And we cannot

do this, on the other hand, without realising that we have been apprehending God's presence long before we became aware of it. Since this
can be true of us only if it is true of everybody, the point of communicating our sense of the presence of God to others is not primarily to
tell them about us, but to make them aware of their own life in the
presence of God. We re-present to them what we apprehend in order
to make them aware of what they themselves apprehend.

This is the rationale of all true religious communication. It not
merely informs those whom it addresses about alleged God-experi-
ences of others but seeks to create a sense of God's presence in their
own life. And it creates this sense not by making them believe revelations that were allegedly received by others but by making them aware
of the reality of God's presence to their own life.

Not all agree. Some argue that what all believers need to know is that
God has been present somewhere in the causal ancestry of their particular faith: to Moses, or to Jesus, or to Mohammed; and that all we can
hope for is a reasonably probable belief, on the basis of the evidence
available, that this was more likely than not: But this is wrong. On the
one hand tradition and testimony would be theologically empty without some first-hand revelation, experience or perception of God from
which it originated[17], and then the problem re-occurs with Moses, Jesus, or Mohammed. On the other hand, Christian faith, at least, cannot merely be based on tradition and history in this way. If the content
of revelation is the unfailing presence of God's self-giving love as disclosed in Christ, then it cannot have been true in the past if it is not
true now. To believe it merely on authority is in fact not to believe it.
Either it is a present reality, or it is no reality at all. Its truth cannot be
decided by historical means or the sense of the presence of God enter-
tained merely hypothetically. Faith is not probable belief but trust in
God's presence here and now. And to create the awareness which alone
justifies this trust is the point of religious communication.

Consider Jesus, for example. As presented by the gospels he was viv-
idly aware of living in the presence of God as loving father. God was as
real to him as the people who followed him or as the country in which
he walked and taught. Their reality did not in any way depend on his
awareness of them, but *vice versa*, and so also with God's. »The heavenly father was not for him a mere concept or a hypothetical entity, but
an experienced living reality; and the supposition that there is no

---

[17] Cf. W.P. Alston, *Perceiving God. The Epistemology of Religious Experience*, Ithaca,
N.Y./London 1991, 280-284, 289-292.

heavenly father would doubtless have seemed as absurd to him, as incapable of being taken seriously, as the supposition that a human being
with whom he was talking did not exist.«[18] Accordingly his message
was not that God was close to him and that others could trust him as a
reliable witness of God's reality and love. He did not propagate a religious insight that he had at first hand but which others could only believe at second hand on his authority. On the contrary, his message was
that the Kingdom of God's love was close *to his hearers*, that *they* could
hear and see it *for themselves in their own lives*, that God was *present to
them* irrespective of their social and religious standing, and that therefore they should wake up to this reality and live consciously in God's
presence as instruments of the divine love on earth. His injunction
›Follow me!‹ was in fact the advice ›Find it out for yourself!‹ He told
his audiences about God's presence in *their* lives, not in his; and he did
not turn his own experience or intensity of feeling into the content of
his message but proclaimed God's presence in the everyday lives of
those whom he addressed.

This is also the point of the Christian message: It testifies not merely
to a past revelation but to a present reality. What it propagates cannot
have a past tense (i.e. have been true at some past time) if it has not got
a present tense (i.e. is true now). It proclaims the presence of God's
self-giving love in our lives, and this can only be true if God's love is at
work here and now, i.e. if God *presents himself* to us in ways that we can
apprehend, and if we apprehend his self-presentation *in the present*. We
must not be *conscious* or *aware* of apprehending it, for not all apprehension is conscious apprehension. But, in an externalist sense, we here
and now are the subjects of God's love and self-presentation, and we
cannot be subjects of it without being affected by it and therefore apprehending it somehow. For the Christian message to be true *God's
self-presentation in the workings of divine love and our apprehension of it on
our 1ˢᵗ-person perspective must be co-present components of one and the same
occurrence or situation.*

It is the point of Christian proclamation to make us aware of this
fundamental fact of our life. It refers to Christ because there it finds
disclosed the sense of the presence of God that provides the paradigm
for a profounder understanding of our own situation; and it succeeds if
it helps to make us aware of the presence of God's love in our own life.
Such awareness is more than believing in a general sense that we
would not be here if God were not present, or trusting the more or

---

[18] J. Hick, *An Interpretation of Religion*, London 1989, 216.

less reliable reports of others who claim to have experienced God's presence. We must become aware of the particular ways in which God's presence affects *us*, i.e. *how God is present to our present, and how we are present to God.*

If God is present to us it is because God wants to be present and not simply by chance or accident. For God, to be present is to become present, and God does not simply happen to become present but does so because – to put it in anthropomorphic terms he wills and knows it. How is God's knowledge of his presence to us to be construed? According to Thomas Aquinas, »God sees other things not in themselves, but in Himself, inasmuch as His essence contains the similitude of things other than Himself«.[19] Some have taken this to mean that God knows not things but only inner mental representations of things: »Temporal entities exist in eternity *as represented in the mind of God*«.[20] Others, such as W. P. Alston, have denied this. In God's case there are no inner mental representations since God knows intuitively. For God »knowledge of a fact is simply the immediate awareness of that fact«.[21] But God's knowledge is neither representational nor intuitive. Facts for God are acts – acts to which God is intrinsically related by being present with their present. Aquinas' point is not that God knows by intuition but that God is not externally related to created reality: God's presence is part of the very existence of things, indeed, it is the source and sustaining ground of all there is. Whatever *is* implies God's presence, even evil. This is not because God wants or does evil, but because evil presupposes some good whose privation it is, and there would not be anything good without God.[22] The property of being present to God, therefore, is not a property of things or events but of the *existence* of things or of the *occurrence* of events. It does not help to describe or define anything but to locate its occurrence relative to the divine ground of being.[23]

---

[19] Thomas Aquinas, *Summa Theologica* Ia q. 14, a. 5.

[20] W. Hasker, *God, Time, and Knowledge*, Ithaca, New York 1989, 168.

[21] W.P. Alston, ›Does God Have Beliefs?‹, *Religious Studies* 22, 1987, 287-306, 294.

[22] Thomas Aquinas, *Summa contra gentiles* III, 71: »Si malum est, Deus est. Non enim esset malum sublato ordine boni, cuius privatio est malum. Hic autem ordo non esset, si Deus non esset.«

[23] It is incoherent for Christian theology to be Trinitarian with respect to God and not also with respect to everything else. God's co-presence to the presence of all contingent events in creation must thus be conceived in terms of the internally differentiated Trinitarian activity of God Father, Son, and Spirit. Whereas nothing can occur without God being present, God is not present to everything that oc-

there is no reason to think that God should accommodate his way of becoming present only to the cognitive capacities of the human mind. We alone among all creatures may be able to become aware of God's presence as the presence of God. But if God becomes present to every present, God will be present not just to us but with everything as it occurs whether it belongs to us (i.e. is embedded in our life as part of the highly sophisticated complex of activities with their different time schedules that together constitute our life) or whether our life belongs to it (i.e. is embedded in the more comprehensive processes of the environment and ultimately of the universe to which it belongs). In each case and at each level of activity, God will be present in the way most appropriate to the situation by playing selected possibilities and chances in the way of our life. From these at each present that is selected and becomes realised at the various levels of activities, which together constitutes our life.

3. Cognitive Re-Presentation: Interpreting Possibilities

We must assume therefore that we apprehend God even where we are not aware of it, i.e. even where we do not apprehend God *as* God; and we do so because we live our life by choosing from the possibilities chosen for us by God in becoming present to our present at each level of our life in a specific way. To say this is of course a retrospective judgement from situations in which we have become aware of God. But if God is present to our present and if we apprehend not only the temporal phenomena that are present to us but also the ways in which they mediate to us how God is present to their present, then there is nothing intrinsically impossible about apprehending God without knowing it. The question is not whether we do it but how it is done.

Consider the case of beliefs about our perceptual environment. We often form beliefs caused by that which we apprehend that are not clear beliefs about the true cause of what we apprehend. If I see a tree, the tree causes the belief, but the content of the belief (›This is a tree‹) involves concepts that are due to the way in which this belief is determined by my belief-system (including its linguistic and conceptual components) and »doxastic practices«.[26] If I mistake the tree for a man, the belief is still caused by the tree but I determine its content in a wrong or inappropriate way.

---

[26] Alston, *Perceiving God*, chap. 4. A doxastic practice Alston defines »as a system or constellation of dispositions or habits ... each of which yields a belief as output that is related in a certain way to an ›input‹« (153).

We continuously acquire beliefs through perception, communication and other beliefgenerating mechanisms, and every belief changes
the state of our belief-system on which we act and live our lives. But
this is not a one-way process. The integration of a belief into our be-
liefsystem is a matter of mutual correction and clarification. It involves
determining the content of our beliefs conceptually: We need conceptual determination to be able to make inferences, to compare and correct our beliefs, to detect inconsistencies among them, and to communicate them to others. But our conceptual determinations may be
more or less adequate or even wrong. (Whether perception involves
concepts is a matter of debate; communication does, and perception
too is not atomic but involves patterns.) That is to say beliefs are
caused, but the cognitive content of our beliefs (i.e. that which would
make the belief true if it were the case) is not something given but results from the way in which we determine what we apprehend conceptually when it becomes part of our belief-system.

In this sense all our apprehensions involve interpretation and re-presentation[27]: We apprehend only what is present and presented to us, i.e.

---

[27] Here I part company with Alston. He denies »that all experience of objects
involves interpretation« (*Perceiving God*, 27) since »any sort of interpretation is
something over and above«, for example, »visual perception«: »To perceive a house
is for a house to be directly presented to one's experience« (28). It is not a matter
of S *interpreting* what appears to him *as* a house but simply for the house *to appear*
to S *as* a house (55). But this is a misleading contrast based on an inadequate distinction between subject and object, subjective interpretation and objective appearing. One cannot contrast *to interpret something as something to someone* and *to appear as something to someone* in this way as I have shown elsewhere (*Gedeutete Gegenwart*, 122-132). What »an external object presents itself as may diverge from what
that object actually is« (55) precisely because appearing is not devoid of interpretation but *happens in and through interpretation*: X appears to S as so-and-so precisely
by being interpreted by S as so-and-so. Moreover, interpretation is not to be restricted to a descriptive form of cognition that is mediated by general concepts
and judgement (i.e. »awareness of X *as* possessing some property«), it is also involved in identifying an object (i.e. »direct awareness of an object, X«). *Perceiving*
X (*as X appears to S*) and *describing X as P* are both forms of cognition mediated by
signs, i.e. interpretative processes albeit different ones. The line to be drawn is not
between (non-interpretative) perception and (interpretative) description or judgement but between different levels and sorts of interpretation (cf. G. Abel, *Interpretationswelten. Gegenwartsphilosophie jenseits von Essentialismus und Relativismus*,
Frankfurt 1995). This is not to say that we are caught in an endless chain of interpretations without ever arriving at what really is. We have access to reality, but in
and through interpretation, not apart from it. What we take to be non-interpretative perception is perception in the context of doxastic practices that we have no
reason to question (yet). We do indeed see a tree (if we see a tree) and not something *as* a tree. But to explain this we do not need a »Theory of Appearing« that

presentations of something present (›*This*…‹). We apprehend it *as some-thing*, i.e. re-present to ourselves what is presented to us *in a specific way* (›*This tree*…‹). *What* is apprehended can be seen from the belief that is caused (›*This tree is blooming*‹). But since the content of the belief in-volves concepts, it is to that extent mind-dependent and open to error, correction and improvement. If I see a tree, I form a certain belief on the basis of some visual perception. The cause of this belief is the tree, the causation is mediated through perception, and what is mediated I conceive (perhaps wrongly) as a tree by determining it in terms of the conceptual structure of my particular belief-system.

How can this help us in the case of God? God is not a cause of what we believe about him but the poet of the possible without which we could not live and form beliefs about anything. When we apprehend something in the temporal processes of our life then it is caused by some actuality (event, thing) earlier than our apprehension, and it is its cause if it makes the apprehension more likely than in the circum-stances it would have been otherwise. But when we apprehend *what* the cause is we do not apprehend the actual event or thing in question but how it is present or presented to us. That is to say, we apprehend a *presentation* or sign of the cause in question but not the cause itself. We apprehend signs or complex of signs, not actual things or events, and although signs are something actual themselves they are different actu-alities from the actualities that have caused them or that they signify. They differ not only because the cause is earlier than its presentation to us so that they are different events in time, but also because the presentation presents the cause to us not in its actual form, i.e. as the thing or event in time which it is, but as a sign and hence as a (com-plex) possibility that we can process in sign-processes both in mental and emotional representations (›thoughts‹, ›feelings‹) and in linguistic communications with others (›words‹).

Now signs do not transport presences but presentations of presences, they do not present actualities but possibilities. This is as true of the difference between an actual cause and its presentation to us as it is be-

---

decrees that »the notion of X's appearing to S as so-and-so is fundamental and unanalysable« (55). All we need to say is that there is no need, in a particular situ-ation, to distinguish what we perceive form the way we perceive it, because we can act on it in a sufficiently reliable way. But the distinction can become impor-tant at any time in the cognitive process of processing this perception in beliefs and actions. And if it does, we cannot take refuge to an objective appearing but have to distinguish between what we have perceived and the way we have per-ceived it in terms of the criteria of the doxastic practice in question.

tween the presentation and its re-presentation by another sign or presentation to us or others: In each case the sign, whether it is a *presentation* of something to us or a *re-presentation* of that presentation, is not only a different event in time but also differs from that for which it is a sign in that it presents to us that which it signifies not as an actuality but a possibility. This possibility can be understood, denied, ignored, questioned, analysed, restated etc. and in all these different ways represented by other signs, and this in more than one way or respect so that each sign presents not only something possible to us but is the possible point of departure for different possible series of re-presentation or lines of interpretation.

When we apprehend something, therefore, we do not apprehend its actuality but its *possibilities*. These do not form part of the temporal process of causation but are presupposed by it, and they constitute the cognitive content of our apprehension. But cognitive content always involves (non-conceptual, pre-conceptual or conceptual) interpretation, as we have seen, and this varies not only with the cognitive system into which the content becomes integrated but also with the communicative and cognitive practice in which our apprehending is embedded. Thus if we apprehend and understand what we apprehend in the context of a Christian doxastic practice that provides the relevant cognitive and symbolic means of interpretation, then we can apprehend the possibilities apprehended as *possibilities provided by God*. And if we do so anywhere then, given the understanding of ›God‹ in Christian life and discourse, we cannot do it in only one respect but must do it in all dimensions of our temporal orientation, i.e. retrospectively (past), prospectively (future) and with respect to the present reality of our life (present).

But if we come to apprehend now that the possibilities that we apprehend are possibilities provided by God, then the possibilities that we apprehended earlier must also have been possibilities provided by God whether or not we have apprehended them as such. In a Christian perspective, there never was a time when what we apprehended was not apprehended in the present of God. We may not have apprehended this, and it may not have been relevant in our own 1st-person perspective. But if it is true now, it must have been true then and although we didn't apprehend it under this description (*as* possibilities played into our way by God) so that no beliefs *about* God were caused by what caused our apprehensions, we relied on it in living our life by choosing from the possibilities available in our situation. But not apprehending it doesn't stop it from being true, if it is, and not knowing it then doesn't entail that it cannot be known to be true now. For as we now know retrospectively (believers may claim) these possibilities wouldn't have been available unless God provided them for us by becoming present to our present. Then we knew only possibilities, but now we know them to be possibilities chosen and provided for us by God. And whereas our beliefs then were not beliefs about God (even though we wouldn't have had them without God as we know now), we now see that we missed an important aspect of their meaning: their meaning was under-determined but what we didn't see then about them has now been made explicit. There are still the same possibilities but there is more to them now then there was before. We do not believe something different now but rather believe it differently, namely more fully, more clearly and, so we hope, more adequately.

However, if this was true about our earlier apprehensions and beliefs before we came to see them in the way we see and understand them now, then it is also true of the present apprehensions and beliefs that we have and acquire at the various levels of operations and interchange with our environment in the process of our life. Nothing of what we apprehend, feel and perceive at the various levels of the operation of our physical, organic and sentient life in its differentiated interactions with its various environments does in any way show it to take place in the presence of God; and the same is true of the physical impressions, complex emotions and cognitive beliefs that we acquire as a result of these bodily operations and interactions and which to a considerable extent influence our ways of behaving, acting and reacting in situations. That they take place in the presence of God cannot simply be read off them but shows only when they are placed in the interpretative perspective of the insight of faith that our life is lived in the presence of God.

So the argument sketched applies not only to our earlier apprehensions and beliefs but also to most of our present ones: They apprehend possibilities, but not *as* possibilities provided by God, and for precisely this reason the resulting beliefs are not beliefs *about God*. But to look at them in this way is possible only in a perspective different from their own; the perspective of living in the presence of God. In this perspective everything that we have apprehended and believed earlier as well as everything we apprehend and believe now (but not under this description) is seen and understood differently. It now becomes, or can become, an occasion that mediates to us what wasn't or isn't accessible in its own perspective: that it took or takes place in the presence of God. *For us* it becomes, or may become, a mediation of God's presence, which it wasn't and isn't for itself. In its own perspective it couldn't and can't see it, but in our perspective we can. Not everything can be seen in every perspective, but in some perspectives we see more and better than in others and not merely because we see different things but because we see the same things differently.

Now perspectives involve interpretation, and different perspectives different interpretations. Thus if we apprehend what we apprehend (feel, perceive, experience, believe etc.) within the horizon of the Christian doxastic practice, we apprehend it *in a specific way* and in a specific (re-)interpretation. We do so not in an isolated way restricted to particular apprehensions, feelings, perceptions, experiences or beliefs (or desires, wishes, hopes or fears, for that matter) but in an ongoing interpretative process in which every interpretation is corrected, modified, continued or replaced by others in a continual attempt to relate through what we apprehend, feel, perceive, believe etc. in the best possible way to the realities and possibilities of the changing situations in which we live our lives.[28]

Thus in the Christian doxastic practice we learn how to *use the word* ›God‹ to refer not to anything past, present or future in time but to the one without whom we wouldn't be present in time nor anything that could be past, present or future for us; we apprehend that what we apprehend are contingent *possibilities* that could not have been available and that are not always available or in every situation available in the same way; we interpret the precarious presence and availability of these possibilities as a *gift* without which we could not live by relating them to the presence of the one to whom we refer as ›God‹ and to whom we address our thanksgiving and lament about the possibilities available or not (no more or never) available to us, to those close to us or to others who are our neighbours; we apprehend *how* God becomes present to us or others by forming particular beliefs about the possibilities we apprehend *as* possibilities provided by God's presence for us or for others; we form contingent beliefs about *God* as the poet of the possibilities which we apprehend; and we do so by moving from beliefs about something as God's gift (›Our possibilities are God-given‹) to beliefs about God (›God is the poet of our possibilities‹), and *vice versa* in an ongoing interpretative process in which, on the one hand, our understanding of us and our world is deepened by illuminating it in the light of the presence of God and in which, on the other hand, our

---

[28] I.U. Dalferth, *Evangelische Theologie als Interpretationspraxis. Eine systematische Orientierung*, Leipzig 2004.

understanding of the presence of God is deepened in giving content to it in the light of our experiences of ourselves and our world.

All these beliefs and interpretations are not caused by God but by contingent causes in the temporal order of the situations in which we live. All these beliefs and interpretations are thus open to change, correction and improvement. They all involve specific and contentious interpretations of what we apprehend at the various levels and in the various dimensions of our life. But insofar as they are reality-depicting, they interpret apprehensions of possibilities which are not of our making but which we discover, and often are surprised to discover, to be the contingent chances played into our way and given to our life. They do not point to the presence of God as such or by themselves. But when we come to experience ourselves as God's creatures living in the presence of God, then they disclose in a ›second reading‹ *to us* what is hidden to themselves: that they are possibilities provided by God.

These possibilities may or may not be mediated to us through the natural processes of creation. They may be mediated through nature's novelty and creativity in a general way, through particular occasions in nature, history or our own life in a particular way, or through individual ways that are accessible only in a 1st- and 2nd-person perspective as possibilities opened up for us by God becoming present to my present, or to yours. But the way in which we determine the content of these beliefs depends on the particularities of our belief-system and doxastic practice in which our processes of apprehending possibilities and of forming beliefs about them are embedded. Our beliefs may not involve any explicit reference to God. We may lack the necessary conceptuality because our belief-system is as yet poorly developed; we may unconsciously determine what we apprehend in terms of other concepts that seem more appropriate to us in the light of our body of beliefs and background knowledge; or we may consciously opt for a non-religious, non-theistic or non-Christian re-presentation of it because this looks to us more likely in the light of the evidence available. After all, »the theological interpretation of nature's creativity and complexity is by no means obligatory«[29], and the same is true of the interpretation of particular occasions in history or of my present situation: Even if I cannot otherwise but express it religiously or theologically in terms of God's presence, it is never the only way in which it can be described or expressed. It is a contingent and contentious view, even

---

[29] Davis, ›Teleology without Teleology: Purpose through Emergent Complexity‹, 108.

though I may have no alternative but to see and express it this way. The
situation could always be described otherwise, even if I couldn't do it
otherwise without being untrue to how I experience it in my perspective.

On the other hand, if God presents himself to us by becoming
present to us in a way that we can apprehend as disclosing his present,
then we can also re-present this both to ourselves (in our beliefs) and
to others (in communications, i.e. linguistic re-presentations of our
beliefs) in varying degrees of clarity. We then form *beliefs* about God
on the basis of how we are affected by the way in which we apprehend
the possibilities played into our way by God's becoming present to our
present. We form *conscious beliefs* about God's presence by becoming
aware of our apprehensions and of their content in the context of the
specific doxastic practices in which we participate. And we *communicate*
these beliefs to others by using some socially available system of (religious) communication (language).

4. Multiple Senses: Dependence, Trust and Presence

Now all this presupposes that God becomes present not only in the
mode of creative activity but also in the salvific activity of the Son
which discloses the character of God's dynamic presence to us (love)
and in the perfecting activity of the Spirit who persuades and guides us
to the realisation of the ends of God's love by being totally responsive
to all that happens. God accommodates his love through the Spirit to
the needs of our present by adjusting the possibilities that he makes
present to us to the changing requirements of our various activities and
operations in our specific situations (*principle of divine accommodation*).
But since God does so by becoming present to our present in the
modes of his triune divine activity, it is to be expected that there are
modes of creaturely receptivity that correspond to these *modes of divine presence*.

And so there are. If we focus the sense of the presence of God with
respect to the three modes of divine presence and activity then we can
distinguish between a ›*sense of absolute dependence*‹ (*schlechthinniges Ab-
hängigkeitsgefühl*) or ›sense of createdness‹ (*Schöpfungsgefühl*) corresponding to God's creative presence and activity as Father, a ›*sense of basic
trust*‹ or ›faith‹ corresponding to God's salvific presence and activity as
Son; and a ›*sense of presence*‹ corresponding to God's perfecting presence and activity as Spirit.

Each of these three senses is not just a part or an aspect of the sense of the presence of God as if it were a set of three independent senses but rather each is the whole Christian sense of the presence of God focussed in a specific respect. For us there is no sense of the presence of God that is not experienced as a sense of dependence, trust and presence, even though one sense or other may dominate in determining an actual experience.

These senses are not restricted to us but can also be found in other created agencies although in different degrees. Whereas a *sense of dependence* can be detected in the most basic forms of sentient life that is able to react to its environment, a *sense of presence* appears to be part of the experience of the more complex forms of animal life, whereas a *sense of trust* can be found in higher animals and in human life. But since humans with their complex organisms also live a life of animals and of more basic sentient creatures, human experience incorporates all three senses in differing degrees and emphases.

In human life each of these senses can come in different degrees; each allows for being designed and culturally formatted in different ways; and each can develop forms that are life-enhancing (healthy) or life-obstructing (unhealthy). Just as there are forms of the sense of dependence that impede a proper and self-determining human life (addiction, dependency, impulsive craving, compulsion), so there are forms of trust that hinder human life rather than strengthen it (credulity, gullibility, lack of caution) and forms of the sense of presence that lead astray rather than orient human life (forgetting the past, ignoring the future, despair of empty repetition, loss of the sense of presence).

None of these senses must manifest itself as a religious sense even though in religions there are explicit practices and forms of life and thought which help to express and symbolise these senses in ways that allow us critically and constructive to relate to them in living a human life. Thus all three senses have their special Christian forms of expression: the sense of absolute dependence takes the form of the *sense of createdness*, the sense of basic trust the form of *faith in God*, and the sense of presence the form of the *sense of the presence of God*. In each case the difference is not some additional experiential content which goes beyond a ›mere‹ sense of dependence, trust or presence but a different mode in which these senses are experienced. This mode is due to the fundamental re-orientation of life that Christian traditions symbolise as the existential change form *non-faith* to *faith*. And in the light of this it is claimed that the *sense of createdness* brings out the truth of the sense of dependence, *faith in God* the true character of the sense of trust, and the *sense of the presence of God* the decisive point of the sense of presence. They are not understood to be different senses from the senses of dependence, trust and presence, but rather are these senses in a form that brings out their full meaning and true character.

This Christian conviction does not preclude forms of Christian life and reflection that focus specifically on one of these senses, sometimes at the expense of the others. So there are strands in Christian practice and theology that concentrate everything on the sense of creaturehood or createdness (orders of creation, creation theologies), or on trust alone (theologies of faith), or on the experience of presence (charismatic movements and theologies). But it is obvious that these senses cannot be isolated or played off against each other but require each other. They are all part of every version of Christian life and thought, even though the emphasis may differ.

Moreover, they are also not confined to religious life or to human life alone. Since God as conceived by Christians is *semper ubique actuosus* and present to each and every present, these senses cannot be restricted human life alone but must function in some way or other at all levels of being and existence, from inanimate nature through sentient organisms to the responsive capacities of moral beings. Therefore, if we apprehend God's presence at all, our ways of apprehending are irreducibly plural and comprise all levels of our being and existence, including our *body*.

Our body is central to what we can perceive and experience, and this is also true with respect to God's presence. The body is the medium of receptivity and agency, it provides the perspectival viewpoint of what we perceive, and it is both the target of experience and the represented object of much of what we do. In particular, the body is both agent and object of our acts; it is the locus where often violent, sometimes traumatising experiences take place and where these experiences leave traces. The body is the signifier of gender, it is subject as well as object of desire, subject as well as victim of violence, and in either respect it is the prime locus of presence. In short, we *are* bodies and do not merely have bodies. Therefore our body is best understood as the complex pattern of activity that we are and which to a large extent is immune from direct intentional control.

Central to this bodily activity beyond our control is what Whitehead and Hartshorne have called *feeling*. Bodies feel what is present to them, and only what is an object of feeling is present to a body. Since we can only feel what is causally present to us, and since nothing that is causally present to us is God, God's activity can only be apprehended as present to us if created activity is apprehended as mediating it, that is

to say, if the presence of created activity becomes a sign of God's presence to us. For this to occur that to which we are present must disclose
to us that the contingent possibilities present in its situation are due to
the way in which God becomes present to it; this will only occur if it
provokes us to apprehend how God becomes present to our present;
and unless we apprehend it here we won't apprehend it anywhere. The
place where created presence mediates God's presence to us is our own
presence, and only if we appreciate our own presence as a place and
sign of God's presence we shall also be able to apprehend it elsewhere.
Thus while God is present with every present at every level of creaturely activity, we apprehend what we apprehend as mediating God's
presence only if we apprehend how God is present to our presence:
My 1ˢᵗ-person insight ›Without God's presence I wouldn't be‹ is the
key to the 3ʳᵈ-person confession ›Without God's presence nothing
would be‹.

5. Plurifom Self-Presentation: The Spirit as Mediation

The Christian tradition has always acknowledged this 1ˢᵗ-person insight not to be an inference from observed facts or a deduction from
first principles but a creative insight or ›inspiration‹ by the Spirit. It is
experienced, whether in a long process or a sudden change, as an insight that opened our eyes to what has been before our eyes all along
without us seeing it, but at the same time as an insight that we could
not have brought about ourselves. Our life could have been seen all
along as a life lived in the presence of God but we couldn't see it. It
was a possibility which we failed to realise and whose realisation we
experience as a complete change of perspective on everything, a displacement that we could not have effected ourselves but for which we
thank the one in whose light we now see ourselves and everything
else: God the Spirit.
   The Spirit is God who opens our eyes to how God accommodates
his presence to our presence by investing our situation with the possibilities that determine its contingent character. We did apprehend
(some of) the possibilities before (for otherwise we couldn't have
lived) but we missed their meaning. On the other hand, what in retrospect turns out to have been a possibility all along was neither available
nor noticed as a possibility before our eyes were opened to it. The reason is that the possibility of experiencing our situation in this way is
not a possibility of our situation but of the way in which God relates
to it. It is not one of the possibilities that define the situation in which
we live but the possibility that defines the possibilities of our situations

as possibilities given by God. It is not a possibility inscribed in our situations but the possibility of understanding the possibilities inscribed
in them in a particular way. To ›see‹ our situation in this way is to ›see‹
how God relates to it. But to apprehend our presence as mediating
God's presence we must apprehend God's presence to our presence.
This is not an insight available to us in apprehending what we can apprehend in the causal processes of our world. It is an insight tied to a
special way of apprehending our apprehending, i.e. apprehending it as
a possibility which we owe to God.

This insight only occurs in our 1st-person perspective, and when it
occurs we credit not ourselves but the Spirit for opening our eyes to it.
Yet it is not just a private opinion or a mere ›subjective‹ view of our
life and situation. If it is true at all, then it is true for everyone, and
whether it is true is not decided by *fiat* or just by us but open to public
debate. However, it cannot be true unless it occurs in our 1st-person
perspective. There is nothing whose truth or falsity could be discussed
independent of it. On the other hand, if what the Spirit discloses is
true of us, then it is true of all created reality; if the Spirit opens our
eyes to how God relates to our presence, then the Spirit discloses how
God accommodates his presence to the presence of all created reality;
and since created reality differs endlessly, the presence of the Spirit
takes on an endless plurality of forms.

Thus whereas God's creative activity is time-free, the same for everyone, and in principle beyond experience since it is presupposed in all
experiencing, God's spiritual activity is different for everyone and as
pluriform as the realities to whose present God becomes present because it relates to everyone in a singular way by making those possibilities available that define this specific situation. On the one hand,
therefore, God is time-free present as creator; but this cannot be experienced because it is the necessary precondition of all experiencing.
On the other hand, God not only creates by becoming present to each
present in a specific way but also makes his presence accessible to creation; and since this requires adjusting his ways of becoming present to
the changing situations of his creatures, he is not only time-free
present as creator but also multi-present to every created present as
Spirit.

But then, just as God's creative presence is presupposed in all that occurs, so God the Spirit actively relates to everything as it occurs. This

---

[30] God is not *interacting* with created agencies but in his acting as Spirit *re-presenting* created realities to God and *presenting* divine activity to creatures. He remains

divine activity has two directions.[30] On the one hand, the Spirit accommodates God's life to the changing present of created realities, and on the other the Spirit mediates the present of created realities to the creative present of divine life. This makes the Spirit the medium of divine mediation and communication and the divine activity in which creation is made present to God and God's present made present to creation: The world is not God's body (as some have argued) but the working of the Spirit is God's ›embodied‹ relation to created reality and at the same time the ›embodiment‹ of created reality in the divine life. God is not a bodiless agent[31]; rather the Spirit is the functional equivalent to God's body, i.e. the pattern of activity through which God relates to creation in ›presenting‹ God's presence to it and ›re-presenting‹ its presence to God. God does not need »any further medium for his self-expression«[32]. In particular there is no need to insist, as Sallie McFague does[33], that God is enfleshed by all bodies, i.e. that the multiple yet interrelated bodily beings of the world are the inspirited embodiment of God. God is present to all bodies as they occur, but he is present to them as Spirit and not embodied by them. God accommodates his activity to bodies, but this neither makes God a body nor the totality of bodies (the universe).

Similarly God does not become incarnate in the totality of human beings (but in Jesus Christ[34]), yet he accommodates his presence and activity to the peculiarities of human existence. Human beings are not just bodies; they live in social and not merely causal relationships. Causal relationships are a purely asymmetrical affair in that the cause can initiate the relationship while the »other partner in a purely causal relationship is an object of causal manipulation and therefore lacks the freedom of will to be able to say ›no‹ with respect to what happens to

---

the sole author of his activity but he moulds it by taking into account the situation of his creation for determining how to relate to it *now*.

[31] Cf. T.F. Tracy, *God, Action and Embodiment*, Grand Rapids, Mich. 1984; Swinburne, *The Christian God*, 125 passim.

[32] As Spirit, Owen rightly holds, God »does not require any further medium for his self-expression« (217). Yet this does not imply that »God ... is bodiless« but that the activity of the Spirit is God's embodiment of creation and in creation, most clearly so in Jesus Christ.

[33] S. McFague, *The Body of God*, Minneapolis, Minnesota 1993.

[34] That is to say, God discloses (as Spirit) the nature of his presence to every presence (love) in his unique presence to the presence of Jesus (Son). What is at stake in God's presence to the presence of Jesus is the nature of his presence to our presence, i.e. God's saving presence with us and not his special presence with Jesus.

him or her«[35]. But God's acting with respect to creatures must be understood in such a way that God becomes present to their present without interfering with their activities precisely because they are made possible by his becoming present. God enables and enhances the operations of his creatures[36] by playing the possibilities into their way from which they choose in creating the continuities and the character of their lives, and just as God does what he does in the mode of his free and unconditional love for his creatures, so they are hoped to do what they do in the mode of a free and unforced love of their creator.

This is why God's relationship to creation is to be conceptualised or represented in theology not only in ontological but also in personal terms. Personal relationships are symmetrical in that the initiative of both partners in the relationship is necessary to establish them. Therefore creation, which is asymmetrical, cannot be a personal relation but must be ›ontological‹ and the same for all created beings. But we differ from other creatures in that God creates us as beings that can freely enter into the personal relationship that God freely establishes with us by being present to us as Spirit. This relationship is mutually dependent on the *freedom* of the other who chooses freely to enter into this relationship. It not only depends on God choosing it freely (personal relationship is not something into which anyone has to enter) but our free choice is equally a necessary condition for establishing it. This is why becoming aware of God's presence is not to enter automatically into a personal relationship to God: since it is a personal relationship we can refrain from doing so. If however we do react to the love of God by love in God, we enter into a *living relation* to God which Christians call *faith*. To live a life of faith is to live consciously in the presence of God, i.e. to *worship God* in the widest possible sense of integrating all our »thoughts and purposes, all valuations and meanings, all perceptions and conceptions« into a »consciously unitary response to« God.[37]

In short, as living organisms we cannot live in our world without forming unconscious and conscious beliefs about it. All our beliefs, in-

---

[35] V. Brümmer, *Speaking of a Personal God. An Essay in Philosophical Theology*, Cambridge 1992, 75.

[36] Thomas Aquinas, *Summa Theologica* Ia q. 105, a. 5.

[37] Ch. Hartshorne, *A Natural Theology*, 4-7. – This, according to Christian faith, is not something we can do by ourselves. Unless God enables us to realise the presence of his love we do not enter into a loving relationship to God. But God's saving action in Christ opens our eyes to the presence of his love so that we can freely enter into a personal relationship with God the Spirit in our own life and thus fully develop our potential as persons.

cluding our beliefs about God, are acquired through our causal and communicative interactions with our environment. For the information embodied in our beliefs is gathered through perception and communication, stored in our memory, and a guideline for our acting. But while it is true that we rarely form conscious beliefs about God before we are told about God, this does not entail that all our beliefs that embody information about our life in the presence of God have been acquired in this way. Hearsay is not the only source of belief about God. If God is present to each and every present, we all have first and not merely second hand beliefs acquired in God's present, although they need not be conscious and, if brought to consciousness, need not explicitly refer to God. Much of what we believe about God is based on our senses of dependence, trust or presence, which we do not experience as God's present but in God's present, whether we know it or not. But then most of the beliefs on which we act and live are tacit beliefs disposing us to certain kinds of actions rather than to others. Most of these tacit beliefs are inscribed in emotions and are present to us in the form of emotional and cognitive dispositions on which we act without much further reflection. They form the background knowledge to the more sophisticated states of our conscious and rational life, and it is often difficult to make them explicit and become aware of them. But we can only become aware of them by making them explicit, and we can do this only by restating and interpreting them against the background of all that we do not understand, understand, and misunderstand at a given time. We shall never fully elucidate this complex background of our more explicit forms of knowledge for in elucidating it in one respect we rely on it in others. And neither can we restate our tacit beliefs without continually re-interpreting their content and determining their meaning in a new way. We become aware of them by interpreting them differently; we do so in order to understand them better as we did before, and we hope that this will help us to relate in more adequate ways to the world in which we live.

6. Understanding the Change: Becoming Present in the Present

This is also true of our beliefs about God. We live in the presence of God long before we can identify God's activity and divine presence with our life. But when we learn to do so we do not simply enlarge our stock of beliefs by adding some beliefs about God but rather put everything we believe about anything in a new and different perspective. We re-orient our life, change our attitude to the world and our-

selves, and view all our views differently. What is at stake here is not
acquiring a new belief about God but changing from believing something about God to believing in God. This is not an epistemic or cognitive but an existential change although it will result in new beliefs
about God also. But these beliefs are secondary, not primary, and they
depend on the difference between epistemic and existential change
and do not overcome it. We may, rightly or wrongly, believe all sorts of
things about God without believing in God. It is true that we cannot
believe in God without holding some beliefs about God. But this
doesn't obliterate the fundamental difference between them. Belief in
God is different from other beliefs in that you cannot come to belief in
God and leave everything else at it is but rather believing in God
changes your views of yourself, of the world and – if you have some –
of God. It is still the same world in which you live but it looks completely different. It has changed not in substance but in mode. You still
eat bread and drink wine but in doing so you now communicate with
Christ (which you didn't do before) and you do it in the present of
God (which you didn't notice before).

On the on hand, therefore, the change from non-faith (not believing
in God) to faith (believing in God) is not a matter of acquiring some
additional new beliefs but of believing everything in a new way. On
the other hand, what we have believed before is not simply discarded,
extinguished or superseded. It becomes the medium and means for
making sense of the change of life and orientation that has occurred. It
does so by being interpreted and re-interpreted in the light of the new
orientation of life. It thus brings out what can and should be continued in the new situation and what cannot and must not. This creates
retrospectively a clarity that wasn't accessible to us before. And this in
turn helps us prospectively to orient ourselves in our life in a way that
wouldn't have been accessible to us without that existential change. We
still know what we knew before, but we know it differently. We still
believe some of what we believed before but what we haven't
changed, corrected or replaced we believe differently. There are plenty
of cognitive continuities across the abyss of the existential change. But
even what is continued in the new life is continued differently and has
a new significance, and what is not continued is done so for reasons
that were not available to us then but are only available now. We still
live in the same world and have feelings, apprehensions, perceptions,
emotions, desires, beliefs etc. as before but we understand them differently and interpret them critically in the light of a difference (non-
faith/faith; not believing in God/believing in God; ignoring the pres-

ence of God/understanding everything in the light of the presence of God) that becomes available to us only through the existential change of becoming aware of the presence of God. In short, the decisive change is not in *what* we believe but in *how* we believe. And just as the *how* helps us to gain a better understanding of the *what,* the *what* helps us to gain a clearer understanding of the *how.*

So we must distinguish between beliefs about God and belief in God: the first comes in many forms, contents and degrees of clarity, the second is a strict Either/Or: Either you believe in God, or you don't. Of course, beliefs *about* belief or lack of belief in God are not different from other cognitive beliefs. They are as vague or clear as others. And belief in God (faith) just as non-belief in God (unfaith) can be lived in an endless variety of ways. But none of this dissolves the Either/Or between faith and non-faith (each of them comes in degrees but the difference between them doesn't) or obliterates the difference between cognitive and existential problems, and while the presence of God may be an interesting cognitive problem to discuss, it becomes a serious challenge only in the light of the existential alternative of believing or not believing in God. For the believer holds that both believing and not believing in God are only possible in the present of God, and this is why the believer sees the non-believer living in a fundamental self-contradiction: He denies or ignores what he has to presuppose in denying or ignoring it. The non-believer denies this, of course. He cannot be shown that *what* he believes or doesn't believe implies this contradiction, or that his *denying* assumes what he denies: If there is no God who is present, there is no contradiction in denying the presence of God, neither in what is said nor in the saying of it. Both positions are coherent as far as they go; both can adduce evidence that is sufficient for the one who adduces it but not for the other, and none is in a position to show conclusively why he is right and the other must be wrong: There is no way to refute conclusively the sense of the presence of God as a mere delusion, for this judgment in a 3rd-person perspective can never do justice to a sense that is tied to a 1st-person perspective. But neither is there a way to refute the non-believer for no amount of evidence for the sense of the presence of God will ever be enough to bar him from giving different interpretations of the sense of dependence, sense of trust or sense of presence pointed out to him. He does not need to deny those senses to make his point but only that they are senses *of the presence of God.* Conversely, no amount of evidence about the senses of dependence, trust and presence, their importance in human life and their universal distribution is sufficient to convince the non-believer or to warrant the believer that they are modes of the *sense of the presence of God*. Both can (or can be construed to) offer complete descriptions of their common world and life, both can integrate all the information to which one or the other can point, and yet both interpret them in a different perspective and horizon, and both will live incompatible lives in incompatible views of the world.

So while the cognitive differences between believer and non-believer are not to be denied, the important difference is the existential difference between faith and non-faith and the different perspective on everything that goes with them. This difference cannot be reduced to a cognitive problem without missing its point. Belief in God is not a belief about God, and neither beliefs about God nor the belief in God are caused by God. God is not a (physical) cause in the world, nor the (metaphysical) cause of the world. Just as there are no negative causes for what we do not believe, so there are no divine causes for what we believe about God. And just as there is no sufficient reason for not believing in God, so is there a sufficient reason for doing so. The non-believer may point out that his reason for not believing in God is that there is no reason to do so, and the believer may emphasize that his reason for believing in God is that doing so is reason enough. In either case it is not the reason adduced that makes them believe or not believe but they hold their beliefs prior to it. The one lives his life with a sense of the presence of God, the other doesn't. Either of them can adduce much in support of his views and much that seems to account against them (evil for the believer, for example, or the existence of believers for the non-believer). But either can find enough arguments to rebut the criticism.

However, in this way of presenting the situation a decisive aspect is missing: For every believer there was a time when he or she was not a believer. We are not born believers but become believers, if we do, in the course of our life. (Some even call themselves ›re-born Christians‹, and they do not mean that they were not born as Christians but became Christians in the course of their lives but that they were Christians who had to be re-born to become believers – and that is a different story altogether.) But if believers *become* believers, they are not believers before they become so, and then the question is how the existential change in a life from non-faith to faith (from not believing in God to believing in God) is to be understood.

It is not, as we have seen, a case of acquiring a belief about God but a change of one's whole life and outlook on life. Where it occurs, believers find questions answered which they may never have asked themselves: *How do we become present in the present?* What is it not merely to be *here* in the same room together with someone who is here at the same time, but *to become present to someone present*? What is the difference between a temporal and local co-presence of persons, and their being present to each other? *Being present* is not enough. What is needed is *becoming present* in the present, and this only occurs when we become present *to the other* present. I may be here, but I am not present as long as I am not open to the other present in such a way that the presence of the other person is apprehended as a gift that enriches me. We become present in the present when we are opened up to the other's present. But this is not something we can do by *fiat*. We cannot make ourselves to become present by deciding so because we cannot open ourselves to the other if we do not find ourselves already being open to him or her. We do not become present by what we do but by what happens to us in doing what we do or before we do anything at all. We become present by being made present. This is precisely the experience of believers when they find themselves no longer living just in the present, but in the present of God. Their *sense of presence* intensifies to a *sense of the presence of God* because they find themselves to be not only present but open to the presence of others in new and unexpected ways: The other becomes a gift to them which he wasn't before, and they become present in the present by receiving the presence of the other as a gift for which they cannot help thanking God.

Where this occurs, believers thank God for the gift of this present and ascribe it to the Spirit and not to themselves or to other persons present. But this ascription is not an explanation of their experience by a non-natural cause but rather the rejection of all possible explanations as sufficient to explain this fundamental change in their life. Whatever explanation is given, and there are plenty psychological attempts and proposals, it doesn't fit their own 1st-person experience of a completely contingent event with an inexhaustible meaning that puts everything in a new light. The event may be experienced as an unexpected rupture of the continuities of a life that results in the need for a complete new orientation in life, or it may be experienced as a slow transformation that takes place over a long period of time in which a particular understanding of the world and of oneself grows on someone until it has become virtually impossible for him or her to look at the world and oneself in any other way. In either case the experience is of a completely contingent event whose significance for a person cannot be exhausted by any explanation, and this inexhaustible contingency is expressed and symbolised in ascribing it to the Spirit. The Spirit, therefore, is not referred to by the believer as a super- or non-natural explanation of a natural event but as the one who safeguards both the utter and inexplicable contingency of the change from non-belief to belief in God and its inexhaustible significance and meaning for the believer. There is more to a life than the events of which it is made up: There is God's creative view and salvific and perfecting judgement of this life. The Spirit mediates this to a life by disclosing its present to be the present of God and God to be the one who out of his love gives us the chance of living in the present of his love: God becomes present to us by making us become present to God. We live in the present but it is the present of God, a gift that we have no reason to receive but which is the chance of our life, as the Spirit makes us see in changing our life from non-belief to belief.

On the other hand, this change takes place in life, and it results in a new attitude to all aspects and dimensions of our life; to our apprehensions, feelings, perceptions and emotions as much as to our beliefs, wishes, hopes and desires. However, if in the new life we experience not just one thing differently but everything differently, then not *what* we experienced but *how* we experience it is the difference to be understood: The believer changes to a *different mode of life* when he becomes a believer, and this change of mode is expressed in the sense of the presence of God. The sense *of the presence of God* is not an additional sense to the sense of dependence, trust or presence, which both believer and non-believer share in their different ways. It rather is *the new mode* in which the believer experiences what he as non-believer had experienced as the sense of dependence, trust and presence. He had all the experience before, but he had missed its meaning. Conversely he has now a new meaning of experiences that he had also had before: The believer and the non-believer do not differ in their experiences (what) but in their mode of experiencing (how), and this is why there is a biographical continuity across the change from non-faith to faith in the life of a person who becomes a believer.

But then it is not merely the believer but also the non-believer who experiences what the believer expresses as the sense of the presence of God even though the non-believer doesn't experience it in this mode. The mode is a deepening and intensifying of the *sense of presence* to the *sense of the presence of God*: Believers come to see that living in the present is living in the present of God. This is not an inference from a sense to its (putative) cause but a more intense experience of the *sense of presence*: To have a present to live is a gift, and God is the one to whom we address our thanks for this gift. So believers do not merely ascribe their change to this new *mode* of experience to the presence of the Spirit, but their very experience of presence: Without God becoming present they wouldn't be and live in the present, and without the Spirit they wouldn't realise that to live in the present is to live in the present of God. God is to be thanked not only for making them experience their present in this new mode by becoming present to them as Spirit, but also for the gift of presence which they now experience in this new way as God's present to their present.

So we must not confuse what we learn about God from others with what we know from experience: If God is really present as Spirit, as Christians believe he is, then we know God not merely by hearsay but because he is at work in our lives, whether we are aware of it or not. However we, and as far as we know we alone, can become aware of it and form conscious beliefs about God's presence to our lives. Where this occurs we begin to realise God's present to our present as persons, and the possibility of a *personal relation* to God that is opened up by this; and we cannot realise this, according to Christian experience, without describing the relation in terms of sin and grace, law and gospel, the way we live it in fact, and the way we could and should live it if we would be true to God's love.

Now personal relationships differ from causal ones in that for the realisation of a personal relationship the initiative of both partners in the relationship is necessary: It is a symmetrical relation – not to the Creator but to the Spirit. Our ontological relation to the Creator is asymmetrical. But God creates us as beings that can freely enter in the personal relationship that he freely establishes with us by being present to us as Spirit. This relationship is mutually dependent on the *freedom* of the other to choose freely to enter in this relationship. It not only depends on God choosing it freely (i.e. it is not unavoidable for God to enter in personal relationship with us) but our free choice is equally a necessary condition for the relationship to be brought about. Hence even when we become aware of God's presence we do not automatically enter into a personal relationship to God; rather just because it is a personal relationship we can refrain from doing so, i.e. continue to live a life of sin.

However, if we do react to the love of God by love in God, then the change of life and orientation occurs and we enter into a *living relation* to God in faith. We then live all our life consciously in the presence of God; that is we turn from ignoring God in sin to worshipping God in its widest possible sense.

This, according to Christian faith, is not something we can do by ourselves. Unless God enables us to realise the presence of his love by opening our eyes to it we cannot form right beliefs about God or enter into a loving relationship to God. But only if we enter in it we fully develop our potential as persons; therefore God's saving action in Christ through which he opens our eyes to the presence of his love is the necessary condition for freely entering into a personal relationship with God the Spirit. God shows us in Christ how we can apprehend and respond to the presence of his love, and he thus provokes us to discover this presence also in our own life by relating to the Spirit and by living a conscious life *coram Deo*, in the presence of God – at all levels of our existence from body to spiritual love. Hence the sense of faith sees God becoming present as creative, saving, liberating love. This divine presence is not restricted to those who react to it by faith in God's self-giving love. It includes everything created and permeates all levels (the ›whole person‹) of our being whether we are aware of it or not. It aims at reciprocity, but its reality does not depend on it. Divine love waits for a free return by us; it works for it by waiting for it; and it waits for it by creating occasion after occasion in which we can become aware of the love in the presence of which we live.

7. Religious Communication

It is a central aim of religious communication in Christian life to help us to achieve such awareness. It seeks to raise our sense of presence to a conscious sense of the presence of God by provoking us to see and express what we apprehend in a way true to the significance of the present in which we live. And it does so by providing a language and well-established criteria in terms of which we can symbolise, conceptualise, scrutinise and criticise our apprehensions in the present and the beliefs about the present built on them.

However, it is not the task of religious communication to create a sense of the presence of God *ex nihilo* in those who become involved in it but to open our eyes to the sense of presence which we all have, to provide the means to interpret it as a sense of the presence of God, and to show that looking at it in this way sheds a light on our life that helps to make more sense of what we experience than it would make otherwise.

All this is not to be confused with doctrinal instruction. Doctrines state the grammar of faith. They explicate the rules and structures of a religious way of life, but they do not create it. Nobody is religious by knowing the doctrines of a religion but only by living the way of life that they govern. Religious grammars can help us to get a clearer understanding of a religion, but they presuppose a religious life and, beyond it, some rudimentary apprehension of living in the present of God already, even though it is not explicit or thematic as such.

This pre-reflective or un-thematic sense of the presence of God is not created by verbal religious communication alone, if at all. If God really is present as Spirit who presents the possibilities to us from which we choose, then we all have some first hand experience of God and apprehend God at all levels of our being, not merely through linguistic re-presentations or explicitly religious communications. When we have become aware of it we may even find that we feel and have felt God's presence more strongly in contexts that we would not describe as religious at all. And it should not surprise us that many today find poetry, painting or music more effective means to create a sense of the presence of God than most traditional religious activities.

On the other hand, we must be careful not to draw wrong conclusions from this and denounce theological reflection and the scrutiny of critical reason in matters of faith and religion as barren rationalism and improper intellectualism. There can be no doubt that verbal communication is particularly apt to engage our cognitive faculties, whereas other means of communication are more effective in reaching deeper levels of feeling and emotion: and it is quite wrong to think (as some Reformed traditions have done) that all this has nothing to do with the preaching of the gospel. But it is as mistake to believe that we could dispense with cognitive communication in religious matters altogether as it is to suggest that art or music should take the place of traditional religion or that truly religious persons need not to worry about the conceptual subtleties of theology. The alternatives are quite misleading: Experience and reason in religion cannot be opposed in this way. On the contrary, they mutually require each other.

7.1 Religious Communication in the Mode of Music

Let me illustrate what I mean with a contemporary example. It has been the life-long conviction of the French composer Olivier Messiaen that music is particularly apt to create a sense of the presence of God. He pursued this idea in most of his compositions, from the earliest works for organ to his chamber music and his orchestral works. In 1938 he issued a manifesto in which he outlined the mystical ends of his music and also the technical means by which they were to be achieved: »The emotion and sincerity of musical work« he writes,

»shall be at the service of the dogmas of Catholic theology«. They »shall be expressed by melodic and harmonic means ... rhythmic means...« and »above all by modes of limited transposition«. And he has followed and worked out this program with highest artistry and care throughout his career.

To many the religious end of Messiaen's music has looked highly idiosyncratic if not bizarre. Even critics who value the outstanding quality of his musical achievements have suggested that »Messiaen's treatment of religion remains extremely personal, even subjective«.[38] But nothing could be further from the truth. Of course Messiaen's music conveys his personal apprehension of God's presence in nature and human culture; and we have seen that there is no other way to become aware of God's presence than to apprehend one's own involvement in it. But while Messiaen's treatment of religion is personal, it is by no means subjective. Being a religious subject does not make Messiaen subjectively religious trapped in his own subjective world of religion. On the contrary, the whole emphasis of Messiaen's music is on the one objective world, the unique creation of which each of us is part, which we all experience in a myriad of ways, and of which we can share our experiences just because we are all equally part of it.

Messiaen shows this by the musical techniques that he employs and the materials that he uses. His melodic, harmonic and rhythmic means are all taken from our natural world of experience. As melodic means he uses bird song from all over the world; as rhythmic means in particular the complicated rhythmic patterns of Hindu music, which he has studied extensively; and as harmonic means the many shades of colours which we experience in the world around us and which he transposes into the magnificent harmonies of his music. It has been said that »he composes sounds just as a painter mixes his colours«[39], and he has often stated himself that he sees colours when writing his harmonies. His extraordinary feeling for timbre can be seen e.g. by the importance he assigns to both instrumentation and harmonic structure in producing his colours, and he may even describe sections of his music as ›violet‹ or ›milk-white‹ etc. In short, his musical materials are taken from the world of inanimate nature (colours), sensitive nature (bird song) and human nature (Hindu rhythms); and he combines those in a remarkably artistic manner[40] to convey a sense of the presence of the

---

[38] A. Boucourechliev, ›Messiaen‹, *The New Grove* XII, 1980, 207.
[39] Ibid., 206.
[40] The section entitled ›Epode‹ of his *Chronochromie* (1960) for example is written for 18 strings each playing a different bird song.

supernatural in the natural and to create a sense of the presence of God in the world of nature and human culture.

Can, however, combining and re-combining the materials mentioned really do more than express Messiaen's own religious feeling and sentiment? How does he achieve his avowed end to compose music »at the service of the dogmas of Catholic theology«?

By employing, I suggest, one of the basic doctrinal principles of this tradition: *grace perfects nature*. He re-combines his materials from the book of nature in such a way that they become transparent to God's hidden presence in our world by interpreting them in the light of the book of scripture and the theological doctrines derived from it. That is, he uses theological doctrine as the grammar that allows us to decipher the religious significance of natural phenomena such as bird song, sunsets or Hindu rhythms. He thus not only shows that the whole of creation praises the glory of God but at the same time that seemingly abstract theological doctrines can be used to disclose the religious significance of natural phenomena. Thus nature is shown to be transparent to God's presence with the help of theological doctrine, and theological doctrine is shown to be true to experience by enabling us to perceive God's presence in nature. Messiaen's music is a magnificent, detailed and highly accomplished attempt to transform theological truth from an object of thought into an object of feeling, from reflective insight of the mind into experience and emotion. Where it succeeds his music conveys how both thought and sound, theological truth and natural experience manifest the presence of God. How does he achieve it?

Consider his *Méditation sur le Mystère de la Saint Trinité* (1969), which beautifully shows his use of the doctrinal principle *grace perfects nature*. In his explanations and analyses of the nine pieces Messiaen points to the differences between communicating by language and by music.[41] Language, he writes, whether based on sound, letters, pictures, colours or touch can be used to transmit ideas because it is governed by conventions such as »that *this* expresses *that*«. Music on the other hand »does not express anything directly. It can suggest, create a feeling or state of soul, touch the subconscious, enlarge the oneiric (dream) faculties«, but »music cannot absolutely ›speak‹ to inform with precision«. So how can we »find a type of musical language that would communicate«? His ingenious answer is (1) to design a musical grammar for

---

[41] The following quotations are taken from O. Messiaen, *Méditation sur le Mystère de la Saint Trinité*, Paris 1973.

transcribing words into music; (2) to use this grammar to translate passages from Thomas Aquinas' *Summa Theologica* into music; and (3) to employ all this to provide the framework for bringing out the religious significance of the materials which he uses from nature (bird song, colours) and culture (rhythms).

Thus he organises a *musical alphabet* for notes to express letters, the five vowels, the palatals, sibilants, dentals, labials etc. He designates *musical formula* to render the grammatical rules by which we indicate the cases of nouns and adjectives (nominative, genitive, dative, accusative etc.). He uses two *melodic motives* to express the auxiliaries *to be* and *to have*: *to be* is a descending movement because, as he says, »all that exists comes from God«, whereas *to have* is an ascending movement »because we can always have more by raising ourselves to God«. And finally he lays down a *theme* for the name of God. »I have thought that I should bring to the attention of the listener the only important word of any language ... the divine Name«. And since God is the beginning and end of everything he gives the God-theme in two versions, one straightforward, one in retrograde »just as two extremes that look at each other« so that one could move to and fro between God and God indefinitely.

All this is then used in the way I have indicated to translate such passages from the *Summa* into music as »In relation to the Persons who proceed from Him the Father is qualified so: paternity and spiration« (1st meditation); »God is holy« (2nd med.); »The true relation in God is really identical to the essence« (3rd med.) etc. And his translations utilise materials such as colours, the song of the Wren, the blackbird, the chaffinch, the garden warbler, the black woodpecker, the wood-owl, the yellow hammer and many others and a great variety of provincial rhythms of ancient India, which again have various symbolic meanings. The result is an enormously rich musical tapestry full of symbolic meaning at all levels of musical composition.

However, all this is not immediately accessible to the listener. What we hear is magnificent music, not a musical treatise on (natural) theology. The listener does not hear the elaborate symbolic structures that underlie this music. It is beautiful, it moves the heart and it creates feelings that may be described as religious. But it does not convey the theological information that has gone into its composition, and only those who have studied its ›grammar‹ will actually realise what has gone into this music and what is going on in it.

But this again is theologically significant. It shows that nature, including music, will not disclose its religious significance or the presence of God without a key; and just as Messiaen's musical grammar provides the key to the religious significance of his music, so the book of scripture provides the key to the book of nature. We need some explicit means to open our eyes and ears to the presence of God. This is not to say that without it we cannot enjoy this music. On the contrary, its elaborate art works quite independently of the listener's knowledge of the principles of its construction and the intentions of the composer; and it is open to all sorts of other interpretations. Yet, just as nature, it has a religious and even theological significance that can be understood and brought out if you know the key to it. In this sense Messiaen's music is an impressive analogy and illustration of the nature-grace principle of Roman Catholic theology, and an excellent example of how it works.

However, in order to grasp the theological significance of this music we need some additional linguistic information. Messiaen provides it in the introductions to and interpretations of his works. To combine words and music in such a way that they interpret each other can serve a similar purpose. This is characteristic of much of what Bach has written, and it would be interesting to compare his techniques with those of Messiaen. Bach's music is not so much an attempt to bring out the theological significance of nature, but to interpret the word of Scripture in such a way that God's presence as described there is re-presented to the listener here and now by the melodic, harmonic and rhythmic structures, musical themes, motives and proportions which he uses.

Whereas Messiaen's music is typical of Roman Catholic spirituality and its openness to the richness and beauty of nature, Bach's music utilises the way in which Lutheran liturgy combines word and music with clear priority given to the word. Liturgy provides the interpretative frame of all elements of a service, including silence and music; and the theological significance of this context is made explicit within each service by the readings from scripture and by the sermon. In this way each service re-presents through all the symbolic means used what the gospel narrates about God's presence in Christ to those who are present in the service. It does not relate stories about past events or revelations but seeks to disclose a present reality. Language is important to communicate about this reality in a way that all can understand. But it creates a sense of the presence of God only if those present see the truth of what is said in their own lives, i.e. discover how God has been present and is present to them. Music helps to experience God's presence in ways that go beyond intellectual insights of the mind. But just as it is important to see that apprehending God's presence involves more than understanding words, so we need words and a common language to clarify what we experience.

7.2 Religious Communication in the Verbal Mode

This clarifying activity is the specific task of explicit religious communication. Its prime task is not to generate beliefs about God, but to help us to get clear about them. It does so by talking *about* God. But we must not confuse what we learn about God from others with what we know about God from experience. If God really is present as Spirit, then we all have first hand apprehensions of the present of God and not merely second hand beliefs about God. We know God not only by hearsay, but because God is at work in our lives prior to and independently of our becoming aware of it.

However, our awareness of God will remain at best ambiguous if we do not apprehend God *as* God. For unless God *presents* himself to us, we cannot discern his present; and unless God presents himself to us *as he really is*, we cannot discern the true character of his present. The former takes place all the time, whether we are aware of it or not. The latter however requires both conscious apprehension on our side and self-interpretative mediation on God's side such as Christians claim to find in the history of Israel and, in particular, in Jesus Christ.

Now even if Christians were wrong about Jesus, they could still be right about God: mistaken beliefs about historical fact do not bar from theological insight. But Christians cannot be right about God if what they believe Jesus Christ to have disclosed about God is wrong: the content of their belief would then be incoherent. Yet the content counts, not where it is derived from. Christians believe in a present reality, not in past facts; they believe this reality to be the presence of God's love; and since they find that what this love amounts to has been most fully disclosed in Christ, his mediation provides the paradigm for their understanding of God's love.

To take this paradigm as normative neither implies that it is exclusive nor that Christian faith rests on historical fact nor that salvation depends on historical knowledge nor that only those can be saved who happen to live *post Christum natum*. The point is rather that if Christ interprets and mediates God's presence to us as it really is we must become co-present with Christ, as Kierkegaard put it. He did not mean of course that we must become contemporaneous with something that is past but rather that in order to know God as he truly is we must have first hand knowledge of his presence to our own life and not merely second hand knowledge about his presence to some other life. Christians believe in a *present* reality whose nature they find normatively disclosed in Christ. In this sense Christian faith is historical, but it does not rest on history. God is never more present, or less, than in the present. But God presents himself to us through the Spirit not always and everywhere as unambiguously as in Christ. Therefore just as God's presence is always mediated to us through the Spirit, so God's nature of self-giving love is once and for all disclosed to us through Christ.

All this may be disputed. There are many that have entirely failed to find in Christ any such significance, indeed, most have. »Only a few of those who saw and heard all that transpired in Galilee and Jerusalem, only a few of those who witnessed our Lord's Crucifixion, were alive to the presence of God in these things. They were nothing to those who passed by.«[42] The very same occurrences that to the eye of faith reveal the divine presence are capable of being experienced and explained quite differently – depending on how the beliefs that they cause are conceptualised. But then believers find God's presence revealed not by these occurrences but by God's Spirit who reveals the divine reality hidden in them. This is why they neither require nor can conceive of any further validation of it, and if they are challenged to justify their faith they cannot do it by reference to any historical occurrences but only by reference to the present working of the Spirit. Just as we are aware that we live in a real world, though we cannot prove that it is a real world, so believers are aware that they live in the presence of God's love though they are unable to prove it by any dialectical argument.[43] In either case the reason why it is rational to live in this way is that we have a right to trust our experiences except when we have reason to doubt that they are veridical. Yet if countervailing considerations have been taken into account and challenges taken seriously, then in the absence of adequate grounds for doubt it is rational to trust our putative experiences.[44]

But all this is only true of first hand experiences; and these we cannot communicate. We cannot communicate God's presence to others but only the particular way in which we have apprehended it. We can communicate our feelings and beliefs about God, but not God. We can

---

[42] J. Baillie, *The Sense of the Presence of God*, New York 1962, 213.

[43] Cf. T. Penelum's ›Parity Argument‹ in: *God and Skepticism*, Dordrecht 1983, chs. 67f.

[44] Cf. the principle of credulity as R. Swinburne states it: »How things seem to be is good grounds for a belief about how things are«, R. Swinburne, *The Existence of God*, Oxford 1979, 254; Alston, *Perceiving God*, 194-197.

hope to create a sense of the presence of God in others, but not make God present to them. We cannot do it, and we need not do it: If God is present to our present God is present to their present. So all we can and need to do is to draw their attention to God's presence, but not present God to them. Conversely, whatever we believe about God on the basis of communications by others is only a second hand belief about God, but not a first-hand belief in God based on our own apprehensions of God's presence. In this way we learn how others feel about God, but not acquire ourselves a sense of the presence of God.

But Christian faith is not a set of beliefs about past events but faith in a present reality. The prime interest of Christian communication therefore is to help those with whom it gets involved to develop a sense of the presence of God and to discover how God is present and active in their own lives and world. The Christian Gospel is not a piece of information about the past, but a pointer to a present reality that can and should be discerned by everyone, however, by everyone in his or her own way.

God's presence and activity as mediated by the Spirit to each and every present is singularly unique, and it is particularised only by the myriad of ways in which God's becoming present to our present is perceived, apprehended, believed or consciously noticed. We all have such apprehensions, even if we are not all and always aware of it for we owe our present to God becoming present. Thus in a basic sense nobody has to be taught to be religious, because we all are.[45] What we have to be taught is how to re-present our apprehensions of God both to ourselves and to others in a way that is adequate to what we apprehend. Not everyone is aware of how he or she is involved in God's presence; and not everybody is able to form adequate beliefs, or give adequate expression to one's beliefs, of what he or she has apprehended.

It is the point of religious instruction to enable people to become aware of God's presence and to provide them with the means to re-present it to themselves (in their feelings, emotions and beliefs) and to others (in the communication of their feelings, emotions and beliefs) in ways that are adequate to what they apprehend. Religious instruction is important not because it is interesting to learn about the feelings, emotions and beliefs of other people but because it helps us to

---

[45] If by ›being religious‹ we mean ›living in the presence of God‹ and not in a more restricted way ›participating in a particular religious practice‹ or ›using the symbolic means of a particular religious tradition‹.

discover, clarify and express our own mostly unconscious and vague feelings, emotions and beliefs. Its aim is not to produce religious experiences, but to help people to sort out and clarify the experiences that they all have. For contrary to what current opinion holds the problem of our time is not the lack of religious experience, but the confused state of it and the widespread incapacity to develop vague impressions into clearer insights due to the growing incompetence in using the interpretative resources of our religious traditions.

These resources are not as lightly to be dismissed as many think today. If God really presents himself to us by adapting his ways of becoming present to our ways of apprehending, it is not unreasonable to expect true insights and proper re-presentations of God's presence to be found in our religious traditions. These insights are not to be mistaken for non-debatable dogmas for the faithful to believe and the godless to ignore. But they provide criteria to probe the foundations of our own experiences, to sort out the unacceptable, confused and harmful from the acceptable, humane and helpful in our beliefs, and to achieve a profounder understanding of what we may have apprehended only dimly. The truth of doctrine does not depend on this use. But if it does not help us to achieve a clearer awareness of how God is present with our own lives, it will lose whatever persuasive power it has left; and it will hardly achieve this purpose unless it is part of a religious way of life.

Therefore it is neither romantic traditionalism nor intellectual backwardness to insist on a public practice of religion. We need to cultivate common means of discovering, expressing, communicating and testing our sense of presence to be a sense of the presence of God if we want to move beyond vague intuitions, confused feelings and, perhaps, momentary flashes of insight to a life lived consciously in the presence of God. We need a socially established practice of religious interpretation that enables us to communicate about and critically explore our religious experiences and, perhaps even more importantly, our *sense of presence* in all our dealings with our world and with ourselves. And we need this practice to provide a common language for expressing and communicating our sense of our presence as a sense, or lack of sense, of the presence of God, and we need it to provide criteria for sorting out the helpful from the misleading that have stood the test of time. To make these symbolic means available is the primary task of public religion – not to create religious feelings that we all have.

VII Conflicting Re-Presentations

1. Religions in a World of Many Cultures

The Christian sense of the presence of God is a sense of the change of life that takes place when one becomes aware of living in the present of God. It discloses God's presence to be the creative, salvific and perfecting reality without which neither a life ignoring God nor a life aware of God's presence nor the becoming aware of it would be possible: to be present is to be present to God; to become present is for God to become present to our present; and to become aware of this is to be unable to close one's eyes any longer to the presence of God's presence. This effects a re-orientation of one's life that may occur suddenly or slowly but always involves everything: The sense of the presence of God is not restricted to a particular strand or area of life. It leaves no area of life untouched but affects everything by providing a new direction and mode in which we live our lives.

Now this sense involves both presentation and re-presentation at various levels of symbolisation, as we have seen, and different re-presentations result in different and sometimes opposing versions of the sense of the presence of God. This is true of individual lives as much as of groups and traditions. The sense of the presence of God does not occur independently of a religious practice, and religious practices differ widely and in more than one respect.

This poses problems for a reflective account of the sense of the presence of God, not only in theology but also in philosophy of religion. Conflicting versions of the sense of the presence of God regularly result in conflicting theologies. They cannot be overcome by integrating them into a more comprehensive theology. Each theology, however comprehensive, is tied to a potential or actual conflicting point of view so that the religious and theological conflicts are not overcome but restated.

The same is true of philosophical reflection, especially if philosophy of religion is understood and practiced as »hermeneutics of contemplation«, as D. Z. Phillips has proposed under changing headings for many years.[1] Its aims are neither apologetic nor in principle critical of

---

[1] D.Z. Phillips, *Philosophy's Cool Place*, Ithaca, New York 1999; *Religion and the Hermeneutics of Contemplation*, Cambridge 2001.

religion. Rather it seeks to keep the insights and to avoid the pitfalls of both sides by rescuing »atheism, as much as belief, from distortions of itself«.[2] Its main concern is »with doing justice to possibilities of religious sense«[3] by understanding religions in their own terms. For Phillips is convinced that there are distinctive religious meanings, neither in general to be criticised nor in principle in need of justification, but a constant source of wonder and amazement, and hence an unceasing occasion for philosophical contemplation.

However, few of those who have praised or criticised his approach have paid enough attention to the fact that his belief in distinctive religious meanings is only the first part of the more complex view »that although there are distinctive religious meanings, these cannot be what they are independent of their relation to other aspects of human life and culture«.[4] Religions exist not *in vacuo,* but in cultures. They do so because it is *people* who are religious (or not religious), and people live their lives in complex human cultures. This is why understanding religions *in their own terms* is not a matter of moving in closed circles of religious meanings but requires us to take their relations to other aspects of human life and culture into account, including their relations to other religions. To understand religions in their own terms is to understand the role they play in human life and culture.

This is an endless task, for a number of reasons. We know religion only through religions, which are not independent of cultures. But there are cultures such as ours in which many different religions exist so that it is impossible to understand any religion without taking its relations to other religions into account. And there are religions such as Judaism, Christianity or Islam that exist, or have existed, in many different cultures so that understanding any one of them becomes a very complex issue indeed. For how do these religions, *in their own terms*, relate to other religions in a common culture, or to different cultures in a world of many religions, or to different religions in a world of many cultures? Conflict and dialogue, change and toleration are obvious issues at stake here. Has a contemplative philosophy of religions anything interesting to contribute to these questions?

To contemplate these questions, and some possible answers, I begin with some simple but important truths, first about *culture*, then about *religion*.

---

[2] Phillips, *Religion and the Hermeneutics of Contemplation*, 5.
[3] Ibid, 325.
[4] Ibid, 25.

2. Culture

For the present purpose, I suggest to define *culture* not normatively (›high culture‹ vs. ›common‹ or ›popular culture‹) but descriptively: In the broadest sense possible, culture is that aspect of human common life »which is socially rather than genetically transmitted.«[5] Six points are important here.

1. Culture is *relative to a group or community.*[6] Human beings differ from other primates by having a culture. In this sense »[c]ulture is the defining mark of human life.«[7] But what does it involve? According to recent research in cultural anthropology, the *possibility of culture* is based on the human cognitive capacity to identify with the other, to distinguish between one's own perspective and the perspectives of others, and to understand the intentions of others as being different from one's own. This capacity of taking the place of the other enabled human beings to develop ways of *social and cultural learning in communities*. And this, we are told, made all the difference: Whereas biological progress is tied to slow genetic mutation in individuals, humans have sped up the process of evolution by learning in communities.[8] Human communities have developed reliable means of storing and transmitting knowledge in a generation-transcending way. ›Culture‹ is the summary term for this communal capacity and activity.

2. Since culture is always *a culture of*, it *varies with social group or community*. Whereas all and only human beings have culture, not all human beings have the same culture. Culture comes in the plural, and not every culture is everyone's culture.

3. Cultures are trans-individual, but they *are not based on agreement*. *›Agreement‹* is a way of overcoming differences by argument and decision, and ›consensus‹ is an achievement in the light of opposing opin-

---

[5] Anthony O'Hear, ›Culture‹, *Routledge Encyclopaedia of Philosophy*, London 1998, 746-750, 746.

[6] Some well-known definitions of ›culture‹ miss this point, e.g. L. White, *The Science of Culture*, New York 1949: »Culture is the name of a distinct order, or class, of phenomena, namely those things and events that are dependent upon the exercise of a mental ability peculiar to the human species, that we have termed symbolling [i.e., the invention and use of symbols]. It is an elaborate mechanism, an organization of ways and means employed by a particular animal, man, in the struggle for existence and survival.«

[7] K. Tanner, *Theories of Culture. A New Agenda for Theology*, Minneapolis, Minnesota 1997, 25.

[8] M. Tomasello, *The Cultural Origins of Human Cognition*, Cambridge, Massachusetts 1999.

ions or positions. But a *culture* comprises what we take for granted and what goes without saying, and that is not based on agreement. What we take for granted is neither coherent nor consistent nor accepted by all nor acceptable to everyone in the same way. It is often riddled with inconsistencies and the source of disagreement as much as of agreement. Before we can even begin to agree, or disagree, about anything, we live our lives in the light of the tacit assumptions and highly inconsistent beliefs of our life-world and culture. They may (and need to) be questioned, but not all at once. And it is an open question, which of them will be accepted by whom and to what extent when made explicit.

4. It follows that cultures *are not dependent on social consensus*. Participants in the same culture do not necessarily hold common beliefs and sentiments or behave and act in the same ways. Cultures are not principles of social order that are binding for all their members. As human constructions they form the basis for conflict as much as they form the basis for shared belief and sentiment. They provide common orientation, but they do not enforce identical behaviour.

5. Cultures are *products of historical process,* and they are *contingent*. They have been made by human beings, and are constantly changed by them. Every culture could have been otherwise, and just as communities differ, so do cultures. There is to this day no ›global culture‹ worth that name; there are only *particular cultural traditions*[9], some of which have universal aspirations and define global standards, which they expect others to accept. Other cultures often reject those standards because they have not been involved in formulating and disseminating those views, values and standards. For, as a rule, a culture only incorporates *what it can appreciate in its own perspective as a possible future for itself.* Whatever it cannot see as a possible continuation of its own legacy and tradition, it will not accept but reject, and insist on being different.

6. Cultures are *adaptable* to changing contexts because they are *internally differentiated.* There are not only *differences among cultures* there also are *differences within cultures.* Cultures are not internally consistent wholes; rather they include their own alternatives and have their own internal principles of change. Thus every culture is pregnant with other cultures, and every given state of a culture is in transition to a varie-

---

[9] Living traditions are communities with a (particular) culture of symbolic communication, social organisation, and generation-transcending learning, but there is no TRADITION in capital letters because there is no community of communities that includes all and everyone.

ty of possible other states. In some of these possible futures religion plays a role, in others it doesn't; and which will be the case, depends on how religion makes its present felt in a given culture.

3. Religious Pluralism

There are obvious similarities between *cultures* and *religions*. Just as culture exists only in cultures, so religion – whatever we mean by the term – *exists only in religions*. And just as cultures display a luxuriant diversity of beliefs and practices, so do religions. *Religious pluralism* is a fact, and it can take many different forms, both within and among cultures. There are cultures with a single or a dominant religion, and there are other cultures that are composed of many different religions. Again, there are pluralist religious cultures that superimpose a civil religious structure on religions (Roman religion; Varro's tripartite division of mythical, political and natural theologies). And there are other religiously pluralist cultures, which refrain from organising or evaluating the plurality of religious and non-religious views and ways of life (Western culture; distinction between private and public life).

Attempts at *reducing religious plurality to a single religious outlook or a common core of all religious convictions* have not only failed in fact but fail in principle. This is borne out by all the major accounts of religion that are commonly discussed. Thus *reductive naturalism* claims that religious beliefs about a transcendent reality are all false. *Exclusivism*, whether doctrinal or soteriological, holds that only one religion (one's own) is true and offers an effective path to salvation, whereas all others are believed to be false and to lead astray. *Inclusivism* claims that although one religion (one's own) contains the final truth, others contain approaches or approximations to it. And *pluralism* holds that »a single ultimate religious reality is being differently experienced and understood in all the major religious traditions; they all, as far as we can tell, offer equally effective paths to salvation or liberation«.[10]

All four options fail to convince because they assume something that cannot be shown to be true, i.e. that all religions are false (*naturalism*); that only one religion (one's own) is true (*exclusivism*); that one religion (one's own) contains the final truth of all religions (*inclusivism*); that all religions are about the same ultimate reality (*pluralism*). None of these views can convincingly be argued and defended on neutral

---

[10] Ph.L. Quinn, ›Religious Pluralism‹, *Routledge Encyclopaedia of Philosophy*, London 1998, 260–264, 260.

and universal grounds. Rather, reasonable people can, and do, reasonably disagree on these issues. Moreover, each of these convictions
holds a much-oversimplified view of religion. Religions are much too
diverse and multifaceted, both within and among themselves, to be
judged and evaluated in such a global and indiscriminate manner. A religion may involve, on the one hand, strands that are acceptable to a
culture (but not to others) and, on the other hand, strands that go contrary to some deeply held convictions of that culture (but not of others). There is never a one to one match between a religion and a culture but always agreement as well as disagreement.

   Thus a religion may cease informing a culture by becoming either
too distant or too adaptive to it. It may be on the wane because it has
become too foreign or too familiar. The first is well known, but the
second is not always taken seriously enough. A religion may become
unable to relate to other cultures, or to a changing cultural situation,
by concentrating too exclusively on those (rational or mystical, doctrinal or ritual) strands that are acceptable to a given culture while divesting itself of everything that runs against the grain of that culture (e.g.
Modernist Protestantism and Catholicism). Being too successful in a
culture can do as much harm to a religion as losing all appeal to its cul-
tured despisers.

4. Religions and Cultures

What is important to note, therefore, is that *religions relate differently to
culture.* This is true of *different religions in different cultures* but also of *the
same religion in different cultures* (Christianity in antiquity and modernity) and of a *particular religion in a particular culture* (Christianity in Britain).

   Moreover, whereas all religions have some impact on a culture, not
all religions carry their own culture with them. Some religions are intrinsically allied to a culture; they cannot be transplanted into another
cultural context without being seriously weakened or destroyed. Other religions are vehicles of a particular culture because they are tied to
a holy language, a book or a ritual practice that is part and parcel of a
specific cultural tradition.

   Again, there are religions, which *proselytize* because they are *not* tied
to a particular culture (such as Christianity); and there are others,
which *proselytize* because they are part of a particular culture, which
they seek to disseminate (such as Islam). The Christian faith, for example, is not tied to a particular culture but a way of *transforming, modify-*

ing, improving (in some respects), *and ending* (in other respects) certain strands in a culture. It is not a ›religion of a book‹ but has always existed only in translations. Throughout its history it has attracted interest precisely because of its critical distance to the cultural matrix of the time. This is why it has been able to give direction to a culture and to engage critically with its own and other cultural traditions.

A religion's engagement with a culture results in a particular *configuration*, i.e. a combination of its religious ends with the particularities of the cultural matrix in which it operates. These configurations change over time, and just as sometimes a culture cannot live up to the developments of a religion (cf. the rise of Christianity in antiquity) so a religion may fail to keep up with the changes in a culture. That is why it is important for a religion to relate *critically* to a culture, i.e. distinguish between itself and the cultural matrix in which it operates; otherwise it will be too directly involved in the rise and fall of that culture. On the other hand, as a living religion it must *relate* to a culture. It is always a meaningful question to ask how a culture has been changed by a religion, and how a religion has been changed through engagement with that culture.

There is no single answer to these questions because there is no single role that religions play in a culture. *Religions are not means to a particular cultural end.* If they serve a purpose in culture or society, they do so because of what they *are* and not the other way round. If a religion was nothing but its function in a culture, another could replace it without loss. But that's not how things are. So in a very important respect whether a religion continues or not depends on that religion itself. It keeps going when its interests are strong and it succeeds in (being) convincing. But the motivation must lie within the religion itself, not merely in its cultural surroundings. If it has a message to live by, it will engage in transmitting it. If not, it won't make an impact.

Religions do not all serve the same end but there is an *actual diversity of religious ends*. If differences between religions are to be overcome (and this does not seem to be necessary everywhere, in each case and in every respect) they are not overcome by concentrating on what religions share in common, but on what divides them. A worldwide agreement between religions, for example, will hardly take the form of agreement on common content (on what we all share) but rather on irreducible differences (on the ways in which we differ). But then what must be explored is the distinctive contribution a religion makes to the direction of human life and the resolution of human conflict within and among cultures. Since there is no general answer to this question, it has to be explored and answered in each particular case.

5. Deep Conflict

This is particularly difficult where a religion identifies with a culture or cultural tradition. Then exploring the religion becomes indistinguishable from exploring a particular culture. But if religions were themselves dictated by cultural forces, it would appear that they could have no decisive direction to provide to their cultures.[11] What we normally find, therefore, are differences between the value orientation of a religion and a culture.

These differences can be the source of *deep conflict* between religions and cultures. *Deep conflict* arises from conflict of underlying value orientations that are taken for granted in a religion and in a culture. Where disagreement cuts that deep, where it concerns not merely particular values or styles of life but underlying background convictions, progress can only be made, as some argue, if all parties involved accept the *contingency* of their religious and cultural orientations. Whatever they are, *they could have been otherwise.* Yet isn't this precisely why *what they are,* is so important to them? The difficulty is not that religious believers are asked to accept the contingency of their religion and yet believe that it provides reliable (›true‹) orientation in life, indeed a better and more reliable orientation than any rival religion or world-view. This, or something like this, is a well-known problem in many areas of human life, and we know how to handle it. The religious difficulty is viewing religions in this way at all, i.e., as *options* that we rationally chose because they look more likely to achieve certain ends, or to achieve them better, than any other religious or non-religious alternative. This is not how believers relate to their religion, at least not normally and in traditional religions.

However, we live in a pluralistic culture today, and sociologists keep reminding us that the »pluralistic situation is, above all, a *market situation*«.[12] A »religion«, Peter Berger argues, »can no longer be imposed, but must be marketed«[13]. But this alternative is neither convincing nor compelling. A religion like Judaism, for example, survives neither by

---

[11] Cf. S.M. Heim, *Salvations. Truth and Difference in Religion*, New York ⁵2001, 199.

[12] P. Berger, *The Social Reality of Religion*, Harmondsworth 1973, 142.

[13] Ibid., 148.

being ›imposed‹ nor by being ›marketed as an option‹ but by the way it is lived and practised and handed on in a particular community from one generation to another.

And as in this case, so in many others: Whether and how a religion continues are questions that each religion has to answer for itself, in its own terms and by its own practice. It will not normally see and present itself as a mere option among others but as a way and a view of life that has to be understood and appreciated in its own terms. If a religion »meets the challenges of others purely in terms of pragmatic accommodation what is distinctively its own will be lost[14]«. Religions are forms of life and practice that seek to provide orientation in life. This requires more of them than meeting the challenge of a given culture. They must point beyond it and critically engage with a culture with the aim of *transforming* it in the light of their objectives. At the end of the day a religion survives not by being successfully marketed but by being practised as a way of life that convinces by the orientation it provides and by the example of those whose lives it informs and transforms.

6. Transformative Contemplation

If religions aim at change and transformation, is this also true of philosophy of religion? Philosophy of religion does not pursue the same end as religion, only in a rational, less confused or more defensible way. It contemplates (explores, describes, analyses, imaginatively reconstructs) religious orientations, but it does not itself provide any religious orientation. It talks *about* religions, but it is not itself a *move within* a religion, or a better alternative to it.

Many philosophers have made this point, most prominently L. Wittgenstein, R. Rhees and D. Z. Phillips: Philosophy leaves everything as it is.[15] It has no message for anyone, and *a fortiori* not a religious message. Its task is to contemplate religion, not to meddle with it, and to »contemplate possibilities of sense is different from advocating those possibilities, or of finding a faith to live by in them«.[16] Philosophy of religion is not to be mistaken for a rational substitute of religion and philosophers should stop the futile and misguided attempts to replace

---

[14] Phillips, *Religion and the Hermeneutics of Contemplation*, 269.

[15] L. Wittgenstein, *Philosophische Untersuchungen*, §124, Kritisch-genetische Edition, ed. J. Schulte et. al., Frankfurt 2001, 814.

[16] Phillips, *Religion and the Hermeneutics of Contemplation*, 5.

the alleged confusions of religions by more rational constructions of their own, or to provide us with a message to guide us in life.[17] This ruins philosophy, plays into the hands of religious sceptics[18], fails to improve religion, and doesn't help to sort out conflict, to say nothing of deep conflict, between religions.

But then why engage in philosophy of religion at all? What has been said so far cannot be the whole story. Wittgenstein, for one, »never saw philosophy as an exercise in quietism«.[19] He claimed that philosophy leaves everything as it is, but he also encouraged a certain way of looking at things, and he clearly thought that this way is philosophically more appropriate than other ways.

This does not imply that there is an appropriate way of looking at religions, a way which Phillips has restated as ›contemplation‹. There is no such thing as ›the appropriate view of religion‹, or ›the only adequate way of doing philosophy‹. Sometimes philosophy's task is contemplation and description, at other times criticism, polemics, imaginative invention, apologetics or direction. The way in which we philosophise depends on the questions that trouble, confuse or provoke us. Contemplation is often but not always the appropriate way to respond. But it is not a monolithic activity, and we can do different things through philosophical contemplation. Sometimes it can help us to see what was mistaken in our understanding (or misunderstanding) of a religion. Sometimes it may deepen and confirm our previous understandings. And sometimes it may open our eyes to something we hadn't noticed before. Philosophical contemplation can have different effects: dispel illusions, clarify problems, correct mistakes, change opinions, suggest improvements or confirm views. But it does have effects, not in changing what it contemplates but in changing those who contemplate.

The whole point of doing philosophy, as M. J. Ferreira has rightly pointed out, is to be »working on oneself‹, and ultimately working on oneself is a matter of changing ›one's way of seeing things‹«.[20] Philoso-

---

[17] Cf. ibid., 318.

[18] Cf. L. Ashdown, *Anonymous Skeptics. Swinburne, Hick, and Alston*, Tübingen 2002.

[19] M.J. Ferreira, ›Vision and Love: A Wittgensteinian Ethic in *Culture and Value*‹, in: J. Stout/R. MacSwain (eds.), *Grammar and Grace: Reformulations of Aquinas and Wittgenstein*, London 2004, 214-231, 226. Cf. M.J. Ferreira, ›Normativity and Reference in a Wittgensteinian Philosophy of Religion‹, *Faith and Philosophy* 18, 2002, 443-464.

[20] Ferreira, ›Vision and Love: A Wittgensteinian Ethic in *Culture and Value*‹, 226.

phers may indeed be well advised to aim merely at contemplating the world, not at changing it. They contemplate possibilities of sense even when they think about the actualities of life. They do so by placing the actual against the backdrop of the possible and explore the many ways in which what happens to be the case could have been otherwise. Their experimental thinking does not change the world, but it changes them so that they see the world, and their own place in it, differently. Philosophical contemplation is an exercise in transformation – self-transformation.

So why do we start philosophising, about religion or anything else? Not because we decide to do so, but because we cannot help it. We are confused by what we see, or think we see, in a religion. We cannot understand why others believe what they do, or why they don't believe what we take to be self-evident, or believe what to us looks very strange or quite unacceptable. Not only Locke had occasion to wonder why »religion, which should most distinguish us from beasts, and ought most peculiarly to elevate us, as rational creatures, above brutes, is that wherein men often appear most irrational and more senseless than beasts themselves«. Why are so many believers »led into so strange opinions, and extravagant practices in religion, that a considerate man cannot but stand amazed at their follies, and judge them so far from being acceptable to the great and wise God, that he cannot avoid thinking them ridiculous, and offensive to a sober good man«[21]?

Perhaps we are more amazed about Locke than about what he was amazed about. But there are plenty of reasons to be confused, amazed or wondering about religion. Unless we are, we won't philosophise, and while we are, we cannot stop philosophising. We seek to overcome our own confusions by contemplation, but we cannot tell how it will be possible or whether it can be achieved. We contemplate what we cannot understand or what makes us wonder. But unless *we ourselves* engage in contemplation, we cannot gain anything from philosophy. Philosophical problems cannot be solved by proxy. What others have thought, or said, or written may guide our reflection or provoke our contemplation. But we have to reflect and contemplate it ourselves if we want to overcome our confusions and find answers to our questions. Philosophy is *Selbstdenken*, as Kant has summed up the enlightenment tradition, not because we have no other topic to think about than ourselves, but because we ourselves have to do the thinking if philosophical contemplation is to have any point. *Sapere aude* is a

---

[21] J. Locke, *Essay concerning Human Understanding*, book IV, chap. XVIII, para. 1.

philosophical injunction which each has to follow by herself or himself, in contemplating religion as much as in any other matter.

Philosophy of religion, as all philosophy, is contemplation. It contemplates problems provoked by religions. Not just any problems a religion may pose, and not the problems others may have, but those *we*
have. So *we* have to do the contemplating. We contemplate what
amazes us, why it amazes us, and why it doesn't amaze others. And in
doing so we find ourselves engaged in transformative contemplation –
transformative not by changing the religions we contemplate, but us
who contemplate them.

7. Differences and Conflicts

We live in a world of many religions with many different ends. But *actual religious differences are not a root evil that needs to be overcome in each
and every case.* No one will deny that there are differences between a
Muslim, a Buddhist and a Christian that are not in practice reconcila-
ble. But even if in some respects religious differences amount to value
conflicts, value conflict is not necessarily something to be resolved or
avoided. It is not a form of inconsistency within a single coherent system. Yet only inconsistency, not conflict, needs avoiding, at least with
respect to ideas, beliefs, values and sentiments.

Moreover, conflict among religions, or between religions and culture, cannot be contained by attempting *to integrate all differences into a
rich and more comprehensive whole.* Even within one and the same society
we do not need a common (or the same) ›sense of the whole‹ in order
to live peacefully together but legal, political and juridical structures
that enable us to live together in the light of irreconcilable differences.[22] The stability of culturally and religiously diverse societies does
not depend on a common ideology or on any shared ethical tradition
but on legal, political and juridical institutions that function independently of any particular religion, world-view, ideology or morality.[23]

This is not to say that we should never seek to remove conflicts in
values. But both individuals and communities are capable of tolerating
a considerable amount of value conflict in their personal and communal affairs. So we must be careful. It is not prudent to try to sort out
what doesn't need to be sorted out to solve a particular problem. We

---

[22] See above chap. 1.

[23] Cf. for a similar argument R. Audi, *Religious Commitment and Secular Reason*,
New York 2000, esp. chap. 3.

may even create conflict by trying to reconcile differences that do not, or need not, lead to conflict here and now. Moreover, ways of life such as religions are not systems of belief that stand and fall with being consistent in every possible respect. So insisting on principles and consequences without regard for the particularities of a given situation may do more harm than good. Nobody will deny that peacemaking among religions is desirable and good. But in times of peace, attempts at peacemaking may create conflict rather than help to avoid it. Not every difference is a conflict that needs to be solved, and not every conflict stands in the way of peaceful coexistence.

So we must pay attention to the particularities of a situation, both in our private and public lives. In private life, inconsistency is intolerable only when we recognise conflict among *our own* value commitments, not when ours differ from those of others.[24] Only in the context of public policy formation may it become necessary to sort out value conflicts among different religious orientations.

But for this *we need no common agreement on some shared fundamental values or a common view of the good life.* All we need for peaceful coexistence are legal, political and juridical structures that enable us to live together with different value orientations. This implies institutions that have the right and power to sort out conflicts between us in ways that *have been accepted as acceptable* by all parties involved, and hence justify the use of legitimate coercion if necessary. That is, when conflict arises that needs sorting out we must, in the last resort, be able to fall back on justified ways of coercion that have been accepted, *for whatever reasons*, by the parties involved independently of the particular conflict at stake. *Commitment to law, not a common morality or a shared ethical code* is what is needed for peaceful coexistence. And that commitment may be *justified in a plurality of ways*, religious and non-religious, not merely by public reasons that are not connected to any particular religious or ethical tradition and which any rational citizen would accept.

8. Dialogue

This is why dialogue among religions is important but not enough. Dialogue is not a way of solving conflicts or of overcoming differences but of identifying and clarifying them; it falls short of decision. Dialogue may prepare the way for it, but it cannot end a conflict. This is

---

[24] I. Levi, *The Covenant of Reason. Rationality and the Commitments of Thought*, Cambridge 1997, 237.

true of dialogue among individual believers as much as it is of dialogue among official representatives of religious traditions.

Moreover, dialogue is never ›inter-religious‹ in the sense of being a comprehensive meeting of religions in all their respects. On the contrary, dialogue is always particular and specific, not holistic and general; it is local and not independent of the particularities of a situation; and it is not always effective in the same way. Dialogue among individuals of different religious or cultural traditions may change, for example, a believer's system of beliefs and values (i.e. effect individual changes of outlook and orientation). But for the whole religious community a dialogue becomes effective only if its results are officially received and accepted according to the agreed procedures of the community in question. And while this may occasionally be a way of overcoming past conflicts among religions, it rarely helps to avoid or to solve actual conflict.

What we need, therefore, is not only dialogue among religions but also public debate that paves the way towards decision. In conflicts of value orientation (among religions or among religions and cultures) we must sort out the defensible from the unacceptable in public debate, and this is not something to be left to the religions alone.

What is defensible cannot be decided in advance but will only show in the actual process of making both these differences and their grounds publicly accessible and debatable. Some of these may turn out to be unacceptable to all or most of us for a variety of reasons. Some may be acceptable to some but not be live options for others. And some may turn out to be of much wider interest and relevance than we had expected. Clarifying defensible differences in public debate, therefore, is a means of improving both one's own religious tradition and one's understanding of others. And knowing in which respect one is different, and why, and how others react to it, and why, is a prerequisite for peacefully coexisting in religiously and culturally diverse societies.

What we need, therefore, are not common religious convictions but agreement on public procedures of debate, defence, contest, and decision-making that enable people with different interests, moral codes, and views of the good life to live together without using physical or mental force to sort out their differences.

Our societies are comprised of an increasing number of citizens who lack a common religious background and history. This fact by itself is no reason to worry about imminent culture wars or global clashes of civilisations. But to contain the potentially destructive effects of religious diversity, we must learn to appreciate, not merely what we hold in common, but what makes us differ, and perhaps irreconcilably so. Tolerance is the cement of our societies. But the crucial respect is for persons, not beliefs, moral codes, or practices. We must find out what constitutes the irrevocable otherness of the other, i.e., his or her religious identity, and in the last resort, this otherness is to be found, not in what we share, but in what distinguishes us.

The promising route to take in dealing with religious diversity, therefore, is (1) to make publicly accessible what lies at the heart of religious convictions and traditions and (2) to construct rules, rights[25] and institutions of justified coercion to deal with problems provoked by those differences without expecting these rules to lead to global consensus or a common view of life. After all, common convictions are no guarantee against conflict. On the contrary, even where there is a lot in common (such as in the Christian churches), it is often precisely what is shared in common, which is the basis of conflict. Here as elsewhere it is not *what is believed* but *the way it is believed* which decides on the rationality of these beliefs and the defensibility of the corresponding moral codes and ways of life.

But there is no valid reason why all rational beliefs and defensible views should have to be part of the same more encompassing whole. Different religious beliefs may be reasonable for different persons for different reasons without being part of some larger whole. This admission is not to give in to relativism. Just as there are no beliefs that are not beliefs of someone, so there are no reasons that are not reasons for someone. But there are well-grounded beliefs that are false (e.g. scientific beliefs), there are ill-grounded beliefs that are true, and there are incompatible beliefs that are well-grounded for different persons, although one of them must, or all of them may, be false.

Yet the problem is not merely one of the compatibility or incompatibility of beliefs. Religious beliefs are intimately bound up with ways of life and practices, and just as one cannot love everyone at once in the same way, so a person cannot seriously engage in a plurality of religious activities at the same time. What is at stake here is not the *logical incompatibility of opposing religious beliefs*, but the *factual impossibility of living more than one life at once*. In this respect we have no choice. We live in one way, and thereby exclude other ways. We may change our way

---

[25] »Human rights are historical constructions, not natural kinds«, as John Clayton has rightly pointed out (›Common Ground and Defensible Difference‹, in: L. Rouner (ed.), *Politics and Peace*, South Bend 1999, 27).

of living, and constantly do. But this doesn't alter the basic situation. We live only one of the lives that we might and could have lived. Life is a series of decisions many of which depend on decisions taken by others, and we cannot know in advance whether what we chose, or find ourselves to have chosen, will turn out to be right. So we must seriously entertain the possibility that we may be wrong and the other right. And this, some have argued, is one of the main and most compelling reasons for us to practice *toleration*.

9. Toleration

Now *toleration*, as I. Berlin has argued, »implies a certain disrespect. I tolerate your absurd beliefs and your foolish acts, though I know them to be absurd and foolish«[26]. This is quite different from genuine respect. Genuine respect differs from both contemptuous toleration and pseudo respect in that I genuinely entertain the other view as a serious possibility. If I really take it seriously, I must be prepared to change my convictions.[27]

This attitude is sometimes but not always appropriate. Our »[b]eliefs ... are resources of deliberation. We use them as a standard for assessing propositions with respect to serious possibility.«[28] We do not change or drop that standard at will, and hence we cannot accept each and every other belief as a serious possibility.

That is to say, we must distinguish between the *etiquette* of debate and controversy and the *ethics* of controversy. Etiquette may require me to I pick my words carefully and to keep my views to myself if not asked. But the ethics of controversy demand of me that I do not pretend to take another view seriously if I am not prepared to entertain the serious possibility of changing my own views in the light of it. And

---

[26] I. Berlin, *Four Essays on Liberty*, Oxford 1969, 184. In a similar way ›toleration‹ is defined by H. Ineichen, Lebenswelt und soziale Welt. Toleranz in einer pluralistischen Gesellschaft (private communication): »›Toleranz‹ meint ... die Duldung von Personen, Handlungen oder Meinungen, die aus religiösen oder moralischen Gründen abgelehnt werden.« However, this does not, as he argues, presuppose »eine von weiten Teilen der Bürger als richtig anerkannte, für richtig gehaltene Auffassung in Glaubenssachen und moralischen Überzeugungen«. It merely requires an *individual conviction* in the matter concerned. Whether my view agrees with others or not, I tolerate the views of others if I do not stop them to hold and propagate what I believe to be wrong and misguided ideas.

[27] Levi, *The Covenant of Reason*, 241.

[28] Ibid., 244.

I can only entertain such a possibility seriously if I respect the authority of the one who propounds the view in question and/or see the point of that view as being important and a serious candidate for consideration in the area under discussion.

For example, if someone tells me that I am a product of a virgin birth[29], I do not show the non dogmatic open-mindedness that is rightly cherished in our societies if I pretend to take this view seriously by assigning it some (weak or very weak) probability rather than dismissing it out of hand. In everyday life as much as in the academy we have a moral obligation to call a stick a stick. If I really follow my convictions and act on that which I am sure to know, that's what I ought to do.

›But doesn't everyone deserve to get a serious hearing?‹ some may ask. Sure, but I am not obliged to accord everyone a serious hearing on every issue. I may pretend do so, but I am not seriously engaging with a view unless I am prepared to modify my own convictions. The »views of the competent ought to be taken seriously – at least concerning matters about which they are competent.« But on issues concerning which they lack authority, »we have no obligation to take them seriously«.[30] And on matters which we know we know better, we must accept that »[c]ontemptuous toleration is sometimes preferable to sceptical respect«.[31] The respect we owe others does not imply that we have to respect their wrong views. Wrong views may be tolerated, but not respected, and toleration does not oblige us to respect, or pretend to respect, what we know to be wrong. This is true in everyday life as much as in religion, as D.Z. Phillips rightly points out. »Nonsense remains nonsense even if we associate God's name with it«[32]. We tolerate it, but we are not obliged to take it seriously.

Similarly, »although it would be wrong to impose a legal ban against the publication of creationist views, there may not be good enough reasons« to take them seriously or to encourage their dissemination«[33]. Not all agree. Even if we are not obliged to open our minds to dissent without good reasons, aren't we obliged not merely to tolerate but to encourage and support the dissemination of dissenting views?[34] Not, I think, as a general rule. The positive desirability of proliferating dis-

---

[29] Levi's example.
[30] Ibid., 251.
[31] Ibid.
[32] D.Z. Phillips, *Belief, Change and Forms of Life,* Basingstoke and London 1986, 13.
[33] Levi, *The Covenant of Reason,* 252.
[34] Ibid.

senting ideas and of taking them seriously has to be justified in each case.

All this is also true with respect to religions. Here as elsewhere an open mind is one thing, an empty mind another. To give every view the same hearing or to take it to be just as important (or unimportant) as any other is to refrain from assessing it and to fall prey to what Isaac Levi has called the *skepticism of the empty mind*. But we never start from scratch. We all live in particular historical settings with contingent preferences for some views, values, and goals rather than others. Those preferences are not completely arbitrary but reflect past or present experiences of our communities that we would be ill advised to ignore. In a changing world we need to assess them critically in order not to fall prey to prejudice, error, and delusion. And we have developed criteria such as justice, goodness, freedom, equality etc. to do so. But we cannot transcend our contingent situations altogether. Our ideas of justice, goodness, freedom, or equality are tied up with specific experiences, practices and background assumptions of our culture. Their content and force can only be illumined and assessed against that background, and they lose their point and persuasive power when they become divorced from the wider cultural tradition to which they belong. Similarly, »although it would be wrong to impose a legal ban against the publication of creationist views, there may not be good enough reasons to take them seriously or to encourage their dissemination«. Not all agree. Even if we are not obliged to open our minds to dissent without good reasons, aren't we obliged not merely to tolerate but to encourage and support the dissemination of dissenting views? Not, I think, as a general rule. The positive desirability of proliferating dissenting ideas and of taking them seriously has to be justified in each case.

Now whereas ideas such as justice or equality provide good reasons for having an open mind for the views of others, they do not justify pretending to have an empty mind. We need to have good reasons for opening up our minds up so as to entertain seriously the dissenting religious or non-religious views of others. »The mere presence of disagreement is not such a good reason. If it were, it would equate toleration and respect for the views of dissenters. Since there will be a dissenter for virtually every substantive view, advocates of toleration who conflate it with respect for the views of dissenters must be urging upon us the skepticism of the empty mind«.[35] And whatever the dialogue be-

---

[35] Ibid., 3f.

tween religions and cultures hopes to achieve, this can't possibly be one of its objectives.

Bibliography

Abel, G., *Interpretationswelten. Gegenwartsphilosophie jenseits von Essentialismus und Relativismus*, Frankfurt 1995.

Adams, R.M., ›Religious Disagreement and Doxastic Practices‹, *Philosophy and Phenomenological Research* 54, 1994, 885-888.

-, *The Virtue of Faith and Other Essays in Philosophical Theology*, Oxford 1987.

Adelung, J.Chr., *Versuch eines vollständigen grammatisch-kritischen Wörterbuchs der hochdeutschen Mundart*, vol. 2, Leipzig 1755.

Alanus ab Insulis, *De Incarnatione Christi. Rhythmus Peregans*, MPL 210, 577-580a.

Alston, W.P., ›Christian Experience and Christian Belief‹, in: A. Plantinga/N. Wolterstorff (eds.), *Faith and Rationality*, Notre Dame, Indiana 1983, 103-134.

-, ›Does God Have Beliefs?‹, *Religious Studies* 22, 1987, 287-306.

-, *Perceiving God. The Epistemology of Religious Experience*, Ithaca, N.Y./London 1991.

-, ›Religious Experience and Religious Belief‹, *Nous* 16, 1982, 3-12.

Aquinas, Thomas, *Summa contra gentiles,* ed. and trans. K. Albert/P. Engelhardt, Darmstadt 1974ff.

-, *Summa Theologica.* Cura et studio Petri Caramello. Cum texto ex recensione Leonina, ed. P. Marietti, Torino [20]1952.

Ashdown, L., *Anonymous Skeptics. Swinburne, Hick, and Alston*, Tübingen 2002.

Audi, R., ›Liberal Democracy and the Place of Religion in Politics‹, in: R. Audi./N. Wolterstorff, *Religion in the Public Square. The Place of Religious Conviction in Political Debate*, Lanham, Maryland 1997, 1-66.

-, *Religious Commitment and Secular Reason*, Cambridge 2000.

-, ›The Place of Religious Argument in a Free and Democratic Society‹, *San Diego Law Review* 30, 1993, 647-675.

-, ›The Separation of Church and State and the Obligations of Citizenship‹, *Philosophy and Public Affairs* 18, 1989, 259-296.

-, ›The State, the Church, and the Citizen‹, in: P.J. Weithman (ed.), *Religion and Contemporary Liberalism*, Notre Dame, Indiana 1997, 38-75.

Augustinus, A., *De Doctrina Christiana libri IV,* MPL 34, 16-121.

Baelz, P.R., *Prayer and Providence,* New York 1968.
Baillie, J., *The Interpretation of Religion,* New York 1928 (reprint 1977).
-, *The Sense of the Presence of God.* Gifford Lectures, 1961-1962, New York 1962.
Barnes, J., *The Presocratic Philosophers,* London ²1982.
Berger, P., *The Social Reality of Religion,* Harmondsworth 1973.
Berkeley, G., *The Principles of Human Knowledge* (1710), ed. G.J. Warnock, Glasgow 1962.
Berking, H., *Schenken. Zur Anthropologie des Gebens,* Frankfurt am Main/New York 1996.
Berlin, I., *Four Essays on Liberty,* Oxford 1969.
Berry, Ph./Wernick, A. (eds.), *Shadow of Spirit: Postmodernism and Religion,* London/New York 1992.
Blumenberg, H., *Lebenszeit und Weltzeit,* Frankfurt am Main ²1986.
-, *Zu den Sachen und zurück,* Frankfurt am Main 2002.
Boethius, A.M.S., *Philosophiae consolationis,* in: H.F. Stewart/E.K. Rand (eds.), *Boethius: The Theological Tractates,* New York 1926.
Boeve, L./Leijssen, L. (eds.), *Sacramental Presence in a Postmodern Context,* Leuven 2001.
Boeve, L./Ries, J.C. (eds.), *The Presence of Transcendence. Thinking ›Sacrament‹ in a Postmodern Age,* Leuven 2001.
Boucourechliev, A., ›Messiaen‹, *The New Grove* XII, 1980.
Brown, H.I., *Rationality,* London/New York 1990.
Brümmer, V., *Speaking of a Personal God: An Essay in Philosophical Theology,* Cambridge 1992.

Caputo, J.D., ›Apostles of the Impossible‹, in: J.D. Caputo/M.J. Scanlon (eds.), *God, the Gift, and Postmodernism,* Bloomington, Indiana 1999, 185-222.
Carroll, L., *Through the Looking-Glass,* 1887.
Cartwright, J., *The English Constitution Produced and Illustrated,* London 1823.
Chauvet, L.-M., ›The Broken Bread as Theological Figure of Eucharistic Presence‹, in: L. Boeve/L. Leijssen (eds.), *Sacramental Presence in a Postmodern Context,* Leuven 2001, 236-262.
Clausen, G., *Schenken und Unterstützen in Primärbeziehungen. Materialen zu einer Soziologie des Schenkens,* Frankfurt am Main 1991.
Clayton, J., ›Common Ground and Defensible Difference‹, in: L. Rouner (ed.), *Religion, Politics and Peace,* Notre Dame, Indiana 1999, 104-127.

Collingwood, R.G., *An Essay on Metaphysics*, Oxford 1940.

Comay, R., ›Gifts Without Presents: Economicas of »Experience« in Bataille and Heidegger‹, *Yale French Studies* 778, 1990, 66-89.

Craig, W.L., ›God and Real Time‹, *Religious Studies* 26, 1990, 335-347.

-, *God, Time and Eternity. The Coherence of Theism II: Eternity*, Dordrecht 2000.

-, *The Tensed Theory of Time. A Critical Examination*, Dordrecht 2000.

-, *The Tenseless Theory of Time. A Critical Examination*, Dordrecht 2000.

-, *Time and Eternity. Exploring God's Relationship to Time*, Wheaton, Illinois 2001.

Dalferth, I.U., ›Alles Umsonst. Von der Kunst des Schenkens und den Grenzen der Gabe‹, in: M.M. Olivetti (ed.), *Le don et la dette*, Padova 2005, 53-76.

-, ›Becoming a Christian according to the *Postscript*. Kierkegaard's Christian Hermeneutics of Existence‹ (forthcoming).

-, *Die Wirklichkeit des Möglichen. Hermeneutische Religionsphilosophie*, Tübingen 2003.

-, *Evangelische Theologie als Interpretationspraxis. Eine systematische Orientierung*, Leipzig 2004.

-, *Existenz Gottes und christlicher Glaube. Skizzen zu einer eschatologischen Ontologie*, München 1984.

-, *Gedeutete Gegenwart. Zur Wahrnehmung Gottes in den Erfahrungen der Zeit*, Tübingen 1997.

-, ›God's Real Presence‹, in: T. Koistinen/T. Lehtonen (eds.), *Philosophical Studies in Religion, Metaphysics and Ethics. Essays in Honour of Heikki Kirjavainen*, Helsinki 1997, 35-59.

-, *Gott. Philosophisch-theologische Denkversuche*, Tübingen 1992.

-, ›Paradigm Lost. From the Sense of the Whole to the Sense of the Presence of God‹, in: D.A. Crosby/CH.D. Hardwick (eds.), *Religion in a Pluralistic Age. Proceedings of the Third International Conference on Philosophical Theology*, New York 2001, 21-48.

-, *Religiöse Rede von Gott*, München 1981.

-, ›Representing God's Presence‹, *International Journal of Systematic Theology* 3, 2001, 237-256.

-, ›Theological Fallacies. A Contribution‹, *The Heythrop Journal* 16, 1975, 389-404.

-, *Theology and Philosophy*, Eugene, Oregon 2001.

-, ›Time for God's Presence‹, in: M. Volf/C. Krieg/Th. Kucharz (eds.), *The Future of Theology. Essays in Honor of Jürgen Moltmann*, Grand Rapids, Michigan 1996, 127-141.

Damasio, A.R., *The Feeling of What Happens. Body and Emotion in the Making of Consciousness*, New York 1999.

Davis, C.F., *The Evidential Force of Religious Experience*, Oxford 1989.

Davis, P., ›Teleology without Teleology: Purpose through Emergent Complexity‹, in: P. Clayton/A. Peacocke (eds.), *In Whom We Live and Move and Have Our Being. Panentheistic Reflections on God's Presence in a Scientific World*, Grand Rapids, Michigan 2004, 95-108.

Davis, S.T., *Logic and the Nature of God*, Grand Rapids, Michigan 1983.

Dean, W., *The Religious Critic in American Culture*, New York 1994.

Derrida, J., *Donner le temps: 1. La fausse monnaie*, Paris 1991 (*Given Time: 1. Counterfeit Money*, trans. P. Kamuf, Chicago 1992).

-, *Sauf le nom (Post-Scriptum)*, Paris 1993.

-, *Speech and Phenomena and Other Essays on Husserl's Theory of Signs*, trans. D.B. Allison/N. Garver, Evanston 1973.

DeWeese, G.J., *God and the Nature of Time*, Burlington, Vermont 2004.

Dewey, J., *Human Nature and Conduct*, Middle Works Bd. 14, Carbondale and Edwardsville 1983.

Dressel, G./Hopf, G. (eds.), *Von Geschenken und anderen Gaben. Annäherungen an eine historische Anthropologie des Gebens*, Frankfurt am Main 2000.

Dummett, M., ›A Defense of McTaggart's Proof of the Unreality of Time‹, *Philosophical Review* 69, 1960, 497-507.

Ebeling, G., ›Cognitio Dei et hominis‹, in: *Lutherstudien I*, Tübingen 1971, 221-272.

Fales, E., ›Mystical Experience as Evidence‹, *International Journal for Philosophy of Religion* 40, 1996, 19-46.

Farrer, A., *Finite and Infinite. A Philosophical Essay*, Glasgow 1943.

-, ›The Prior Actuality of God‹, in: *Reflective Faith. Essays in Philosophical Theology*, ed. C.C. Conti, London 1972.

Ferreira, M.J., ›Normativity and Reference in a Wittgensteinian Philosophy of Religion‹, *Faith and Philosophy* 18, 2002, 443-464.

-, ›Vision and Love: A Wittgensteinian Ethic in *Culture and Value*‹, in: J. Stout/R. MacSwain (eds.), *Grammar and Grace: Reformulations of Aquinas and Wittgenstein*, London 2004, 214-231.

Godelier, M., *Das Rätsel der Gabe. Geld, Geschenke, heilige Objekte*, München 1999.

Gondek, H.-D./Waldenfels, B. (eds.), *Einsätze des Denkens. Zur Philosophie von Jacques Derrida*, Frankfurt am Main 1997.

Green, R.M., *Religious Reason. The Rational and Moral Basis of Religious Belief*, New York 1978.

Greenawalt, K., *Religious Convictions and Political Choice*, New York/Oxford 1988.

–, *Private Consciences and Public Reasons*, New York/Oxford 1995.

Gregersen, N.H., ›Three Varieties of Panentheism‹, in: Ph. Clayton/A. Peacocke (eds.), *In Whom We Live and Move and Have Our Being. Panentheistic Reflections on God's Presence in a Scientific World*, Grand Rapids, Michigan 2004, 19-35,

Griffin, D.R., ›Panentheism: A Postmodern Revelation‹, in: Ph. Clayton/A. Peacocke (eds.), *In Whom We Live and Move and Have Our Being. Panentheistic Reflections on God's Presence in a Scientific World*, Grand Rapids, Michigan 2004, 36-47.

Grotefeld, St., ›Distinkt, aber nicht illegitim. Protestantische Ethik und die liberale Forderung nach Selbstbeschränkung‹, *Zeitschrift für Evangelische Ethik* 45, 2001, 262-284.

Gutting, G., *Religious Belief and Religious Scepticism*, Indianapolis 1982.

Hart, J.G., ›Michel Henry's Phenomenological Theology of Life: A Husserlian Reading of *C'est moi, la vérité*‹, *Husserl Studies* 15, 1999, 183-230.

Hart, K., Response to Graham Ward, in: Boeve, L./Leijssen, L. (eds.), *Sacramental Presence in a Postmodern Context*, Leuven 2001, 205-211.

Hartshorne, Ch., *A Natural Theology for Our Time*, La Salle, Illinois 1967.

–, *Omnipotence and Other Logical Mistakes*, Albany, New York 1984.

–, *The Darkness and the Light: A Philosopher Reflects Upon his Fortunate Career and Those Who Made It Possible*, Albany, New York 1990.

–, ›The Logic of Panentheism‹, in: Ch. Hartshorne/W.L. Reese, *Philosophers Speak of God*, Chicago 1953, 499-514.

Hasker, W., *God, Time, and Knowledge*, Ithaca, New York 1989.

Heim, S.M., *Salvations. Truth and Difference in Religion*, New York ⁵2001.

Helm, P., *Eternal God. A Study of God Without Time*, Oxford 1988.

Henry, M., *Philosophie et phénoménologie du corps: essai sur l'ontologie biranienne*, Paris 1965.

Hick, J., *An Interpretation of Religion*, London 1989.

–, *Arguments for the Existence of God*, London 1979.

Hicks, G.D., *Critical Realism. Studies in the Philosophy of Mind and Nature*, London 1938.

Hocking, W.E., *The Meaning of God in Human Experience*, 1912.

Horner, R., *Rethinking God As Gift. Marion, Derrida, and the Limits of Phenomenology*, New York 2001.

Husserl, E., *Logical Investigations*, transl. by J.N. Findlay, 2 vol., London 1970, vol. 2.

–, *Logical Investigations, Introduction to Volume 2*, trans. J.N. Findlay, ed. D. Moran, London/New York 2001.

Ineichen, H., ›Lebenswelt und soziale Welt‹, in: E. Hufnagel/J. Zovko (Hg.), *studia hermeneutica*, Neue Folge, Bd. 1, 2004, 69–85.

Jäger, Chr. (ed.), *Analytische Religionsphilosophie*, Paderborn 1998.

–, ›Religious Experience and Epistemic Justification: Alston on the Reliability of »Mystical Perception«‹, in: C.U. Moulines/K.-G. Niebergall (eds.), *Argument und Analyse*, Paderborn 2002, 403–423.

Jorgenson, A. G., ›Luther on Ubiquity and a Theology of the Public‹, *International Journal of Systematic Theology* 6, 2004, 351–368.

Jüngel, E., *God as Mystery of the World. On the Foundation of the Theology of the Crucified One in the Dispute Between Theism and Atheism*, transl. by D.L. Guder, Edinburgh 1983.

Kant, I., *Kritik der reinen Vernunft* (1787), AA III, Berlin 1911. (Kant, I., *Critique of Pure Reason* (1787). Trans. N.K. Smith, London 1933).

Kant, I., *Opus postumum. Kant's handschriftlicher Nachlaß*, Vol. 8, AA XXI, Berlin/Leipzig 1936.

Kellenberger, J., *The Cognitivity of Religion. Three Perspectives*, Berkeley/Los Angeles 1985.

Kelly, Th.M., ›Experience, Language and Sacramental Theology. George Steiner and Karl Rahner on the Postmodern Critique‹, in: L. Boeve/J.C. Ries (eds.), *The Presence of Transcendence. Thinking ›Sacrament‹ in a Postmodern Age*, Leuven 2001, 61–78.

Kierkegaard, S., *Works of Love* (1847), in Kierkegaard's Writings, vol. 16, ed. and transl. by H.V. Hong and E. H. Hong, Princeton, New Jersey 1995.

Klemm, D., ›The Autonomous Text, the Hermeneutical Self, and Divine Rhetoric‹, in: *Hermeneutics, the Bible and Literary Criticism*, ed. A. Loades and M. McLain, London 1992, 3–26.

Kneale, W., ›Time and Eternity in Theology‹, *Proceedings of the Aristotelian Society* 61, 1960–1961, 87–109.

Kusch, M., *Knowledge by Agreement. The Programme of Communitarian Epistemology*, Oxford 2002.

Leftow, B., *Time and Eternity*, Ithaca, New York 1991.

Levi, I., *The Covenant of Reason. Rationality and the Commitments of Thought*, Cambridge 1997.

Luther M., ›De servo arbitrio‹ (1525), *WA* 18, 551-787.

-, ›Daß diese Wort Christi »Das ist mein Leib« noch fest stehen, wider die Schwärmgeister‹ (1527), *WA* 23, 38-320.

-, ›In epistolam S. Pauli ad Galatas Commentarius ex praelectione D Martini Lutheri (1531) collectus 1535‹, *WA* 40/1.

-, ›Vorlesungen über 1. Mose von 1535-45‹, *WA* 43.

-, ›Tischreden aus den Handschriften Bav. und Oben‹, *WAT* 5, 355-369.

-, ›Vom Abendmahl Christi. Bekenntnis‹ (1528), *WA* 26, 241-509 (›Confession Concerning Christ's Supper‹, *LW* 37).

-, ›Wochenpredigten über Joh. 6-8‹, *WA* 33.

Mackie, J.L., *The Miracle of Theism. Arguments for and Against the Existence of God*, Oxford 1982.

Macquarrie, J., *In Search of Deity: An Essay in Dialectical Theism*, London 1984.

Mahler, M.S./Pine, F./Bergman, A., *The Psychological Birth of the Human Infants: Symbiosis and Individuation*, New York 1975.

Maier, H., ›Die Überwindung der Welt. Auf dem Christentum liegt kein Fluch. Eine Antwort auf Herbert Schnädelbachs Polemik‹, *Die Zeit* 27, 2000 (http://zeus.zeit.de/text/archiv/2000/27/200027. replik_.xml).

Mannermaa, T., *Der im Glauben gegenwärtige Christus: Rechtfertigung und Vergottung. Zum ökumenischen Dialog.* Arbeiten zur Geschichte und Theologie des Luthertums, Neue Folge, Band 8, Hannover 1989.

Marcel, G., *Geheimnis des Seins*, Wien 1952.

Marion, J.-L., *Being Given. Toward a Phenomenology of Givenness*, Stanford, California 2002.

-, *Etant donné. Essai d'une phénoménologie de la donation*, Vendôme ²1998.

-, ›La raison du don‹, *Philosophie* 78, 2003, 3-32.

-, *Réduction et donation. Recherches sur Husserl, Heidegger et la phénoménologie*, Paris 1989.

Mauss, M., *The Gift. The Form and Reason for Exchange in Archaic Societies*, trans. W.D. Halls, London 1990.

Mavrodes, G., *Belief in God. A Study in the Epistemology of Religion*, New York 1970.

-, ›Rationality and Religious Belief - a Perverse Question‹, in: C.F. Delany (ed.), *Rationality and Religious Belief*, Notre Dame, Ind./ London 1979, 40f.

McCall, St., *A Model of the Universe. Space-Time, Probability, and Decision*, Oxford 1994.

McCormack, B.L., *For Us and Our Salvation: Incarnation and Atonement in the Reformed Tradition*, Princeton, New Jersey 1993.

McFague, S., *The Body of God*, Minneapolis 1993.

McTaggart, J.E., *The Nature of Existence*, Cambridge 1927, vol. II.

-, ›The Unreality of Time‹, *Mind* 17, 1908, 457–474.

Mellor, D.H., *Matters of Metaphysics*, Cambridge 1991.

-, *Real Time*, Cambridge 1981.

-, *The Facts of Causation*, New York 1995.

Messiaen, O., *Méditation sur le Mystère de la Saint Trinité*, Paris 1973.

Milbank, J., *Being Reconciled. Ontology and Pardon*, London 2003.

Min, A., *The Solidarity of Others in a Divided World. A Postmodern Theology after Postmodernism,* New York 2004.

Mill, J.S., *On Liberty*, London 1859.

Mitchell, B., *The Justification of Religious Belief*, London 1973.

Morris, Th., *Anselmian Explorations*, Notre Dame, Indiana 1987.

Moxter, M., ›Wie stark ist der »schwache Realismus«?‹ In: J. Schröter/ A. Eddelbüttel (eds.), *Konstruktion von Wirklichkeit. Beiträge aus geschichtstheoretischer, philosophischer und theologischer Perspektive*, Berlin/ New York 2004, 119–133.

Newberg, A., d'Aquili, E., Rause, V., *Why God Won't Go Away. Brain Science and the Biology of Belief*, New York 2001.

Nielsen, K., ›Wittgensteinian Fideism‹, *Philosophy* 42, 1967, 191–209.

O'Hear, A., ›Culture‹, *Routledge Encyclopaedia of Philosophy*, London 1998, 746–750.

Owen, H.P., *The Christian Knowledge of God*, London 1969.

Padgett, A.G., ›Can History Measure Eternity? A Reply to William Craig‹, *Religious Studies* 27, 1991, 333–335.

-, *God, Eternity and the Nature of Time*, New York 1992.

Pailin, D.A., ›Panentheism‹, in: S. Andersen, D.Z. Phillips, *Modern Theism and its Alternatives*, Aarhus 1994, 95–116.

Parnas, J./Bovet, P./Zahavi, D., Schizophrenic Autism: Clinical Phenomenology and Pathogenetic Implications, *World Psychiatry* 1, October 2002, 131–136.

Peirce, Ch.S., *Collected Papers of Charles Sanders Peirce II*, hg. v. Ch. Hartshorn/P.Weiss, Cambridge, Massachusetts 1932.

Penelhum, T., *God and Skepticism*, Dordrecht 1983.

–, *Problems of Religious Knowledge*, London 1971.

Peterson, M./Hasker, W./Reichenbach, B./Basinger, D. (eds.), *Reason and Religious Belief. An Introduction to the Philosophy of Religion*, New York/Oxford ³2002.

Phillips, D.Z., *Belief, Change and Forms of Life,* Basingstoke and London 1986.

–, *Faith and Philosophical Enquiry*, London 1970.

–, ›On Really Believing‹, in: *Proceedings. Seventh European Conference on Philosophy of Religion*, Utrecht 1988.

–, *Philosophy's Cool Place*, Ithaca, New York 1999.

–, *Religion and the Hermeneutics of Contemplation*, Cambridge 2001.

–, *Religion without Explanation*, Oxford 1976.

Phillips, P., ›George Steiner's Wager on Transcendence‹, *The Heythrop Journal* 39, 1998, 158–169.

Piaget, J./Inhelder, B., *The Psychology of the Child*, New York 1969.

Pierce, J., Review of *God and Time: Four Views*, ed. Gregory E. Gansle; contributors: W.L. Craig, P. Helm, A. Padgett, and N. Wolterstorff, Downer's Grove, IL 2001, *Faith and Philosophy* 20, 2003, 504–509.

Plantinga, A., ›Is Belief in God Properly Basic?‹, *Nous* 15, 1981, 41–51.

–, ›Is Belief in God Rational?‹, in: C.F. Delany (ed.), *Rationality and Religious Belief*, Notre Dame, Ind./London 1979.

–, *Warranted Christian Belief*, New York/Oxford 2000.

Popper, J., *Objective Knowledge. An Evolutionary Approach*, Oxford 1972.

Quinn, Ph.L., ›Religious Pluralism‹, *Routledge Encyclopaedia of Philosophy*, London 1998, 260–264.

–, ›Towards Thinner Theologies: Hick and Alston on Religious Diversity‹, *International Journal for Philosophy of Religion* 38, 1995, 145–164.

Rawls, J., *Political Liberalism*, New York 1996.

–, ›The Domain of the Political and Overlapping Consensus‹, *New York University Law Review* 64, 1989, 233–255.

Rescher, N., *Pluralism: Against the Demand of Consensus*, Oxford 1993.

-, *Rationality: A Philosophical Inquiry into the Nature and the Rationale of Reason*, Oxford 1988.

-, *The Coherence Theory of Truth*, Oxford 1973.

Ricken, F., ›Religiöse Erfahrung und Glaubensbegründung‹, *Theologie und Philosophie* 70, 1995, 399–404.

Ricoeur, P., *Soi-même comme un autre*, Paris 1990.

Riesebrodt, M., *Die Rückkehr der Religionen. Fundamentalismus und der ›Kampf der Kulturen‹*, München 2000.

-, *Fundamentalismus als patriarchalische Protestbewegung. Amerikanische Protestanten (1910-28) und iranische Schiiten (1961-79) im Vergleich*, Tübingen 1990

-, *Protestantischer Fundamentalismus in den USA. Die religiöse Rechte im Zeitalter der elektronischen Medien*, Stuttgart 1987.

Rochat, P., *The Infant's World*, Cambridge 2001.

Root, H.E., ›Beginning All Over Again‹, in: A.R. Vidler (ed.), *Soundings. Essays Concerning Christian Understanding*, Cambridge 1962.

Rost, Fr., *Theorien des Schenkens. Zur kultur- und humanwissenschaftlichen Bearbeitung eines anthropologischen Phänomens*, Essen 1994.

Saarinen, R., *Gottes Wirken auf uns: Die transzendentale Deutung des Gegenwart-Christi-Motivs in der Lutherforschung*, Stuttgart 1989.

-, ›The Presence of God in Luther's Theology‹, *Lutheran Quarterly* 3, 1994, 3ff.

Sabatier, A., *Esquisse d'une Philosophie de la Religion d'après la Psychologie et l'Histoire*, Paris ⁴1897.

Schellenberg, J.L., ›Religious Experience and Religious Diversity: A Reply to Alston‹, *Religious Studies* 30, 1994, 151–159.

Schlesinger, G.N., *Timely Topics*, New York 1994, 70–77.

Schmied, G., *Schenken. Über eine Form sozialen Handelns*, Opladen 1996.

Schrag, C.O., *The Resources of Rationality: A Response to the Postmodern Challenge*, Bloomington, Indiana 1992.

Schwöbel, Chr., *God: Action and Revelation*, Kampen 1992.

Sider, Th., *Four Dimensionalism. An Ontology of Persistence and Time*, Oxford 2001.

Smith, Q., *Language and Time*, Oxford 1993.

Steiner, G., *After Babel. Aspects of Language and Translation*, London 1975.

-, *Errata. An Examined Life*, New Haven/London 1997.

-, *No Passion Spent: Essays 1978-1996*, London 1996.

-, *Real Presences*, Chicago 1989.

-, ›Real Presences‹, in: G. Steiner, *No Passion Spent*, London 1996, 20-39.

Stenmark, M., *Rationality in Science, Religion, and Everyday Life*, Notre Dame, Indiana 1995.

Steup, M., ›William Alston, Perceiving God – The Epistemology of Religious Experience‹, *Nous* 31, 1997, 408-420.

Stoellger, Ph., *Metapher und Lebenswelt. Hans Blumenbergs Metaphorologie als Lebenswelthermeneutik und ihr religionsphänomenologischer Horizont*, Tübingen 2000.

Swinburne, R., *Space and Time*, London ²1981.

-, The *Christian God*, Oxford 1994.

-, *The Coherence of Theism*, Oxford ²1993.

-, *The Existence of God*, Oxford 1979.

Taliaferro, Ch. (ed.), *Contemporary Philosophy of Religion*, Oxford 1998.

Tanner, K., *Theories of Culture. A New Agenda for Theology*, Minneapolis 1997.

Taylor, Ch., *Sources of the Self. The Making of Modern Identity*, Cambridge, Massachusetts 1989.

Tomasello, M., *The Cultural Origins of Human Cognition*, Cambridge, Massachusetts 1999.

Tooley, M., *Time, Tense and Causation*, Oxford 1997.

Tracy, T.F., *God, Action and Embodiment*, 1984.

van Huyssteen, J.W., *The Shaping of Rationality. Toward Interdisciplinarity in Theology and Science*, Grand Rapids, Mich./Cambridge 1999.

van Inwagen, P., ›Four-Dimensional Objects‹, *Nous* 24, 1990, 245-255.

Wagner, F., *Was ist Religion? Studien zu ihrem Begriff und Thema in Geschichte und Gegenwart*, Gütersloh 1986.

Wagner-Hasel, B., *Der Stoff der Gaben. Kultur und Politik des Schenkens und Tauschens im archaischen Griechenland*, Frankfurt am Main/New York 2000.

Waldenfels, B., ›Das Un-ding der Gabe‹, in: H.-D. Gondek/B. Waldenfels (eds.), *Einsätze des Denkens. Zur Philosophie von Jacques Derrida*, Frankfurt am Main 1997, 385-409.

Ward, G., ›The Church as The Erotic Community‹, in: L. Boeve/L. Leijssen (eds.), *Sacramental Presence in a Postmodern Context*, Leuven 2001, 167-204.

Ward, K., *Holding Fast to God. A Reply to Don Cupitt*, London 1982.

-, *Rational Theology and the Creativity of God*, Oxford 1982.

Weber, M., *Wirtschaft und Gesellschaft. Grundriss der verstehenden Soziologie*, Tübingen ⁵1972.

Weder, H., ›Komparatives und ein parataktisches kai. Eine neutestamentlich orientierte Skizze zur transzendierten Notwendigkeit‹, in: I.U. Dalferth/J. Fischer/H.-P. Grosshans (eds)., *Denkwürdiges Geheimnis. Beiträge zur Gotteslehre. Festschrift für Eberhard Jüngel zum siebzigsten Geburtstag*, Tübingen 2004, 555-579.

Wentz, R.E., ›The Domestication of the Divine‹, *Theology Today* 57, 2000, 24-34.

Westphal, M., ›Faith as the Overcoming of Ontological Xenophobia‹, in: O.F. Summerell (ed.), *The Otherness of God*, Charlottesville and London 1998, 149-172.

White, L., *The Science of Culture*, New York 1949.

Whitehead, A.N., *Adventure of Ideas* (1933), New York 1967.

Wiles, M., *Faith and the Mystery of God*, London 1982.

Winch, P., *The Idea of a Social Science and its Relation to Philosophy*, London 1958.

-, ›Understanding a Primitive Society‹, in: D.Z. Phillips (ed.), *Religion and Understanding*, Oxford 1967, 9-42.

Wittgenstein, L., *Lectures and Conversations on Aesthetics, Psychology and Religious Belief*, ed. C. Barrett, Oxford 1970.

-, *Philosophische Untersuchungen*. Kritisch-genetische Edition, ed. J. Schulte et. al., Frankfurt 2001.

Wolterstorff, N., ›Can Belief in God be Rational If It Has No Foundations?‹, in: A. Plantinga/N. Wolterstorff (eds.), *Faith and Rationality. Reason and Belief in God*, Notre Dame, Indiana 1983, 135-186, 163.

-, ›The Role of Religion in Decision and Discussion of Political Issues‹, in: R. Audi/N. Wolterstorff, *Religion in the Public Square. The Place of Religious Convictions in Political Debate*, Lanham, Maryland 1997, 67-120.

-, ›Why We Should Reject What Liberalism Tells Us about Speaking and Acting in Public for Religious Reasons‹, in: P.J. Weithman (ed.), *Religion and Contemporary Liberalism*, Notre Dame, Indiana 1997, 162-181.

Zahavi, D., *Husserl's Phenomenology*, Stanford, California 2003.

-, *Subjectivity and Selfhood. Investigating The First-Person Perspective* (forthcoming).

Zelechow, B., ›God's Presence and the Paradox of Freedom‹, in: A. Loades, M. McLain (eds.), *Hermeneutics, the Bible and Literary Criticism*, London 1992, 162-176.

Name Index

Abel, G. 222
Adam 208
Adams, R.M. 104, 121
Adelung, J.Chr. 57
Alanus ab Insulis 90
Allison, D.B. 175
Alston, W.P. 15, 114, 121–125, 216, 218, 221f, 249
Andersen, S. 165
Aquinas, Th. 124, 159, 202, 218, 234, 246
Aristotle 160
Ashdown, L. 262
Audi, R. 7, 8, 264
Augustine, A. 90, 92, 149, 156, 168, 220

Bach, J.S. 247
Bacon, F. 2, 113
Baelz, P.R. 141
Baillie, J. 113, 116, 137, 249
Barnes, J. 12
Basinger, D. 3
Berger, P. 260
Bergman, A. 66
Berkeley, G. 102
Berking, H. 194
Berlin, I. 268
Berry, Ph. 158
Blumenberg, H. 179f, 183, 191
Boethius 81, 164
Boeve, L. 39, 45, 86

Boucourechliev, A. 244
Bovet, P. 61, 3, 66
Brown, H.I. 10
Brümmer, V. 128f, 142, 160, 234

Calvin J. 2, 121, 136
Caputo, J.D. 176
Carroll, L. 102
Cartwright, J. 3
Caravaggio, M. de 208
Chauvet, L.M. 39
Christ 146, 155, 166, 168, 173, 216f, 236, 242, 247, 249
Clausen, G. 194
Clayton, J. 3f, 7–9, 18, 23f, 267
Clayton, Ph. 168, 220
Cobb-Stevens, R. 180
Collingwood, R.G. 36, 76, 82
Comay, R. 194
Craig, W.L. 53, 78
Crosby, D.A. V, VI

d'Aquili, E. 101
Dalferth, I.U. 1, 3, 11–13, 28, 37, 57, 100f, 113, 117, 154, 205, 207, 219, 226
Damasio, A.R. 59
Davis, C.F. 101, 105
Davis, P. 220, 227
Davis, S.T. 56, 164f
Dean, W. 19, 25, 34

:NT • GEDRUKT OP DUURZAAM PAPIER - ISO 9706

50, B-3020 HERENT